HOW THE
SPITFIRE
WON THE
BATTLE OF
BRITAIN

For all who served in RAF Fighter Command during the Battle of Britain.
On 20 August 1940 Churchill said that they had the 'gratitude of every home in
our island'. Seventy years later, and forever more, that should remain the case.

HOW THE
SPITFIRE
WON THE
BATTLE OF
BRITAIN

DILIP SARKAR
MBE FRHistS

Author's Note

Throughout the text I have referred to German *Messerschmitt* fighters by the abbreviation 'Me' (not 'Bf', which is also correct), or simply by their numeric designation, such as '109' or '110'. This, in my view, not only reads better but is authentic: during the Battle of Britain, Keith Lawrence, a New Zealander, flew Spitfires and once said to me 'To us they were just 109s or 110s – simple.' The purely numeric designations are also frequently found in contemporary documents.

Also, many of the survivors whose accounts are included in this book ultimately retired from the RAF with senior, even Air, rank. In the text, however, I have used their ranks as per 1940.

First published 2010

Amberley Publishing plc
Cirencester Road, Chalford,
Stroud, Gloucestershire, GL6 8PE

www.amberleybooks.com

British Library Cataloguing in Publication Data.
A catalogue record for this book is available from the British
Library.

ISBN 978 1 84868 868 1

Typeset in 10pt on 13pt Adobe Caslon Pro.
Typesetting and Origination by Amberley Publishing.
Printed in the UK.

Contents

Other Books by Dilip Sarkar
(in order of publication)

Glossary

AASF: Advance Air Striking Force

A&AEE: Aircraft & Armament Experimental Establishment

ACM: Air Chief Marshal

AOC: Air Officer Commanding

ASR: Air Sea Rescue

BEF: British Expeditionary Force

E/A: Enemy Aircraft

CAS: Chief of the Air Staff

CFI: Chief Flying Instructor

CFS: Central Flying School

CO: Commanding Officer

FTS: Flying Training School

CFS: Central Flying School

LDV: Local Defence Volunteer, the Home Guard

OTU: Operational Training Unit

RAFVR: Royal Air Force Volunteer Reserve

RN: Royal Navy

RNAS: Royal Naval Air Service

R/T: Radio Telephone

RDF: Radio Direction Finding, radar

SASO: Senior Air Staff Officer

Schwarm: A section of four fighters

Rotte: A pair of fighters, comprising leader and wingman, into which the *Schwarm* broke once battle was joined

Katschmarek: Wingman

Staffel: A squadron

Staffelkapitän: The squadron leader

Gruppe: A wing, usually of three squadrons

Gruppenkommandeur: The wing commander

Geschwader: The whole group, usually of three *gruppen*

Geschwader Kommodore: The group leader

Jagdgeschwader: Fighter group, abbreviated JG

Kampfgeschwader: Bomber group, abbreviated KG

Jagdbomber: A fighter-bomber, or *Jabo*

Jagdflieger: Fighter pilot

Kampffleiger: Bomber pilot

Lehr Geschwader: Literally a training group, but actually a precision bombing unit, abbreviated LG

Stuka: The Ju 87 dive-bomber

Zerstörer: Literally 'destroyer', the term used for the Me 110

Zerstörer Geschwader: Destroyer group, abbreviated ZG

Jagdwaffe: The fighter force

Freie jagd: A fighter sweep

Stab Schwarm: The staff flight

Luftflotte: Air Fleet

Gruppenkeil: A wedge formation of bombers, usually made up of vics of three

Oberkommando der Wehrmacht (OKW): The German armed forces high command

Oberkommando der Luftwaffe (OKL): The German Air Force High Command

Each *geschwader* generally comprised three *gruppen*, each of three *staffeln*. Each *gruppe* is designated by Roman numerals, i.e. III/JG 26 refers to the third *gruppe* of Fighter Group 26. *Staffeln* are identified by numbers, so 7/JG 26 is the seventh *staffel* and belongs to III/JG 26.

Rank comparisons may also be useful:
Unteroffizier: Corporal, no RAF aircrew equivalent
Feldwebel: Sergeant
Oberfeldwebel: Flight Sergeant
Leutnant: Pilot Officer
Oberleutnant: Flight Lieutenant
Hauptmann: Squadron Leader
Major: Wing Commander
Oberst: Group Captain

Introduction

Seventy years ago this summer there was a great air battle in which the German *Luftwaffe* fought to achieve aerial supremacy over England as a prelude to a seaborne invasion. RAF Fighter Command prevented this, and so won what Churchill called 'The Battle of Britain'. There were two main British single-engined fighters that fought and won this victory: the Hawker Hurricane and the Supermarine Spitfire. The latter, it has been said, was lesser in number but, being somehow altogether more charismatic than the Hurricane, walked off with all the glory – glory, some still say, it did not deserve. Group Captain Peter Townsend, who flew Hurricanes in the battle, wrote that the *Luftwaffe* put so much store in being shot down by Spitfires, rather than Hurricanes, that they suffered from 'Spitfire Snobbery'. 'But', he argued, 'figures were to prove that during the Battle of Britain, machine for machine, the Hurricane would acquit itself every bit as well as the Spitfire and in the aggregate (there were more than three Hurricanes to two Spitfires) do greater damage among the *Luftwaffe*.[1] This comment has passed into legend and has become one of the many myths of the Battle of Britain.

The intention of this book is to contextualise the Hurricane, Spitfire and Me 109 stories, anchoring them accurately in time and space against the backdrop of the inter-war period. Those were days when disarmament ruled and the depression hit pockets hard. But they were also exciting times in aviation, not least because of the Schneider Trophy being won outright by the British S.6B. This was a very fast monoplane, designed by Reginald Joseph Mitchell of Supermarine, and would lead, in due course, to the biplane being replaced by monoplanes with superior performance. They were also days in which the dread of air power was immense: an immeasurable global fear of the bomber and its unstoppable 'knock-out blow'. Then, after years of tension, came the Second World War. In 1940, Hitler's unprecedented advance conquered most of Europe, until the Germans stood at Calais, within sight of England. The eyes of the world then became focussed upon the air battle over south-east England – and on the Spitfire in particular, which excited popular enthusiasm and became the symbol of freedom and defiance.

Did the iconic Spitfire deserve this adoration? In this book is presented a balanced view, based entirely upon evidence – all sources being clearly referenced and available for inspection. The fact is that the Battle of Britain would not have been won without the Spitfire. And Hurricanes did not destroy more enemy aircraft than all other defences combined, as legend would have us believe. So this book – driven by evidence and not emotion or prejudice – represents an important new interpretation. It is not simply another narrative regurgitating the same old theme – and predictably plenty of those have been published in this seventieth anniversary year. Nonetheless I suspect that it will provoke much argument and debate. For that is what we historians do – argue and debate – and long may that remain the case.

Dilip Sarkar MBE, FRHistS, Worcester, August 2010

The Bomber Will Always Get Through

To fully appreciate the contribution made to the aerial defence of Britain in 1940 by the Supermarine Spitfire and Hawker Hurricane fighters, it is first necessary to contextualise their creation and development. In so doing we must travel back in time to a world still shocked by the enormity of the First World War, determined not to repeat the unprecedented scale and horror of that conflict. Given that globally casualties during that so-called Great War were 37 million, arguably this was perfectly understandable. Indeed, as Charles Loch Mowat wrote, 'When the war ended in November 1918, there were few who did not hope that the losses and sufferings it had brought might be redeemed in a better world – a happier society at home, the nations on earth living in peace and unity.'[1] The American President, Woodrow Wilson, visited Manchester in December 1918, and spoke of the beginning of not necessarily 'a golden age', but at least a 'brightening one.'[2] Tragically the next twenty years would see such hopes completely dashed, leading to George Orwell writing in *The Lion and the Unicorn* that 'as I write, highly civilised human beings are flying overhead, trying to kill me'.[3] Clearly, therefore, peace ultimately failed and air power played an increasingly significant role in armed conflict.

It was on Christmas Eve 1914, in fact, that the first German bomb was dropped on England – the small device exploded harmlessly in a Dover garden.[4] From that point onwards, though, Britain could no longer rely upon the security provided by being an island nation and, of course, the Royal Navy (RN). These primitive air attacks, however, soon intensified, culminating in the dropping of a one-ton bomb on London on 16 February 1918.[5] By the Armistice, German airmen had raided Britain over 100 times, killing 1,413 people.[6] These attacks were carried out largely at night by zeppelins and twin-engined bombers. This quite unanticipated development in air warfare meant that no shelters had been built. For the first time in history, London's deep underground network provided a safe haven for terrified Londoners. According to Angus Calder, the bombing provoked 'mass panics and near riots'.[7] Although the total number of casualties involved would later equate to those suffered in just one night of the infamous *Blitz*, they were enough to generate an understandable fear of and respect for air power. Moreover, the air power doctrine that emerged between the wars confirmed the bomber as supreme. These two factors are vitally important to understanding events concerning attitudes to aerial warfare in Britain between the wars.

In his masterful study *The Shadow of the Bomber*, Uri Bialer considered that 'the fear of aerial bombardment in inter-war Britain was unprecedented and unique'.[8] This indicates how shocking those early air raids were. Britain was, in fact, particularly vulnerable to air attack. Although surrounded by water, the British Isles are nonetheless close to the continent – from where any future threat was likely to be launched. Due to the relative smallness of the islands, no point within it was beyond a bomber's range – including not only crucial manufacturing centres and ports, but also the all-important capital: London. The successful attacks by German bombers in the Great War had made clear that British aerial defences were inadequate. Consequently the Prime Minister, Lloyd George, commissioned the South African General Jan Smuts to investigate the matter, his conclusion being that an Air Ministry should be formed immediately, responsible for all aspects of British air power, and that the existing air services should be amalgamated into an independent service.[9] Hitherto British military aviation had been shared by the army-controlled Royal Flying Corps (RFC) and the Royal Navy Air Service (RNAS). In spite of loud protests by both the Admiralty and War Office, the Royal Air Force (RAF) was born on 1 April 1918. By the Armistice, the RAF was the largest air force in the world and also enjoyed technical superiority. The new service boasted 22,000 aircraft and 188 operational squadrons.[10] After the Paris Peace Conference in 1919, however, the world was eager to disarm. In the quest for Wilson's 'brightening' age, Britain lost no time in reducing the size of all three services. By the end of 1919, the RAF had been stripped to just 371 aircraft of all types and a mere twelve squadrons.[11] These figures hardly justified the RAF's status as an independent service. The RAF's first Chief of the Air Staff (CAS), however, Air Chief Marshal (ACM) Sir Hugh Trenchard, believed strongly that a powerful air force could deter a potential aggressor. He therefore set about creating sound foundations upon which to build the RAF. On 11 December 1919, Trenchard's proposal concerning every detail of how his service should be developed was delivered to Parliament as a White Paper. The memorandum was entirely comprehensive, covering all aspects necessary to create an effective modern air force. According to Derek Wood and Derek Dempster, Trenchard's plan proved to be 'a model for most air forces of the world and stand the test of time'.[12]

Fortunate for the RAF though Trenchard's appointment and intervention was, it was not good news for Britain's fighter force. Trenchard was a 'Bomber Baron'. Many influential people in both the services and in civilian life, in fact, believed in the so-called 'knock-out blow'[13] – which could only be delivered by bombers. Indeed, such was the bomber's perceived power, Trenchard considered it unnecessary 'for an air force, in order to defeat the enemy nation, to defeat its armed forces first. Air power can dispense with that immediate step, can pass over the enemy navies and armies, and penetrate air defences and attack direct the centre of production, transportation and communication from which the enemy war effort is maintained. It is on the destruction of enemy industries and, above all, in the lowering of morale of enemy nationals caused by bombing that the ultimate victory lies'.[14] In 1932, Stanley Baldwin, then Prime Minister, emphasised the all pervading fear of bombing: 'I think it is as well for the man in the street to realise that there is no power on earth that can save him from being bombed. Whatever people may tell him, the bomber will always get through. The only defence is offence, which means that you have to kill more women and children more quickly than the enemy if you want to save yourselves'.[15] What precious little spending there was on British air power between the wars, certainly until 1935, was overwhelmingly focussed on the bomber force. This is unsurprising considering Trenchard's view in 1921 that the aeroplane was 'a shockingly bad weapon for defence' and that the use of fighters was 'only necessary to keep up the morale of your own people'. Trenchard's doctrine revolved almost entirely, therefore, around offensive operations. Defence was side-lined with the absolute bare minimum of resources.

Although reduced to a shadow of its former self in the immediate wake of the First World War, it was always intended that Trenchard's RAF could easily be expanded – in the unwelcome event of that being required. The first half of the 1930s saw Britain and other nations 'hell-bent', according to Sir Maurice Dean, 'for collective security and prepared to accept incalculable risks in that cause'.[16] In 1932, Britain abandoned what was a miniscule re-armament programme. A year later, Adolf Hitler and the Nazis came to power in Germany. Essentially Hitler's main aims were to overthrow the hated 1919 Treaty of Versailles, which severely restricted Germany's armed forces, and achieve 'living space' for the German people by territorial expansion. The *Führer* immediately set about contravening both the military restrictions and what were seen in Germany as territorial injustices, re-building the *Wehrmacht* in the process. In 1934, Britain revisited rearmament, but given the restricted spending involved Dean charged that 'even now Britain was not taking its problems seriously'.[17] It was not just a reluctance to rearm that had contributed to this sorry scenario, however. According to Calder, the 1930s were 'the best of times, the worst of times'.[18] In 1929 the world had been plunged into an economic crisis when the Wall Street stock market infamously crashed. The resulting fiscal chaos directly affected the next decade. Indeed, the British novelist and broadcaster J. B. Priestley famously made his celebrated *English Journey* in 1934, finding 'three Englands': the old and traditional, green and pleasant land; that of Victorian industrialisation and finally a new, American-inspired, revived England of 'motor coaches, wireless, hiking, factory girls looking like actresses' and belonging 'far more to the age itself than to this particular island'.[19] Prosperity was largely confined to the 'New Britain' of the area south of a line between the rivers Severn and Humber. North of that line was the demoralized and declining 'nineteenth-century Britain'. The countryside too was hard-hit by the depression. In 1932, unemployment stood at 2,750,000.[20] The British government between the wars, therefore, had serious social issues at home to deal with. Against this calamitous backdrop Nazi Germany busied itself with re-armament, while Churchill later wrote that so far as British military spending was concerned the years 1931-35 were those of 'the locust'.[21]

Locusts or not, in November 1934 Stanley Baldwin told the House of Commons that Britain would 'in no conditions … accept any position of inferiority with regard to what Air Force may be raised in Germany in the future'.[22] According to Dean, though, 'the plan of air re-armament adopted was quite inadequate to fulfil the pledge, and was indeed little more than a façade'.[23] The simple truth was that neither the government nor British people were yet ready to pay the price required for aerial parity with Nazi Germany. Moreover, the price would now be paid for Trenchard's offensive doctrine. In the mid-1930s the Air Staff still believed in a strict numerical ratio of fighters to bombers. This was, however, meaningless, because, again as Dean wrote, 'the requirements of defence' should be 'determined by the area to be defended and the nature of the probable attack'.[24] The size of the bomber force, of course, was dictated by quite different factors. In sum, the complete lack of substantial re-armament and deficiencies in doctrinal thinking were caused by three things: financial constraints, the indifference of or opposition by politicians, and Trenchard's offensive thinking. Information received in Britain during 1935, however, confirmed that although Germany was unlikely to be ready for war until 1939, Hitler's preparations towards that end were so substantial that the threat could no longer be ignored.[25] So it was that, albeit tentatively, Britain at last began to rearm.

On 25 February 1936, Expansion Scheme 'F' was approved by the Treasury: 124 squadrons (1,736 aircraft of all types) by April 1937. Intelligence, however, suggested that Germany's target was 2,000 front line aircraft.[26] Light bombers were dropped from the RAF programme, which concentrated on bombers with increased range and performance. The previous expansion plan, Scheme 'C' of 1935, proposed 800 bombers to 420 fighters. While Scheme 'F' increased the number of bombers to 1,000, it maintained the existing fighter strength.[27] Significantly, though, Scheme 'F' led directly to the formation of the RAF Volunteer Reserve (RAFVR), which planned to recruit and train a total of 8,100 pilots, observers and wireless operators (air gunner) by the end of 1938. From the regular service, 4,000 more pilots and 1,264 observers were required in the years 1936-39. Things had at last started moving in the right direction.

2

Schneider Trophy Racers

Hugh Caswall Tremenheere Dowding was born at Moffat on 24 April 1882. In 1899 he entered the Royal Military Academy at Woolwich, subsequently being commissioned as a second lieutenant. In 1912 he attended the Military Staff College at Camberley and learned to fly privately. A qualified pilot, Dowding served in France with the Royal Flying Corps (RFC) during the First World War. By July 1915 he was a major and commanding 16 Squadron at Merville, spotting for the big guns. During that period of his career, Dowding quarrelled for the first time with Trenchard, then Major-General commanding the RFC. His squadron having received the wrong type of propellers, Dowding complained. Trenchard resented Dowding's 'pernickety primness', ordering him to fit the propellers as supplied. Dowding did so but was nearly killed when his propeller failed on a test flight. Trenchard considered the incident typical of Dowding's 'self-righteous stubbornness'. Dowding thought it 'typical of Trenchard's stupidity', which, according to Orange, 'earned Dowding's contempt'.[1] During the Battle of the Somme in 1916, Dowding commanded a wing of four squadrons. Heavy losses were suffered due to the so-called 'Fokker Scourge', leading to Dowding once more being at odds with Trenchard and being posted back to England in 1917.[2] By the Armistice, Dowding was a temporary brigadier general in the RAF, of which, of course, Trenchard was the first CAS. This may explain why Dowding was not permanently commissioned into the new service until 1 August 1919. On 1 September 1930, Dowding was elevated to the Air Council of the Air Ministry, with responsibility for supply and research. From this point onwards, according to John Ferris, although Dowding's contribution 'has been the subject of mythologization', he did not, in fact, have much 'impact on the design and procurement of new equipment, nor did he single-handedly create air defence'; nonetheless, he 'did oversee the greatest recalibration in British strategic air defence between 1915-1930'.[3] Arguably that process began with his appointment as Air Member for Supply & Research. From that point onwards, therefore, Dowding became inexorably linked with the defence of Britain, and, indeed, the Spitfire and Hurricane legend.

Financial constraints and, of course, disarmament, severely restricted the resources made available to the RAF for research and development in the 1920s. Similar restrictions applied to the British aircraft industry generally, which by the early 1930s Orange considered 'was surviving on the smell of an oily rag'.[4] Paradoxically though, it was in some ways an exciting time for aviation. There were many and various flights of endurance. In April 1919, for example, Major Keith Park and Captain Stewart completed a non-stop circuit of the British Isles in a Handley-Page 0/400. The route of 1,880 miles was flown at an average speed of 66 mph in 28 hours and 30 minutes flying time.[5] In 1939, Alex Henshaw, flying a single-engined Percival Mew Gull, flew non-stop from England to Cape Town. Most exciting of all, however, was the Schneider Trophy. Seven tenths of the world's surface is covered by water. The Frenchman Jacques Schneider, son of an armament manufacturer, could not understand why, this being so, marine lagged so far behind land-based aviation. He saw the seaplane as being possessed of massive potential, with water providing cheap airports. As an incentive for aircraft designers to invest in seaplanes, Schneider presented his famous trophy for an international air race. The winner would be the nation whose seaplane flew the fastest over a measured water course. Whichever country won the trophy three consecutive times would keep it. This was a time of emerging nationalism on a global basis, and so what undoubtedly remains the most emotive air race to date developed into a competition of immense national pride. More importantly, the races led directly to the Spitfire and Hurricane.

Between 1919 and 1931 the Schneider races were spectacular, competitions being held at low-level over water, giving spectators on the ground an excellent view of events. Schneider's trophy – a silver nymph kissing the sea – became coveted. Both aircraft manufacturers and governments spent large sums of money designing, developing and racing their entrants. The first race, in 1913, was won, perhaps appropriately, by a Frenchman, whose top speed was 45.75 mph.[6] Importantly, the winning design was not, as might be assumed, a biplane: it was a monoplane. Although Britain's first win came the following year, Sopwith's victorious design was a biplane. This achieved, however, a new seaplane speed record of 86.78 mph.[7] Given that the speed involved was almost double that of the previous winner, the biplane's supremacy appeared both assured and justified. The biplane, of course, dominated the war of 1914-18, that conflicting interrupting the Schneider races until 1919. That year saw an entry submitted by the Supermarine Aviation Works, whose factory was situated on the Itchen estuary at Southampton. With no time to produce a new machine, Supermarine's Chief Designer, Reginald Joseph Mitchell, and the company's owner, Hubert Scott-Paine, modified the Supermarine Baby, a biplane seaplane produced during the First World War.[8] The resulting machine – the Sea Lion – competed over Bournemouth Bay, but sank when the pilot was forced to land due to poor visibility. The Sea Lion was more flying boat than seaplane, as were subsequent developments of that design which competed in later races. Significantly, however, when the Sea Lion competed in the 1922 race, held at Naples, Britain's was the only entry not government funded. Nonetheless, that year Mitchell's team won with a top speed of 145.7 mph – just 2.5 mph faster than the Italians in second place.[9] In 1923, however, the Sea Lion was beaten – by 20 mph – by the American government sponsored Curtiss CR-3 seaplane.[10] Inspired, Mitchell went back to Southampton – and designed a monoplane.

The Curtiss, Mitchell had noted with interest, boasted a number of new features, including a liquid-cooled engine, wing surface radiators and a metal airscrew. Mitchell's new monoplane – the S.4 – was even more advanced than the American machine. Instead of employing the usual external bracing struts and wires, Mitchell's monoplane's wing was cantilevered.[11] This represented both an important juncture in both Mitchell's personal career and aircraft design generally. Interestingly, the Air Ministry funded the design and construction of both the S.4 and the Gloster Aircraft Company's entry. The S.4 looked stunning. The single wing was made in one piece, covered not in doped fabric but in plywood. The fuselage was similarly covered and was of a monocoque construction which included both fin and tailplane. The nose – housing the Napier Lion engine – was covered in aluminium and the two-bladed propeller was also metal. On 13 September 1925 the S.4 set a new air speed record over Southampton Water: 226.75 mph. Unfortunately, the aircraft failed to meet expectations when it crashed during the Schneider race a month later. Fortunately the pilot survived, but the reason for the crash remained unclear. Aileron flutter was thought most likely. 'Aviation experts', wrote Gordon Mitchell, 'believed that Mitchell's ambitious use of the cantilever wing had exceeded the bounds of aerodynamic and structural knowledge available at the time'.[12] Nonetheless, Mitchell still believed that the monoplane still represented the best chance of preventing America winning once more and therefore keeping the Schneider Trophy.

Mitchell had no time to produce an entrant in the 1926 race, which was won by the Italians, meaning that the contest remained ongoing. In a bright red Macchi M.39, Major de Barnardi set a new air speed record of 258.87 mph.[13] Mitchell set-to and designed the S.5, which had a metal covered fuselage much smaller in cross-section than the S.4. In fact everything about the S.5 was intended to reduce drag, including flush rivets and a highly polished surface. Most importantly, this 1927 entry was Air Ministry funded and flown by an RAF pilot of the High Speed Flight, which had been formed specifically for the race. Two S.5s competed, winning first and second place, the victor setting yet another speed record at 281.66 mph.[14] Quite rightly, Mitchell and his triumphant team returned from Venice to a heroes' welcome in Southampton.

In March 1928, Flight Lieutenant S. M. Kinkead was killed in a finely tuned S.5 while making an attempt on the world air speed record over the Solent. Mitchell was devastated. That month also saw the Italian, de Barnardi, push the boundaries further still in a Macchi M52R and increase the record to 318.57 mph. Speeds were now being reached which were unimaginable back in 1913. Towards the end of the year, Flight Lieutenant D'Arcy Greig hit 319.57 mph in an S.5 – but the margin over de Barnardi was insufficient to be accepted as a new record.[15] By now the contest was being held every two years, giving Mitchell more time to develop his existing – excellent – racing seaplane into the S.6. One thing the gifted designer was uncertain about, though, was the Napier engine. This led to him enquiring about the Derby-based firm Rolls-Royce. Sir Henry Royce's Chief Designer and engineers assured Supermarine that they could deliver a new engine of 1,900 hp – 500 hp more powerful than the Italian engine. Mitchell then designed the S.6 around the potent new Rolls-Royce engine. His new machine featured further revolutionary improvements: the wings and fuselage were completely constructed of duralumin, and the heavy copper radiator internals replaced with much lighter alloy. The 1929 race, described as 'The World's Greatest Aerial Spectacle', took place at Calshot on the Solent. Flight Lieutenant H. R. D Waghorn won, flying an S.6, at an average speed of 328.63 mph.[16] Mitchell was ecstatic: Britain had now won the Schneider trophy twice. Shortly afterwards Squadron Leader A. H. Orlebar reached speeds of 336.3 and 357.7 mph, setting new world records in the process.[17] The S.6 was now confirmed as both the fastest and most technologically advanced aircraft in the world.

That same year, however, also saw the Wall Street Crash. As the effect of this severe economic depression resounded throughout the world, people had more important things on their minds than fancy air races. In spite of pressure upon the Treasury exerted by many influential individuals and organisations sympathetic to Mitchell's plight, in January 1931 Prime Minister Ramsay MacDonald announced his Labour government's understandable decision: there would be no money made available from the public purse to finance Britain's Schneider Trophy that year.[18] This decision was immediately attacked by the press, which accused the government of being anti-British. MacDonald remained unmoved. Italy, however, which had also won twice, was competing and at this time looked set for a third and final victory in the S.6's enforced absence. Then an astonishing and inspirational thing happened: Lady Houston – a tremendous patriot and nationalist – paid the £100,000 necessary for Mitchell to compete. With the race but seven months away, there was no longer time for Mitchell to produce his proposed S.7. Instead he improved the S.6 – now powered with a 2,350 hp 'R' engine.[19] So was born the S.6B. Gordon Mitchell, son of 'R. J.', colourfully described what this meant to many people: 'People who were sick and tired of the hopeless struggle to find work and the humiliation of the dole queues, longed for some excitement to relieve the monotony of everyday life. The sight of Mitchell's seaplanes thundering across the sky at breathtaking speeds raised a cheer from lips which had forgotten to smile. England might be in a depression, but in the world of aviation she still had something of which to be proud'.[20] On 12 September 1931, Flight Lieutenant J. N. Boothman flashed over the cheering crowds at 340.08 mph – with the throttle not even fully open – winning the Schneider Trophy outright for Britain. That afternoon, Flight Lieutenant G. H. Stainforth took up another S.6B in which he set a new world record: 379.05 mph.[21] The depressed nation was delighted, British aviation supreme, and Mitchell was deservedly made a Commander of the Most Excellent Order of the British Empire (CBE).

Although Schneider's original concept was that the first nation to win three consecutive times would keep the trophy – and thus bring an end to the famous air race – after Britain's win many people wanted the competition to continue with a new prize. According to Orange, Britain's 1931 win was, in fact, 'a hollow one because no rival machine got to the starting line', although conceding that Britain did win the trophy five times.[22] Dowding, however, disagreed with continuing the race: 'I was strongly opposed to this', he wrote, 'because the float-planes we had developed were perfectly useless for any military purpose. There was absolutely no value in them as a combat machine, and what value they did have was limited to flying from sheltered waters in light wind conditions. What I wanted to do was invite private tenders from two firms to cash in on the experience that had been gained in aircraft construction and engine progress so that we could order two of the fastest machines which it was possible to build with no restriction except landing speed, and that had to be on grass airfields.'[23] The far-sighted Dowding's proposal was agreed by the Air Ministry. Another important landmark in the Spitfire and Hurricane story had been reached.

3

Monoplanes and Machine-guns

When Dowding became Air Member for Supply and Research in 1930, and when Mitchell's S.6B won the Schneider Trophy in 1931, the Air Defence of Great Britain was entirely dependant upon biplanes, such as the Bristol Bulldog, Hawker Fury and Demon fighters.[1] These lightly armed fighters, however, were already being outpaced by new biplane bomber variants. For example, the Bulldog's top speed was 174 mph – but the Hawker Hart light bomber, introduced in 1929, was 10 mph faster. Bombers were also of an increasingly substantial construction. Stephen Bungay wrote of two problems arising, therefore: firstly, fighters looked unlikely to actually be able to intercept bombers because 'They could not even catch them', and secondly their existing twin rifle-calibre machine-guns provided insufficient firepower to 'knock them down'.[2] Dowding quickly realized that drastic advances were required to both airframes and aero-engines – particularly where fighters were concerned. The major improvement evident to him at that time was the monoplane. Experts, however, advised him that biplanes were superior – to which argument Dowding countered that if that was so, why had Mitchell chosen to develop a monoplane to win the Schneider Trophy?[3] The use of more metal parts in his designs was also noted by Dowding. Hitherto biplanes had largely been constructed from seasoned wood and fabric. Dowding feared that in the event of war, it would no longer be possible to import sufficient quantities of such timber, favouring, therefore, the elimination of as much wood in aircraft manufacture as possible.[4] From this point onwards, therefore, Mitchell's influence on the development of military aviation can clearly be seen.

Dowding's belief that the experience gained by designers during the Schneider Trophy races should be applied to military land-based aircraft led to the Air Ministry issuing Specification F.7/30 on 1 October 1931. The intention was for British aircraft designers to produce a new single-seat day and night-fighter intended to replace the Bristol Bulldog. The actual specification required was documented in detail by the Air Ministry's Directorate of Technical Development. The main requirements were:

1. Highest possible rate of climb.
2. Highest possible speed at 15,000 feet.
3. Fighting view.
4. Manoeuvrability.
5. Capability of ease and rapid production in quantity.
6. Ease of maintenance.

The machine had to be armed with four machine-guns, carry four twenty-pound bombs and powered by any British produced engine.[5] The Air Ministry required that the new fighter achieved a speed of at least 250 mph.[6] Over the next three years eight very different designs were submitted, five of which were biplanes. Among these was the Hawker P. V. 3, a direct development of the existing Hawker Fury, also designed by Sydney Camm, but with a Goshawk engine and four machine-guns grouped together in the nose. The Bristol Aircraft Company, however, produced an unusual monoplane with a pusher Mercury engine. The Westland tender – also a monoplane – was never seriously considered with a top speed of only 185 mph. Although not accepted for production, according to Francis K. Mason 'the most direct and significant end product of the F.7/30 venture was R. J. Mitchell's Goshawk-powered Supermarine Type 224 monoplane'. This, he wrote, 'formed an essential link between the successful Schneider Trophy racing seaplanes and the Spitfire'.[7] That may be so, but Gordon Mitchell described his father's Type 224 as 'a near disaster – with a maximum speed of only 230 mph, its performance in general fell short of what had been considered an "easy to achieve" specification'.[8] R. J. Mitchell himself was never happy with the Type 224, a low-winged monoplane completely constructed of metal – an innovation described by Alfred Price as 'a considerable novelty at that time'.[9] The aircraft's main failing, in fact, was that the Goshawk engine was prone to overheating and the overall performance was poor: with a top speed of 238 mph it took eight minutes to reach 15,000 feet. Gloster Aircraft won the competition with a radial engine biplane, the SS37, developed from the existing Gauntlet. The winning machine's top speed was 242 mph and reached 15,000 in six-and-a-half minutes.[10] This further delayed the RAF's entry into the monoplane age. Nonetheless, it was an unexpected turning point so far as fighter development was concerned, and as will now be explained.

Although the SS37 was the winning tender, it failed to enter production. The Air Ministry realised that its edge in performance was insufficient to warrant an order because it would doubtless soon be obsolete. An aircraft was required that had a considerably greater margin of superiority. Mitchell, it has been argued, had found Specification F.7/30 'too restrictive and insufficiently advanced in concept to produce an aircraft of the highest possible performance'.[11] The Air Ministry, however, wanted Supermarine to replace the problematic Goshawk with a Napier Dagger engine, but both Sir Robert McLean, Chairman of the Vickers (Aviation) Board which owned Supermarine, and Mitchell were convinced that the Type 224 could be developed no further. On 6 November 1934, the Air Ministry's proposal was therefore turned down. Sir Robert and his opposite number at Rolls-Royce, A. F. Sidgreaves, decided that their companies would be better advised to collaborate not on F.7/30 but on 'a real killer fighter'.[12] Sir Robert later wrote that 'The Air Ministry was informed of this decision, and were told that under no circumstances would any technical member of the Air Ministry be consulted or allowed to interfere with the designer'.[13] In November 1934, therefore, Mitchell was given permission to begin work on his Type 300 fighter. Concurrently Rolls-Royce continued improving its new PV XII engine – later called Merlin.

It is a little known fact the initial design and development work on both the Spitfire aircraft and Merlin engine began as a privately funded venture. The Air Ministry has been blamed for a lack of foresight regarding the new fighter's specification. This is not entirely justified. Sir Robert McLean made it formally quite clear that this was a private venture and that Air Ministry involvement was unwelcome. On that basis the Air Ministry was unable to do anything other than permit Vickers Armstrong (Aviation) and Rolls-Royce to privately fund their new project. It could perhaps be argued that had the Air Staff been properly familiar with the developments in single-seat and single-engine performance wrought by the Schneider Trophy, it would have issued an appropriate requirement from the outset in 1931. Clearly, however, the Air Staff were prepared to listen and learn. McLean's actions obviously represented a lack of confidence in the Air Staff's ability to write an appropriate specification. Just one month later, however, the Air Ministry – stimulated by news of the Type 300 and PV XII combination – commissioned Supermarine to produce an 'improved F.7/30' design.[14] From that point onwards, therefore, the venture was no longer privately funded. The reason that it was ever privately funded appears due to the attitude of Vickers Armstrong (Aviation) and Rolls-Royce – not any reluctance or antipathy on behalf of the Air Ministry, which was quick off the mark to recognise the potential of the new design and provide government funding. On 3 January 1935, the Supermarine Aviation Works sent the Air Ministry details of the new 'Experimental High Speed Single Seat Fighter'. The document confirmed that the Supermarine submission would 'conform to all the requirements stated in Specification F.7/30'. Furthermore, a tail wheel (as opposed to the traditional skid) was to be fitted and the four machine-guns wing-mounted to fire beyond the propeller arc. This was progress indeed.

In April 1935 the Air Ministry issued its 'Requirements for Single-Engine Single-Seater Day and Night Fighter (F.10/35)'. The main points were that the new fighter:

1. Had to be at least 40 mph faster than contemporary bombers at 15,000 feet.
2. 'Have a number of forward firing machine-guns that can produce the maximum hitting power possible in the shortest space of time available for one attack'. The Air Ministry 'considered that eight guns should be provided'.
3. Had to achieve 'the maximum possible and not less than 310 mph at 15,000 feet at maximum power with the highest speed possible between 5,000 and 15,000 feet'.
4. Have the best possible climbing performance to 20,000 feet, although this was considered of secondary importance to 'speed and hitting power'.
5. Be armed with at least six but preferably eight machine-guns, all forward firing and wing mounted outside the propeller arc. These were to be fired by 'electrical means'. In the event of six guns being used, 400 rounds per gun was necessary, 300 if eight were fitted.
6. Had to be 'a steady firing platform'.
7. Had to include the following 'special features' and equipment:
   a. Enclosed cockpit.
   b. Cockpit heating.
   c. Night flying equipment.
   d. Radio Telephony (R/T).
   e. Oxygen for two-and-a-half hours.

f.   Easily accessed and maintained guns.

g.   Retractable undercarriage and tail wheel.

h.   Wheel brakes.

Such an aircraft would indeed be a 'real killer fighter'. Interestingly, however, the Air Staff did not dictate that it must be a monoplane. This indicated that monoplanes were not yet considered supreme in the corridors of Whitehall – although thanks to both R. J. Mitchell and Sydney Camm that would soon change.

The requirement for eight machine-guns and situating these beyond the propeller arc was significant. Existing fighters' guns were nose-mounted and fired through the propeller arc via an interrupter gear. A study in 1932 suggested that more guns were required to destroy a modern bomber, and that interrupter gear should be dispensed with to both save weight and permit the guns to fire at their own rate. Eight machine-guns were decided upon because it was believed that a fast monoplane would provide its pilot with only one high speed attack – consequently as much lead had to be delivered in that limited time as possible. Dowding, however, knew that most pilots were poor shots, frequently opening fire at far too great a range. Moreover, tiny rifle calibre bullets were not always sufficient to bring down an enemy aircraft – even at close range.[15] The answer was exploding 20 mm cannon shells, but although such a cannon – the Hispano-Suiza – was available, it remained unreliable and experimental even by the forthcoming Battle of Britain. As will be explained, this would prove significant.

Nonetheless, with rearmament now underway at last and both Hawker and Supermarine working on new fighters, prospects for Britain's air defence were more optimistic now than at any time since 1918. It was just in time. Adolf Hitler and the Nazis came to power in Germany in 1933, the clouds of war thickening rapidly thereafter. Significantly, in 1934 the RAF's annual air exercise had been, according to Orange, 'a fiasco'.[16] Only two of the five bombers used in the mock air attack were successfully intercepted. Incredibly, the air defences at that time were only capable of intercepting a total of five raiders simultaneously. The new 'real killer fighter' was needed desperately – and in numbers.

4

The Hawker Hurricane

Whilst the 1934 air exercise highlighted the great deficiencies in Britain aerial defences, Winston Churchill was becoming increasingly concerned and vociferous regarding the threat posed by Nazi Germany. In November 1934 Churchill criticised the government's efforts in respect of air re-armament. This programme was intended purely to preserve parity with Germany.[1] In Churchill's view this was not enough. His information suggested that within a year the *Luftwaffe* would be equal to the RAF, and two years later would be twice as strong. The Prime Minister, Stanley Baldwin, rejected Churchill's assertions while confirming that his government would 'not accept any position of inferiority with regard to what air force may be raised in Germany in the future'.[2] The threat from across the Channel, however, was clearly growing and no longer being ignored. The 1934 air exercises indicated the importance of improving both the systems and aircraft involved. Work by British designers on new monoplane fighters was now of crucial importance.

According to Bungay, one designer had 'set the pace of military aircraft development in the early 1930s'[3]: Sydney Camm of Hawker. Two of Camm's designs were already in service with the RAF: the Hart light bomber and Fury fighter. The latter provided the RAF's first fighter with a speed over 200 mph, and, according to Richard Hough and Denis Richards, 'marked the fine flowering of the biplane, in-line engined, single-seat fighter, graceful, manoeuvrable, a delight to fly'.[4] But monoplanes were needed now. Having a greater wing surface area, biplanes develop more lift and so are highly manoeuvrable. The two wings, however, together with rigging and struts, reduce speed. It was speed that was important now, and so arguably the Fury represented the ultimate biplane fighter. Nothing could be done to significantly improve its performance. Camm knew this. He was also inspired by Mitchell's Schneider Trophy success, recognising that monoplanes represented the future. Inevitably, therefore, Camm responded by designing the 'Hawker Interceptor Monoplane'. This was just in time – as Francis K. Mason wrote, 'Britain's recognition of the monoplane's superiority over the biplane' was indeed 'belated'.[5]

A one-tenth scale model of Camm's proposed fighter was built in June 1934 and began wind tunnel tests. By August the model had withstood speeds of up to 350 mph. A proposal for the new machine, armed with eight machine-guns, was then put to the Air Ministry, which consequently issued Specification F.36/34. This required a top speed of 320 mph in level flight at 15,000 feet. By November Hawker's Experimental Shop was producing the jigs required to build the new fighter's fuselage. In the past Camm's fuselages were of a fabric-covered tubular metal framework. The Interceptor Monoplane was no different in that respect, although the undercarriage was retractable and the pilot's cockpit enclosed. The weight of eight Browning machine-guns also dictated that the wings not be covered in fabric, as was traditional, but with stressed metal. This would prove significant. By now the Rolls-Royce PV XII engine had been renamed 'Merlin' in the tradition of naming the company's aero-engines after birds of prey. The Merlin was to become the most famous engine of all time and Camm designed his fighter around it. On 21 February 1935 the Air Ministry received detailed performance calculations from Hawker, resulting in a contract being issued for the production of a prototype: K5083.[6]

On 6 November 1935 the company's chief test pilot, P. W. S. 'George' Bulman, complete with trilby and watched by an anxious Sydney Camm, made the Hawker Hurricane's first flight from Broooklands.[7] Pulled along by a comparatively basic Watts Z33 fixed-pitch, two-bladed wooden propeller, Camm's Hurricane revealed no major deficiency. After this historic flight, the Hawker team began the hard work of rigorously testing every aspect of their creation. Bulman soon initiated minor improvements, but after his flight on 7 February 1936 declared K5083 ready for evaluation by the RAF Aircraft & Armament Experimental Establishment (A&AEE) at Martlesham Heath. These brief trials largely concerned performance and handling. A maximum speed of 315 mph was recorded at 16,200 feet at 2,960 rpm and six pounds boost. The silver fighter soared from the runway to 15,000 feet in just 5.7 minutes. The pilots concerned were generally satisfied with K5083, other than reporting heavy aileron and rudder controls at high speed. The enclosed cockpit was popular and the retractable undercarriage commended.[8] Having passed these initial service trials, Camm's proto-type returned to Brooklands for further development.

On 3 June 1936, the Air Ministry issued Contract 527112/36 for 600 aircraft – later that month officially approving the name 'Hurricane'. As Mason wrote, 'This was the largest production order ever placed at a single time for a military aircraft in Britain during peacetime and undoubtedly reflected the growing anxiety now being felt at Air Ministry for the re-equipment and expansion of the RAF'.[9] It was just in the nick of time, as future events would confirm. In November 1937, 111 Squadron at Northolt received the first production Hurricane, L1547.[10] By Christmas the squadron boasted four of the new monoplanes. One by one the squadron's Gloster Gauntlet biplanes were replaced and under the command of Squadron Leader John Gillan 111's pilots converted to the Hurricane. They found the Hurricane extremely fast, being nearly 100 mph faster than the Gauntlet. The monoplane increased visibility enormously without compromising manoeuvrability. In sum, the Hurricane was a revelation. Nonetheless, the conversion was sadly not without incident: during the first few weeks there were several accidents, one of them fatal.

On 14 January 1938, by which time 111 Squadron had been equipped with the Hurricane for four weeks, Gillan reported comprehensively on the new fighter's 'operational characteristics':

FLYING CHARACTERISTICS
(i) The Hurricane is completely manoeuvrable throughout its whole range, though slow at speeds between 65 mph and 200 mph controls feel a bit slack.

Owing to its weight and speed, some time is taken in coming out of a dive and at high speed the turning circle is large.

On the ground the Hurricane is as manoeuvrable as is possible and has the additional advantage of feeling secure across wind or a strong wind due to its high wing loading.

(ii) Cross-wind landings are particularly easy in the Hurricane. Simplicity in cross-wind landings is a characteristic of aircraft with a high wing loading.

(iii)

(a) Taxying with the seat full up and the hood back is exceptionally good all round, far better in front and above than the fighter aircraft before in the service, and just as good in all other directions.

(b) Taking-off. The view is considerably better than the Gauntlet and better than the Demon, both individually and in formation.

(c) Landing. The view is considerably better than the Gauntlet and better than the Demon both individually and in formation.

(d) Flying in Formation. The view is better than the Gauntlet or Demon with the hood open or closed, though at present no experience is available of flying in formation, in bad rain or damp cloud when it is thought the hood may fog or ice up.

(e) The view is better than the Gauntlet or Demon.

(iv) Formation flying at height at speeds in excess of 200 mph is very simple. It is thought the reason being that air resistance at this speed is considerable and that the power used by the engine at this speed the pilot can slow his aeroplane up or accelerate it very quickly indeed.

At slow speeds in the neighbourhood of 100 mph when only a small proportion of the engine power is in use and the resistance to the air of this clean aeroplane is comparatively small, some difficulty is found in decelerating the aircraft, though no difficulty is found in accelerating.

Landing in formation is similar to landing in formation in any other type of aircraft.

Taking off in formation is simple, but immediately after leaving the ground when pilots retract their undercarriages and flaps aircraft cannot keep good formation as undercarriage and flaps retract at different speeds in each aircraft. It is recommended, therefore, that take-off should be done individually, in succession.

(v) The Hurricane is a simple aircraft to fly at night. There is no glare in the cockpit, either open or closed, from the cockpit lamps or luminous instruments.

The steady steep glide at slow speed, which is characteristic of this type, makes landing extremely simple.

The take-off run being longer than has been experienced in the past, it is recommended that the landing light should be at least 600 yards away from the beginning of the run, instead of the normal 250 yards on ordinary flare paths.

(vi) The minimum size of aerodrome from which the Hurricane can be operated in still air in England must depend on obstructions surrounding the aerodrome. With good approaches and inexperienced pilots the Hurricane could be operated from an aerodrome 800 x 800 yards and with experience could probably be reduced to 600 yards.

(vii) The Hurricane without its engine running has a very steep glide and to the pilot inexperienced on this type judging the flattening may be difficult. Therefore it is recommended for initial training that pilots should come in with their engines running. After they have become accustomed to an aeroplane of high wing loading and steep glide they should be able to land efficiently off the glide in the Hurricane as in any other aircraft. It follows that landing with an engine lengthens the period of holding off, making landing easier, and in the event of flattening out too high gives the pilot time to stop the aeroplane falling heavily on the ground as speed falls off.

(viii) The cockpit is large and comfortable and there is room for the largest man inside with the hood shut and by using the adaptable seat the smallest man can see everything comfortably.

It is thought that from an operational point of view that the system of having a selector box and a lever which must be operated to move either the undercarriage or the flaps is unsatisfactory and furthermore it occupies for a period of perhaps half a minute the right hand of the pilot whilst he flies with his left and neglects the throttle. Should it be essential to take-off in formation or as in conditions of bad visibility the difficulties of the system are obvious, and it is recommended that two simple controls, one which moves the flaps to full up and full down position, and the other which would move the undercarriage from full down to full up and vice versa could well be substituted.

All other controls are easily accessible and efficient and the instrument layout is good and not complicated.

OPERATIONAL CHARACTERISTICS

With more experience on this type of aeroplane further figures will be submitted, but as far as can be seen at present the indicated airspeed at 2,000 feet is 270 mph, at 10,000 feet indicated airspeed 260 mph and at 15,000 feet indicated airspeed 240 mph.

The petrol consumption at 15,000 feet and economical cruising speed of 160 mph indicated correcting to 200 mph is 25.08 gallons per hour. At + 2½ lbs boost is the maximum permissible cruising speed-petrol consumption approaches 60 gallons per hour.

At 2,000 feet an indicated air speed of 200 mph petrol consumption is 30 gallons per hour at an indicated boost of +1lb.

The remaining operational characteristics have yet to be investigated, but as yet the windscreen has shown no sign of oiling up and the cockpit is weather-proof so far as can be seen at present.[11]

It was a good start, Gillan's report revealing no major problems.

On 10 February 1938 Gillan took off from Northolt, bound for Turnhouse near Edinburgh. Having experienced high winds while outward bound, after refuelling the pilot decided to use those 80 mph winds to his advantage and return south at maximum speed. He took off shortly after 5 p.m. and climbed to 17,000 feet – the altitude most favourable to the performance of his machine. Forty-eight minutes later he landed at Northolt – having covered 327 miles with an average ground speed of 408.75 mph [12]. The feat was publicised, it being conveniently forgotten that a considerable downwind had significantly assisted Gillan achieve his colossal speed. Nonetheless, in Air Force circles Gillan was forever after known as 'Downwind'.[13] On 3 May 1938 the Hurricane was displayed to a delighted public for the first time at the Hendon Air Pageant. *The Times* subsequently described the aircraft as 'the fastest 'plane in service anywhere in the world … outstanding in its class in respect of duration as well as speed'.[14] This was an impressive reaction, and one with which Camm and Hawker's were no doubt well pleased.

Understandably rearmament in Britain accelerated after the Munich crisis over Czechoslovakia in September 1938. On 5 October, Churchill told the House of Commons that, 'We are in the presence of a disaster of the first magnitude. And do not suppose that this is the end. It is only the beginning of the reckoning'.[15] Top priority was at last given to producing defensive fighters. Peter Townsend had flown Hawker Fury biplanes with 43 Squadron at Tangmere; in November 1939 he found himself converting to the new Hurricane:

> By mid-December we had our full initial equipment of sixteen aircraft. The Fury had been a delightful play-thing; the Hurricane was a thoroughly war-like machine, rock solid as a platform for its eight Browning machine-guns, highly manoeuvrable despite its large proportions and with an excellent view from the cockpit… At first the Hurricane earned a bad reputation. The change from the light and agile Fury caught some pilots unaware. The Hurricane was far less tolerant of faulty handling, and a mistake at low altitude could be fatal. One day a sergeant pilot glided back to Tangmere with a faulty engine. We watched him as with plenty of height he turned in – too slowly – to land. The Hurricane fell out of his hands and before our eyes he dived headlong into the ground. The unfortunate pilot died as the ambulance arrived.[16]

Nonetheless, conversion from biplane to the new monoplane continued apace. Townsend wrote that, 'And so we came to know ourselves and our Hurricanes better. There grew in us a trust and an affection for them and their splendid Merlin engines, thoroughbreds and stayers which changed our fearful doubts of the Munich period into the certainty that it would beat all comers'.[17] Peter Brothers was another experienced pre-war fighter pilot who found himself flying Hurricanes in 1938:

> We were shown over the aircraft. We then familiarised ourselves with the controls and instruments – no Pilot's Notes were available at that time! Then it was start-up and taxi over the grass to the boundary fence and take off. These Mk I Hurricanes had a fixed pitch two-bladed propeller which gave rapid acceleration. It was the first type I had ever flown with a retractable undercart and closed canopy – both great improvements. On my first flight I performed a few aerobatics and was impressed by the aircraft's immediate and smooth response. I knew straightaway that going to war in this machine was preferable to doing so in a biplane which – as the record of the Polish Air Force in 1939 would show – would have been suicidal.[18]

The fixed-pitch propeller, however, required improvement. This did not just concern the Hurricane but applied to every service aircraft. German aircraft designers had recognised the benefits of the variable-pitch propeller the previous year. The pilot had a control with which he could change the pitch – or angle that the blade bit into the air – while in flight.

The effect was similar, in fact, to changing gear in a car and therefore provided more power for certain situations – including take-off and combat. In August 1938 trials began on the de Havilland two-pitch propeller. This was constructed of duralumin and had three blades. Fitted with the new variable pitch airscrew, a marked improvement was recorded in tests on Hurricane L1582. Fine pitch, which is to say 30.5°, was used for take-off, coarse pitch, 42.5°, in flight. Even given a weight increase of 300 lbs, L1582 reduced the time climbing to rated altitude by one minute. From January 1939 onwards, therefore, production Hurricanes were fitted with the new two-pitch propeller.[19] This was, however, only a half-way house. Rotol Ltd had been developing a constant-speed (CS) propeller. Also three-bladed and made of duralumin, the pilot could rotate the blades through 360° and therefore fly in the optimum pitch for any given circumstance. On 24 January 1939, Hurricane L1606, fitted with the experimental CS propeller, achieved 328 mph – 13 mph faster than Bulman's maiden flight in K5083 – and took 6.2 minutes to reach 15,000 feet.[20] These improvements would soon be desperately needed on all operational RAF fighters.

Speed was all-important and the most notable difference for pilots converting to the new fighter. Douglas Grice converted from the Gloster Gauntlet biplane to Hurricanes with Peter Brothers on 32 Squadron: 'It meant flying an aircraft which at cruising speed did about 240 mph – about 100 mph faster than you were used to flying. The flaps did not worry me but what was rather worrying was the Merlin engine. It was so powerful that it took a bit of getting used to … What a thrill to be flying so fast. There were no vices with the Hurricane at all. And it was so rugged. You could virtually fly it into the ground and it would just bounce up and land by itself.'[21]

In 1938 it became known that German fighters were armed not just with machine-guns but also with the heavier 20 mm cannon. This led to the fitting of more armour plate to British fighters, protecting the pilot and fuel-tank. These improvements included a thick armoured glass windscreen. Of course this increased weight decreased performance slightly, but such modifications were essential. Although metal stressed-skin wings for the Hurricane had been mooted back in 1935, they did not become a reality until 1940. The process to address this deficiency began in April 1939. Existing Hurricanes in service were slowly fitted with new metal wings, but the factories were still producing fabric-covered wings until March 1940.[22] Eventually all Hurricanes enjoyed the benefits of metal wings, bringing the Hurricane in line with both the Supermarine Spitfire and Me 109 – of which much more later. It has often been argued that because the Hurricane relied upon traditional construction techniques with which the Hawker workforce was familiar, it was easy to produce and henceforth why the Air Ministry initially ordered Camm's fighter in larger numbers than the Spitfire. That may be so, but the lack of a metal-covered wing was a design deficiency. Moreover, the reason that it took so long to rectify was because construction of all-metal wings required the workforce to learn new construction techniques. This slowed production, in fact. Fortunately by the time shooting began, all operational Hurricanes enjoyed the benefits of metal-skinned wings. This is an early indication, however, that the Hurricane was technically inferior to the other two principal single-engine single-seat fighters of the day.

By the outbreak of war on 3 September 1939, though, 400 Hurricanes had been delivered to the RAF, equipping eighteen fighter squadrons.[23] At the time of Munich, just a year before, Fighter Command mustered a total of 759 fighters – only ninety-three of which were Hurricanes.[24] Although the RAF received its first production Spitfire one month before Munich, the first Spitfire squadron would not be fully operational for another three months. Had Britain gone to war over Czechoslovakia in 1938, therefore, the outcome would have been disastrous. The British Prime Minister of the day, Neville Chamberlain, is often condemned by history for his policy of appeasing Hitler during the late 1930s. But had Chamberlain not bought time for Britain to prepare for war, the country's weak aerial defences of 1938 would have been exposed. Indeed, as Calder wrote, 'the day of the bombers, Armageddon, was palpably at hand'.[25] One year later – largely thanks to the Hawker Hurricane – the situation was rapidly changing – albeit at the eleventh hour.

5

The Supermarine Spitfire

After the experience of producing the Type 224, with which Mitchell was dissatisfied, Supermarine was soon hard at work producing the new Type 300 fighter to meet Air Ministry Specification F.37/34. Mitchell's Type 224 failure is the principal reason that the Hurricane flew before the Spitfire and was therefore available in larger numbers by the summer of 1940. Had there been no Type 224 but a Type 300 from the outset, things would have been very different. Nonetheless the experience gained in producing the Type 224 was useful to Mitchell when he retired to his drawing board to design an infinitely better aircraft. Hitherto, it must be remembered, unlike Hawker's Sydney Camm, Mitchell had no previous experience creating fighter aircraft. Excepting the Schneider Trophy winning machines, his work had largely revolved around the production of biplane flying boats. Now Supermarine's Chief Designer faced the greatest challenge of his career. Time, he knew, was running out for two reasons. Firstly the threat from a revitalised and jingoistic Nazi Germany was clear. Secondly Mitchell was dying. In August 1933, while working on the Type 224, his doctors diagnosed rectal cancer. An operation saved him but left a permanent legacy: a colostomy. Advised that the cancer could well return – and that should it do so nothing could save him – Mitchell briefly convalesced in Bournemouth with his wife and nurse before returning to work. As Gordon Mitchell wrote, 'He could not and would not accept the life of a semi-invalid or think of retiring for the rest of what years he might have left'.[1]

Mitchell returned to work and even began learning to fly himself. Throughout 1935, never knowing whether fate would grant him sufficient time to complete the project, he worked on the Type 300. Mitchell did not, of course, create the Spitfire single-handedly. His work was supported by one of the best and most experienced teams of aeronautical engineers in the world, including the likes of Supermarine's Chief Draughtsman Joe Smith and aerodynamicist Alan Clifton. The Air Ministry, RAF A&AEE and the Royal Aircraft Establishment (RAE) at Farnborough were also involved. Mitchell was, though, the Chief Designer from whose genius the Spitfire was born. Supermarine's new fighter was immediately striking with an elliptical wing and, like the Hurricane, had retractable undercarriage and a sliding cockpit hood. Another similarity was that the Spitfire – so-called after Sir Robert McLean's nickname for his daughter – was also powered by the Rolls-Royce Merlin engine. By March 1936 the new fighter was ready to fly. The prototype – K5054 – was transported by road to Eastleigh airfield near Southampton and reassembled. The historic flight was made on 5 March 1936 by the Vickers Chief Test Pilot, Captain Joseph 'Mutt'

Summers.[2] The Assistant Test Pilot, Jeffrey Quill, was present and recalled that '"Mutt" did not retract the undercarriage for the first flight on, I believe, Mitchell's instructions. The take-off run was short because the aircraft was fitted with a special fine pitch propeller specifically for the first flight. "Mutt" took the aeroplane up to about 3,000 feet, checked the low speed handling and then came straight back to land'.[3] After this successful first flight of some twenty minutes, Summers famously said 'I don't want anything touched'.[4] This remark has passed into legend. 'Some of those present', wrote Quill, 'misunderstood his meaning and thought that he had said that the aircraft was absolutely right as it then stood. As I know well that was not the case. "Mutt" simply meant that he had found no major snag, the thing was functioning all right as a piece of machinery and he didn't want the controls or anything else altered before the next flight … nevertheless everyone was elated by his comment'.[5] So it was that Mitchell's Spitfire flew at last.

On 3 June 1936 the Air Ministry ordered 310 Spitfires at a cost of £4,500 each (excluding engine, guns, instruments and radios).[6] It was expected that the first production aircraft would be delivered in October 1937, but it soon became apparent that Supermarine – a small company of 500 employees – lacked the capacity to fulfil this large order. By the time those Spitfires were ready, the individual cost had risen to £6,033.[7] In 1937 a further order was placed for another 200 Spitfires. Jeffrey Quill wrote that the cause of problems in mass producing the Spitfire 'lay in the years of neglect of the aircraft industry by successive governments up to 1936. At the last possible moment they initiated the re-armament programme and expected an industry starved of orders since 1919 suddenly to increase production capacity by four or five times, and change over to building far more complex types of aircraft, all within a space of just two or three years. Of course there were going to be enormous problems and with the best will in the world mistakes were going to be made. It was all very well for the Air Ministry to say to Supermarine "What you can't do yourselves you must sub-contract". But where were the sub-contractors to be found with the necessary experience, on the fringes of an industry which hitherto had hardly sufficient orders to keep itself alive'.[8] These observations put to perspective the old accusations that the Spitfire, being technically advanced, required the workforce to learn new production techniques and hence the delay in delivery to the RAF. More accurately the problem lay in a simple lack of resources. Nonetheless, as Richard Overy commented, 'a Spitfire did take two and a half times the man hours that it took to produce a Hurricane fighter'.[9] The first Spitfire, K9788, was eventually delivered to the RAF on 19 July 1938.

On 4 August Jeffrey Quill delivered the first aircraft, K9789, to 19 Squadron at Duxford – nearly a year later than was originally anticipated. By then the Spitfire had been extensively tested with various improvements made. In September 1936, for example, service test pilots at the RAF A&AEE put K5054 through its paces, reporting in detail on every aspect of the new fighter. It was recorded that 'Loops, half rolls off loops, slow rolls and stall turns have been done. The aeroplane is very easy and pleasant to handle in all aerobatics'.[10] In sum the report concluded that:

> The aeroplane is simple and easy to fly and has no vices. All controls are entirely satisfactory for this type and no modification to them is required, except that the elevator control might be improved by reducing the gear ratio between the control column and elevator. The

controls are well harmonised and appear to give an excellent compromise between manoeuvrability and steadiness for shooting. Take-off and landing are straightforward and easy.

The aeroplane has a rather flat glide, even when the undercarriage and flaps are down and has a considerable float if the approach is made a little too fast. This defect could be remedied by fitting higher drag flaps.

In general the handling of this aeroplane is such that it could be flown without risk by the average fully trained fighter pilot, but there can be no doubt that it would be improved by having flaps giving a higher drag.[11]

Tragically Mitchell did not live to see the Spitfire taken on charge by the RAF: the cancer returned and he died, aged 42, on 11 June 1937. Joe Smith succeeded Mitchell as Supermarine's Chief Designer and was subsequently responsible for the Spitfire's development for many years to come. *The Aeroplane* of 12 April 1940 rather summed things up:

True, it all seems simple enough, now that it is done, but it needed the genius of Mitchell to visualise without precise knowledge what had to be done, to reach out into the unknown for something nearer perfection than any other man had been able to reach.[12]

The Spitfire was thus described in *The Aeroplane*:

From the mediocrity of the F.7/30 came the brilliance of the Spitfire, a much smaller aeroplane with greater power … Structurally the Spitfire is a straightforward stressed-skin design. The elliptical cantilever low wing, which tapers in thickness, is built up on a single spar with tubular flanges and a plate web. Forward of the spar the wing is covered with a heavy-gauge light aluminium sheet which forms the torsion box with the spar. Aft of the spar the covering is of thinner gauge sheet with light-alloy girder ribs. The wing tips are detachable for ease of maintenance and repair. Split flaps are between the ailerons and the fuselage.

The fuselage is an all-metal monocoque, built on four longerons with transverse frames and a flush-riveted light-alloy skin. The front frame forms the fireproof bulkhead and is built as an integral part with the centre portion of the main wing spar. To help in maintenance the tail portion of the fuselage with fin and tailplane is detachable.

The tail unit is of the cantilever monoplane type. The fin is integral with the rear fuselage. The tailplane is of metal with smooth metal covering. The elevator and rudders have light alloy frames and fabric covering. There are trimming tabs on elevator and rudder.

The undercarriage is fully retractable outwards into the under-surface of the wings. There are two Vickers cantilever oleo-pneumatic shock absorber legs which are retracted hydraulically. An emergency hand system is fitted to lower the wheels should the hydraulic system be damaged.

The rather uneven spacing of the guns is explained by the fact that the Spitfire was originally designed for only four guns, and not until it was in an advanced stage were eight guns decided upon. If it had not been for this then the installation would have been neater.

Probably the Spitfire could never have come to life had it not been for the relative failure of the F.7/30. For the Spitfire's thin wing we thank the F.7/30's thick wing. For the Spitfire's smoothness, the F.7/30's corrugations and roughness. For the Spitfire's sweet lines the F.7/30's angularities. For the Spitfire's simple basic structure, the F.7/30's complex structure of tubes and stressed skin.[13]

The Spitfire was undoubtedly stunning in appearance, akin to a flying bullet. Its elliptical wings provided a unique signature, and the Spitfire soon excited the general public as its inspirational shape and sound was seen and heard in British skies. According to Gordon Mitchell, however, his father 'was heard to say on a number of occasions that "A Spitfire without a pilot was a lump of metal", which was meant to show the high regard and respect he had for the pilots whose job it was to fly his "lump of metal"'. The first service pilots to fly Mitchell's 'lump of metal' were those of 19 Squadron, commanded by Squadron Leader Henry Cozens and based at Duxford. Amongst them was Flight Sergeant George Unwin:

Before the Spitfire arrived we flew Gloster Gauntlet biplanes, which were good so far as biplanes went. But of course the Spitfire was in a completely different league. We were naturally very proud to have been chosen to be the RAF's first Spitfire squadron and it was our job to learn to fly it operationally and iron out any teething troubles along the way. There were a few accidents. Flight Lieutenant Clouston and Pilot Officer Ball collided, but neither was hurt. Clouston forced-landed on Newmarket racecourse, causing quite a stir! On 9 March 1939 I had to make a forced-landing at Sudbury in Essex due to a broken coolant pipe, which caused the engine to partially seize up. I decided to land on a large playing field and was doing fine with undercarriage down until the schoolchildren who were playing on the various pitches saw me descending - I was apparently on fire and trailing smoke. They ran towards me and on to the path I had selected for a landing. I was then at less than 100 feet and decided to stuff the Spitfire into the thick hawthorn hedge in front of me. The impact broke my straps and I gashed my right eyebrow on the windscreen but was otherwise unhurt. For this I received an Air Officer Commanding's Commendation. It was the first of many an exciting adventure flying Spitfires – the speed and power after our old Gauntlets was quite something to behold, and the aircraft's aerobatic ability was excellent. This was the fighter that we wanted to go to war in.[14]

There was a gulf of difference in performance between the biplanes that RAF fighter pilots were used to flying at this time and the new, much faster, monoplanes. One technical difference that caused problems was when the original fixed pitch propeller was changed to the two-pitch airscrew. Pilot Officer Michael Lyne flew Spitfires with 19 Squadron during early 1940 and remembered that:

By March the weather was better but we had Flying Officer Douglas Bader to cope with. He had, of course, lost both legs in a flying accident before the war, had overcome this disability and argued his way back into the service. He was having a hard time coming to grips with flying the Spitfire, especially in cloud. More than once my friend Watson and

I, lent to him as a formation by the CO, emerged from cloud faithfully following Bader in a steep diving turn! On one occasion Douglas forgot to put the airscrew in fine pitch for take-off, went off downwind on the shortest run at Horsham and cart-wheeled across the main road and into a ploughed field! Watson and I stuck to him until late on before pulling away on emergency power. I remember just clearing the hedge and seeing clods of earth flying high overhead from my leader's Spitfire. Bader broke a pair of artificial legs and had to send away for another pair! [15]

The initial production Spitfires were not fitted with automatically retracting undercarriage. Retraction was effected via the pilot pumping a lever by hand. The tight confines of the aircraft's cockpit, however, led to many a case of 'Spitfire knuckle'. This advancement also caused Flying Officer Bader problems. Pilot Officer Frank Brinsden:

In his book *Fight for the Sky*, Douglas Bader wrote regarding his first Spitfire flight that a "young pilot officer with little experience, showed me the knobs. He omitted to tell me one important thing about the undercarriage operation which embarrassed me in due course, fortunately without damage". I feel free to elaborate on this comment as he raised the matter and I was there. Any "young pilot officer with little experience" on 19 Squadron assigned to brief Douglas Bader would actually have been flying Spitfires since October 1938. By early February 1940, when Bader came on the scene, that pilot officer would have been qualified to fly operationally by both day and night. Is such a pilot officer therefore likely to have omitted from the briefing the rather important matter of raising the undercarriage? In any case the crew room had an ample supply of Pilot's Handling Notes and anyone who embarked upon his first solo in such a (for that time) radical aircraft without fully understanding its controls was a complete BF! It must be remembered that the biplanes with which Bader had previously been familiar had a fixed undercarriage. Although he had flown a handful of hours in a Hurricane, retractable undercarts remained relatively new to him. [16]

Biplanes had changed little over the years, with fixed undercarriage, fixed pitch propellers and open cockpits. These technical advancements – common to both the Hurricane and Spitfire – would undoubtedly lead to problems during the conversion process for pilots hitherto used to biplane flight. Douglas Bader was a gifted pilot, particularly aerobatics, and with practice mastered the Spitfire as he already had the Hurricane. It is worth quoting here a particular recollection of Wing Commander A. B. 'Woody' Woodhall, Duxford's Station Commander in 1940:

One day Douglas flew over from the Central Flying School in a Hurricane. I was delighted and amazed to see him, as I had not done so since his crash. He was in terrific form, and as it happened the AOC also came to visit us. I introduced Douglas to him and over lunch Douglas used all his charm to persuade Air Vice-Marshal Leigh-Mallory to take him into one of his operational squadrons. After lunch, with the AOC watching, Douglas put on a most finished display of aerobatics. [17]

Of the Hurricane, Bader wrote that it 'was a thoroughbred and looked like it ... it was immensely strong: a pilot had no need to fear the danger of pulling the wings off, no matter how desperate the situation became. When I first flew the Hurricane in June 1940 I was agreeably surprised at the compact feel of the aeroplane. It had seemed big on the ground ... but in the air felt nothing of the sort. You could see out of it better and the controls were perfectly harmonised. Like all pilots who flew and fought in the Hurricane I grew to love it'.[18]

The Spitfire Bader described simply as 'fabulous ... once in the air you felt in the first few minutes that here was the aeroplane *par excellence*. The controls were light, positive and synchronised: in fact, the aeroplane of one's dreams. It was stable; it flew hands and feet off; yet you could move it quickly and effortlessly into any altitude. You brought it in to land at 75 mph and touched down at 60-65 mph. Its maximum speed was 367 mph. You thus had a wide speed range which has not been equalled before or since'.[19]

By the time of Douglas Bader's return to the service, pre-operational training was conducted on the two-seater, single-engined Miles Master monoplane. This had a top speed of some 260 mph and retractable undercarriage. The introduction of both this type and the similar North American Harvard trainer helped train a whole new generation of RAF fighter pilots to fly monoplanes. They would only fly biplanes, such as the Tiger Moth, in elementary training. Monoplanes were their norm, therefore. To these young men the new Hurricanes and Spitfires represented their modern age. Many a young fledgling fighter pilot fell under the spell of Bader's 'fabulous' Spitfire – amongst them Pilot Officer H. R. 'Dizzy' Allen, who joined 66 Squadron at Duxford in April 1940:

> I didn't know where Duxford was and nor was I aware of what aircraft 66 Squadron had – they could have had Hurricanes, which did not appeal to me in any way. On the other hand they might have Spitfires, which appealed to me *very* much. I had seen the Spitfire in flight, had seen many photographs of it, to me it was the very peak of perfection (and after due experience proved to me that it was indeed perfection). When I arrived at Duxford's hangars I could see nothing but Spitfires littering the airfield – not a Hurricane in sight. Wherever Heaven is, St Peter opened the doors when I arrived at Duxford! [20]

A month later 66 Squadron was based at Coltishall, where eighteen year old Bob Morris joined the unit as an engine fitter: 'My first glimpse of 66 Squadron was from the bus as it travelled along the airfield for a short distance. What an absolute thrill to see *Spitfires*! Here was a young man's dream!' [21]

Already the inspirational Spitfire was occupying a unique place in the minds of those who had seen or read of it. Amongst the new generation of RAF fighter pilots being introduced to the Spitfire was Pilot Officer Richard Hillary. An Oxford undergraduate and former member of the University Air Squadron there, after advanced training on the Master and Harvard he first flew a Spitfire during operational training at Aston Down, near Stroud in Gloucestershire, in June 1940:

And we learned, finally, to fly the Spitfire … Kilmartin, a slight dark-haired Irishman in charge of our Flight said "Get your parachute and climb in. I'll just show you the cockpit before you go off"… "Don't worry; you'll be surprised how easy she is to handle."

I hoped so.

The Spitfires stood in two lines outside "A" Flight's Pilots' Room. The dull grey-brown of the camouflage could not conceal the clear-cut beauty, the wicked simplicity of their lines … I noticed how small my field of vision was. Kilmartin swung himself on to a wing and started to run through the instruments. I was conscious of his voice, but heard nothing of what he said. I was to fly a Spitfire. It was what I had most wanted through all the long dreary months of training. If I could fly a Spitfire, it would be worth it. Well, I was about to achieve my ambition and I felt nothing. I was numb, neither exhilarated nor scared.

I ran quickly through my cockpit drill, swung the nose into wind, and took off. I had been flying automatically for several minutes before it dawned on me that I was actually in the air, undercarriage retracted and half-way round the circuit without incident. I turned into wind and hauled up my seat, at the same time pushing back the hood. I came in low, cut the engine just over the boundary hedge, and floated down on all three points. I took off again. Three more times I came round for a perfect landing. It was too easy. I waited across wind for a minute and watched with satisfaction several machines bounce badly as they came in. Then I taxied rapidly back to the hangars and climbed out nonchalantly. Noel, who had not yet soloed, met me.

"How was it?" he said.

I made a circle of approval with my thumb and forefinger. "Money for old rope", I said. I didn't make another good landing for a week.[22]

Another young man filled with promise who first flew the Spitfire that fateful year was Pilot Officer David Crook of 609 Squadron. Afterwards he wrote of being 'almost light-headed with exhilaration when I landed at the end of an hour's flight, and felt that I could ask nothing more of life. Actually once you have done a few hours flying in a Spitfire and become accustomed to the great power and speed, then it is an extraordinarily easy machine to fly and is absolutely marvellous for aerobatics. Practically everybody who has flown the Spitfire thinks it is the most marvellous aircraft ever built, and I am no exception to the general rule. I grew to like it more than any other aircraft I had flown. It is so small and compact and neat, yet possessed of devastating fire power'.[23] Like Crook, Hillary subsequently practised aerobatics in the Spitfire, a process that filled him with a 'sudden exhilarating confidence'. He knew then that he could 'fly a Spitfire … in any position I was its master'. Ominously, however, Hillary wrote that 'It remained to be seen if I could fight in one'.[24]

Although late in the day, the superiority of the monoplane had at last been recognised. The RAF now had not one but two fast modern interceptors – which, in spite of production difficulties, were quickly replacing obsolete biplanes on the front line. This salvation was due to various factors, not least the technical advances achieved by Mitchell in the Schneider Trophy contest, which both he and Hawker's Sydney Camm subsequently applied to the design of fighters. The Camm's Hurricane was good and available in greater numbers than the Spitfire. But Mitchell's fighter was better – which, as will be proven, was fortunate indeed.

6

The System of Air Defence

Given the overwhelming emphasis on bombing between the wars, it is perhaps little short of miraculous that Britain developed effective fighter defence at all. It must be understood, though, why the bomber had been seen as all conquering. At the time Baldwin infamously said that 'the bomber will always get through', as Overy identified 'the disparity in performance between fighter and bomber aircraft was still so low that the prospect of a successful fighter defence seemed correspondingly unlikely'.[1] The new monoplane fighters, however, were so superior in performance to their bomber counterparts that everything changed. The fighters were also comparatively heavily armed. Moreover, the System of Air Defence designed to place them in the best possible tactical position to engage the enemy enjoyed a great advantage: the ability to monitor enemy attacks as they built up and approached the British coastline. This was made possible through a new science known as Radio Direction Finding (RDF) – more commonly known as radar – which helped predict both route and target. The advent of Hurricanes and Spitfires and the creation of a sound defensive structure incorporating the very latest scientific advances owed most to one man: Air Chief Marshal Sir Hugh Dowding.

When Britain belatedly began rearming in 1935, air defence was co-ordinated by the Air Defence of Great Britain (ADGB). In 1936 it was decided to divide this single command into two, thus creating Fighter and Bomber Commands.[2] Thus Fighter Command came into being on 6 July 1936 with its headquarters at Bentley Priory, to the north of London. On 14 July, the first Commander-in-Chief was appointed: Dowding. The re-organisation had a distinct advantage, as Dean wrote: 'the freedom to press ahead with sophisticated techniques of air defence, an opportunity of which everyone from Dowding downwards took full advantage'.[3] According to Malcolm Smith, 'Dowding's recent experience as the man responsible for research and development at the Air Ministry clearly fitted him to oversee the major developments of the next few years'.[4] Dowding had already been involved in both the commissioning and development of the new fighters and radar. He therefore perfectly appreciated the strengths and limitations of these inventions – and how best, therefore, to use them. Immediately Dowding set about ensuring that his new Command received information enabling his fighters to intercept enemy bombers before the raiders reached their targets. As Orange wrote, 'Unlike many senior officers, he was keenly interested in air defence. He had always resisted Trenchard's obsession with offence and argued that "security of the base must come first"'.[5]

In 1937, Dowding found a powerful political ally in Sir Thomas Inskip, the Minister for the Co-ordination of Defence, who asked him to state how many squadrons were required to defend Britain. A committee, chaired by Dowding, decided upon forty-five. It was not until a year later, though, that priority was at last given to the production of fighters. Like Dowding, Inskip believed that the RAF's priority was not the deliverance of a 'knock-out' blow, but to defend Britain from such an attack, permitting the build-up of resources necessary to counter-attack.[6] This made the RAF, in fact, the only air service to place such confidence in the fighter force.[7] Those fighters Dowding coveted, and ensured that his Hurricanes and Spitfires received all the latest technology: armoured glass windscreens, armour plate to protect the pilot, first the two-pitch then CS airscrews, self-sealing fuel tanks and Identification Friend or Foe (IFF), which prevented Controllers from mistaking friendly for enemy fighters. Many pilots would later have occasion to thank their technically minded and aware Commander-in-Chief for these sound improvements. Exactly how the new fighters would be used once war broke out, however, was still guesswork. As Overy argued, 'There was so little experience to draw on about the kind of air war most powers expected to fight ... As powers became more aware of what potential air enemies were preparing to do the initial guesswork was often modified or abandoned'.[8] Dowding knew exactly where he stood on the issue of an appropriate doctrine, however:

> The best defence of the country is fear of the fighter. If we were strong in fighters we should probably never be attacked in force. If we are moderately strong we shall probably be attacked and the attacks will gradually be brought to a standstill ... If we are weak in fighter strength, the attacks will not be brought to a standstill and the productive capacity of the country will be virtually destroyed.[9]

When Dowding became Fighter Command's first chief, the ADGB already had a system of air defence. This Dowding understood and, according to Orange, 'laboured to improve'.[10] The organisation of Fighter Command and the system perfected by Dowding was described in detail in an Air Ministry Pamphlet published in 1943. As it is necessary to understand the Dowding System, the relevant sections of that official publication are reproduced below:

Fighter Command

At the time of the Battle of Britain, Fighter Command was organized into four Fighter Groups. Each group was, for purposes of tactical control, subdivided geographically into a number of sectors. A sector consisted of a main fighter station and airfield, sector head-quarters and operations room, also one or more satellite or forward airfields upon which were based a number of squadrons varying in accordance with the situation and the need for good dispersal.

No. 11 Group's area covered South-East England and, consequently, it was this group which bore the brunt of the fighting, although other groups extensively reinforced the air battle from time to time and, in addition, fed into No. 11 Group a regular supply of fresh squadrons to relieve those worn down by intensive air fighting.

Operations Rooms

The heart of each headquarters at command, groups, and sectors, was its operations room. This varied somewhat in size and complexity depending upon the scope and function of the headquarters and upon the amount of detail regarding our own squadrons that it was necessary for the commander to have before him; but the ultimate object of all operations rooms remained the same, namely, to ensure the utmost rapidity in the issue of orders. For time was the essence of the problem; with machines of war moving at the rate of 5 miles a minute, the issue of written orders was out of the question and the only possible course was to cut the length of orders to a minimum and to use direct telephone, whether landline or radio. To effect this, the operations room had, first, to portray physically the movements of enemy aircraft and, where necessary, of our own fighters, over the whole country and the sea approaches thereto (or such part as was appropriate to the headquarters concerned); secondly, to show how soon and in what strength our own squadrons could leave the ground; and, thirdly, to provide an adequate and reasonably secure network of communications both by landline and radio telephony.

Air Raid Intelligence

The essential basis of any air defence system is, of course, a good air-raid intelligence system. In this country, during the Battle of Britain, as now, such a system comprised a chain of radio location stations sited around our coasts. The function of these stations was the detection of all aircraft approaching this country over the sea. This early warning was vital since the German Air Force was in occupation of airfields just the other side of the Straits of Dover, which could be crossed in four or five minutes. It was supplemented over the land by the Observer Corps, whose function was to take over and 'tell on' the tracks of all aircraft as they crossed our coasts and proceeded inland to their targets.

During the Battle of Britain, information received by radio location was transmitted to Fighter Command headquarters and after passing through a 'filter room' was telephoned direct to one of the plotters in the Command operations room and simultaneously to those at the group and sectors affected. Information received from the Observer Corps followed the reverse course, being passed through observer centres to fighter groups and sectors and repeated by the group tellers to Fighter Command and adjacent groups.

Display of Information

In all Fighter Command operation rooms was a large table map upon which this air-raid intelligence could be accurately plotted as tracks, after such tracks had been identified as hostile, friendly or doubtful. Seated round the table map were a number of plotters, each one connected by a landline to the appropriate reporting centre. From these centres the plotters received minute-to-minute information of the progress of enemy aircraft towards and over this country, together with their numbers and height. The plotter displayed, on the table map suitable symbols indicating the identity, numbers, height and track of the aircraft concerned. Thus each RAF commander, from the Commander-in-Chief in his operations room at Fighter Command down to the sector commander in his operations room at a fighter station or airfield, had continually before him the same moving picture of the enemy as the situation continually changed at the speed of modern flight. Naturally the area that had to be covered by the picture presented to a Sector Commander was much smaller than the area required for the command or group operations room, but in so far as their responsibilities were severally affected, it was the same picture.

During the heavy attacks in September it was found that in No. 11 Group Headquarters operations room the table got too congested, so all detail regarding enemy raids and the fighter squadrons detailed to intercept was transferred to a slotted black-board on the wall known as the *Totalisator,* leaving the map clear except for the raid numbers and symbols for our squadrons in the air.

Each operations room contained an elevated dais which might extend much of the way round the room; a gallery was sometimes added between the dais and the floor of the room. On the wall was shown complete meteorological information including wind and clouds and, at groups and sectors, the strength and degree of readiness of our own squadrons. In sector operations rooms arrangements existed whereby the minute-to-minute position of our own fighters was also plotted on the table map.

Transmission of Information and Orders
In the centre of the dais sat the controller with his assistants responsible for the issue of orders. In the gallery or on the dais sat the tellers who passed on the information appearing on the table map to plotters in other operations rooms. Accommodation on the dais was provided for representatives of the Observer Corps, AA guns and searchlights and the Ministry of Home Security. Very complete intercommunication was provided; for instance, the controller in a group operations room could, by moving a switch, speak directly to any of his sectors, and the controller in a sector operations room could speak through R/T with any of his squadrons in the air or at their dispersal points on the ground.

At Fighter Command headquarters was the main operations room. In addition to the Commander-in-Chief Fighter Command and his staff, it contained the Commander-in-Chief AA Defences and the Observer Corps Commandant, or their representatives, liaison officers from the Admiralty, Bomber and Coastal Commands, as well as a Home Security official. It fulfilled many functions. Information from the various sources was co-ordinated and analysed and the reported formation identified as friendly or hostile and, if the latter, was allotted a number. Where any doubt existed as to the responsibility, raids were allotted to groups. The air raid warning system was operated through certain trunk exchanges in direct telephone communication. The Commander-in-Chief Fighter Command exercised general control over the opening of AA gunfire and the exposure of searchlights, through the Commander-in-Chief, AA Command. He also controlled the balloon barrage through his group commanders. Group commanders decided which sector should meet any specified raid and the strength of the fighter force to be employed. Sector Commanders detailed the fighter units.

Responsibility of Commanders
This system enabled RAF commanders at each different level immediately to dispose their air forces to meet any situation as it could be seen threatening or developing before his eyes

on the table map. It enabled the Commander-in-Chief to reinforce groups with fighters from an adjacent group as and when he saw where the weight of the enemy's attack was likely to fall. It enabled a group commander to organize his squadrons in the various sectors at the appropriate states of preparedness to leave the ground and to order his readiness squadrons off the ground at a moment's notice. It enabled a sector commander to carry out interceptions with incoming raids, since he could see on his table map the minute-to-minute position, course and height both of the incoming enemy formation and of his own outgoing intercepting fighters. He could thus, by R/T, issue orders to his formation leaders in the air, giving the compass course to steer and height at which to fly so as to ensure the best chance of interception.

When once visual contact in the air with the enemy raid had been made, the executive control of the fighters passed automatically from the sector commander in the operations room to the man on the spot, the leader of the fighters, who, in turn, issued to his pilots by radio telephony his executive orders for the conduct of the ensuing air battle. Interception depended finally on being able to see the enemy, so although the system worked well by day, it was not sufficiently accurate to effect interception at night against raiders not illuminated by searchlights.

When the battle was joined, it was the function of the sector commander or his representative in his operations room to 'listen-in' and observe radio silence during the fighting, unless it appeared that other enemy fighters or bombers were approaching the area, when the formation leaders were duly informed. Immediately the battle was over, it became the function again of the sector commander to take control and assist his pilots to regain their home base or nearest airfield if necessary, particularly when, as often happened, squadrons became much split up during a dog-fight or when bad weather intervened and petrol was low.

Group, and, in a less degree, sector commanders had many factors to keep in mind: the necessity for holding some squadrons in reserve to meet further attacks that might develop at short notice; recalling squadrons at the right moment to land for re-fuelling and re-arming; petrol endurance; probable expenditure of ammunition. All these had constantly to be weighed up and decisions made very rapidly.

The whole technique of operating fighters in defence of Great Britain and the facilities provided in Fighter Command operations rooms were the result of a steady process of development over many years. Arrangements are never static. Improvements in methods, in layout and in equipment of operations rooms, are constantly being introduced. However, the existing arrangements today are, in their essentials, the same as they were in the days of the Battle of Britain.

AA Guns

The anti-aircraft guns, under the Command of General Sir Frederick Pile, took no small toll of enemy aircraft, and during the heavy attacks on London rendered great service in turning them back, both by day and night, through the weight of their barrage. On some nights as many as 60 percent, of the enemy aircraft approaching London from the South, dropped their bombs in open country or on the fringe of the barrage, and then went home.

They also rendered direct service to our fighter aircraft, first by breaking up enemy formations, thus rendering them more vulnerable to fighter attacks, and secondly by indicating to our pilots in the air the position of enemy aircraft by shell bursts. On the dais are the tellers, passing on plots as they appear on the centre table to fighter group and sector operations rooms and adjacent observer centres.

Where conditions permit, posts are spaced so that all aircraft flying over the country are within sight or sound of at least one post and continuous tracks are therefore obtained at the centres. Each track is given a separate symbol to maintain its identity, and when 'seen' the height and number of aircraft are reported and 'told' forward. The Observer Corps organization was the sole method of tracking enemy aircraft overland during the battle, and its efficiency enabled many successful interceptions to be made and this contributed in no small degree to the result. It was also essential for the air raid warning systems.

In addition to the work in connection with Air Defence the organization was of great value in enabling our own aircraft, lost in thick weather or at night, to be grounded. Any aircraft thought to be in difficulty owing to its erratic course, the sound of its engines or distress signals was specially tracked and told forward. In some cases RAF airfields were asked by centres to light their landing lights and fire pyrotechnics to help the aircraft down.

The organization was a very democratic one, members being drawn from all classes of society, but all were animated by the knowledge that their work was of vital importance to the country and to the Royal Air Force. Their skill at recognition reached an astonishingly high standard. During the severest winter known for half a century, every post and every centre was continuously manned day and night by these civilian volunteers, many of them over sixty years of age. Their motto is *Forewarned is Forearmed*.[11]

Whilst the System was developed and perfected, the tactics Fighter Command's pilots would actually use in battle remained a matter of speculation. This was because the monoplane fighters had appeared so late in the day that the RAF remained inexperienced in their operation. When war eventually broke out on 3 September 1939, for example, the Hurricane had been taken on charge by 111 Squadron less than two years previously and the first Spitfire squadron had been fully operational for only nine months. Most importantly, however, it was understandably not envisaged that Britain would ever come within range of German single-engined fighters. Only twin-engined bombers, flying from bases in Germany, would have the necessary range to intrude over the British Isles, meaning that RAF fighters would only need to intercept these types. The Hurricane's maximum speed was around 320 mph, the Spitfire's 355 mph. The German Do 17 bomber, however, cruised at 236 mph, the He 111 at 225 mph, and the Ju 88 at 286 mph. Bombers, therefore, could not out-run a British fighter, and any evasive action possible was in no way comparable to the aerobatic capabilities of either the Hurricane or Spitfire. For defence bombers had to rely upon armour plate and mutual fire support. Most of the German bombers each had some five machine-guns for defence, located around the aircraft to cover all directions. The RAF fighters, however, each had eight machine-guns, all firing forwards. If these aircraft were operated in sections of three, flying close together in a V-shaped formation called a 'vic', then a total of twenty-four guns would simultaneously be brought to bear upon the target. This tactic, of course, assumed that the aircraft attacked was taking little or no evasive action – and as it was only expected to encounter bombers, this was given. Fighting Area Attacks, in fact, consisted of six set-piece interceptions with whole squadrons flying in sections of three and therefore attacking with a total of ninety-six guns. So much faith did the Air Ministry invest in these tactics that Squadron commanders were officially forbidden to experiment with alternative ideas.[12]

Not all senior RAF officers, however, were satisfied that the Fighting Area Attacks were correct. In July 1938, Air Commodore Keith Park – a tough New Zealander and Great War fighter pilot – became Dowding's Senior Air Staff Officer (SASO) at Fighter Command. Park became specifically responsible for the Command's fighting efficiency.[13] In November he attended a meeting of the Air Fighting Committee at which a report on tactics for the new monoplanes was examined. This emphasised that the vic was the most suitable fighter formation. Park disagreed. On 29 December 1938 he sent a written proposal to the commanders of both 11 and 12 Groups to the effect that the officially dictated formations and attacks were too rigid to be practical, imploring that 'some latitude be left to the leader in the air in order to effect surprise'. This was to no avail: the Air Ministry ruled that fighters should only attack from astern or below.[14] Moreover, in 1938 the RAF *Manual of Air Tactics* stated that 'manoeuvres at high speeds in air fighting is not now practicable because the effect of gravity on the human body during rapid changes of direction at high speed causes a temporary loss of consciousness'. For this reason it was believed that the fast, new monoplanes would be physically incapable of engaging each other. On 10 January 1939 Park wrote to the Air Ministry criticizing the manual. In total contravention of Air Ministry beliefs, he wrote 'The possibility of bombers having fighter escorts even in attacks on London should not be overlooked'.[15] The fact of the matter was that Park understood fighter combat and tactics perfectly – probably more so than Dowding, who concentrated on the system and strategy. Although Park's views on tactics involving the new monoplanes were also based upon speculation, he, more than any other, grasped the most likely principals – the reality of which would be poles apart from the pre-war manual. As Orange wrote, 'Park emphasized that ... formation leaders must use their initiative in air fighting tactics. Good teamwork would be important and pilots would take advantage of blind areas, cloud and sun; above all they should seek to surprise their opponents'.[16] Experience would ultimately prove him right.

In March 1939 Dowding responded to a question concerning tactics by Air Vice-Marshal Gossage, the commander of 11 Group. The Commander-in-Chief explained that if too many fighters were scrambled at once they might be bombed whilst re-fuelling and re-arming. If insufficient fighters were scrambled to meet a threat then losses would be too great. The squadron, directed Dowding, would be the largest unit deployed under normal circumstances, although two or more might fight in pairs against a significantly superior enemy force. Dowding knew that his Command could not even practise or work towards the discovery of ideal tactics because his squadrons were as yet still largely unfamiliar with the new monoplanes, and limited resources dictated the provision of too small a number of 'target' aircraft with which to practise interceptions. Training was, therefore, always undertaken in completely unrealistic conditions.[17] There was no alternative, however. Clarity would only be provided through combat experience, which was hardly ideal.

Before the war, pilots went straight from Flying Training School (FTS) to their squadron, where they were trained on the particular fighter aircraft with which their squadron was equipped, and made combat ready. With the advent of war, it was clear that this could not continue, because hard-pressed squadrons would simply not have the time or resources to train replacements. The Air Ministry therefore revealed plans to create special units which would train fledgling fighter pilots to operational standard prior to them reaching their actual units. Three training 'pools' were proposed, the first of which was the 11 Group Pool at St Athan, which had eleven Fairey Battles (single-engined light-bombers, soon replaced by the North American Harvard monoplane trainer) and twenty-two Hurricanes on strength. Shortly after the outbreak of war, the course length was halved to four weeks, and syllabus hours were reduced from forty-five to thirty hours per pupil. It was hoped that 300 pilots would be trained to operational standard, per pool, per annum. In March 1940, the group pools were renamed Operational Training Units (OTU) and a third such unit was added. Nonetheless, during the forthcoming Battle of France, their combined output was barely sufficient to make good the losses of squadrons fighting on the continent, where the standard of training was harshly criticised: new pilots often had only ten hours flying time on Spitfires or Hurricanes, with no high altitude or fighter attack experience.

An operational fighter squadron comprised twelve aircraft and pilots, excluding reserves, divided into two 'flights', 'A' and 'B', each commanded by a flight lieutenant. The flights were then sub-divided into two sections of three aircraft, each trio of fighters having their own leader and being identified by a colour. 'A' Flight usually consisted of Red and Yellow Sections, whilst 'B' comprised Blue and Green. Each section was numbered from one to three, one indicating the leader. 'Blue One' would therefore identify the leader of 'B' Flight's Blue Section. Each squadron was identified by its own two code letters, which were applied to the fighters' fuselages in medium sea grey. Individual aircraft were then further identifiable by a single letter, choosing from A–K for 'A' Flight, and L–Z for 'B'. Each squadron also had its own radio call sign: 'Luton Blue One' therefore identified the leader of 19 Squadron's 'B' Flight. The squadron was under the overall command of a squadron leader, who, in addition to flying duties, was responsible, through his adjutant, for administration, discipline and the general day-to-day smooth running of his unit. In the air, officers and non-commissioned pilots flew together, but on the ground, whilst off duty, they were segregated in this still much class conscious society. It should not be forgotten that a fighter squadron also included those in behind-the-scenes but nonetheless essential roles: intelligence officers, airframe riggers, engine fitters, instrument fitters, and armourers.

The operational centre of the squadron was 'dispersal', usually a wooden hut on the airfield in which was situated the orderly clerk and all-important telephone. There were also twelve beds on which the pilots rested between sorties. Outside, their aircraft were dispersed as a precaution against bombing, facing the centre of the airfield so that pilots could take off with the minimum of delay. During the daytime, pilots learned to leave their parachutes, which they sat on, not in their bucket seats but on top of either the port wing or tailplane with the straps hanging down, meaning that they could seize the two shoulder straps, pull the parachute pack off the wing and move towards the cockpit, all without pausing. Pilots wore a flying helmet made of leather, containing radio-telephony earphones, the leads of which were plugged into a socket in the cockpit, in which the helmet and goggles were left, usually on the reflector gunsight or control column top. Stout leather flying boots were usually worn, lined with sheepskin, to insulate against the cold in what were unheated cockpits, and a life jacket known as a 'Mae West', after the buxom American actress and for obvious reasons. Oxygen, required at high altitude, was delivered via an oxygen mask, covering the nose, cheeks and mouth, the pilot's eyes being protected by his goggles. With the addition of leather gauntlets, the pilot was thus afforded some protection from fire. What fighter pilots rarely wore, however, in direct contrast to the movies and due to the tight confines of their tiny cockpits, was the bulky, leather and sheepskin flying jacket. Instead they preferred to wear uniform shirts and tunics, although the brightly coloured silk neck scarf was not altogether a pose but necessary to prevent chafing as the pilot constantly screwed his neck around searching for the enemy. Moreover, neck ties shrank in seawater, another valid reason why their use was discarded on operations. On the ground, the fighter pilot famously wore his tunic top button undone.

Most squadrons worked a four day cycle, on the first day of which pilots would be on 'Stand by' and therefore available to fly within the hour; second day would be 'Available', as in ready to fly in fifteen minutes, and day three would see the stakes upped to 'Readiness', when pilots were ready for immediate take-off. On day four came 'Stand down', when pilots, with their flight commander's permission, could leave the aerodrome. One flight of operational pilots had to remain on the airfield, so this was often used as an opportunity for training.

Pilot Officer William Walker was a pilot of the RAF Volunteer Reserve (VR) who joined the auxiliary 616 Squadron shortly before the Battle of Britain began:

> The early days of war were interesting so far as we were unprepared for what was to come. It is my lasting regret that I did not have more operational training – trying to pick it up with the Squadron straight from flying school was a pretty haphazard affair. For instance, I flew my first Spitfire on 23 June 1940, and was declared operational on July 1st.[18]

Across the Channel, however, was a highly trained and well-equipped enemy that had spent some years preparing for war. By the time that Pilot Officer Walker and many other new fighter pilots like him joined their squadrons in the early summer of 1940, their foe also had great experience of aerial combat. Although Fighter Command thanked God and Dowding for not having to go to war in biplanes, it remained disadvantaged in various respects. To put the situation into perspective it is now necessary to examine the threat from Nazi Germany's *Luftwaffe*.

7

German Military Aviation Between the Wars, and the Me 109

The Air Clauses of the Treaty of Versailles in 1919 were intended to end military aviation in Germany, thereby preventing a resurrection of the German Flying Corps which had fought in the Great War. In accordance with these provisions Germany surrendered over 15,000 aircraft and 27,000 aero engines.[1] The Treaty, however, failed to prevent Germany possessing or manufacturing civil aircraft. The opportunity was immediately seized, therefore, to develop and expand civil and commercial aviation, including airlines, flying clubs, and schools to train both air and ground crews. Behind this innocent façade, however, the foundations of a new – illegal – air force were soon being laid. As early as 1920 General von Seeckt, the Chief of the Army Command at the *Reichswehr Ministerium*, was convinced that German military aviation must be revived. Certain officers whose names were later to become famous as commanders in Hitler's *Luftwaffe*, including Sperrle, Kesselring and Stumpff, were given responsibility for various aspects of military aviation and hidden away in von Seeckt's ministry. Thus the first cornerstone was laid of a renaissance of German air power.

By 1926, Germany was widely considered the most air-minded nation in Europe. The German society for aviation enthusiasts, the *Deutscher Luftsportverband*, founded in 1920, exceeded 50,000 by the end of that decade. Again, von Seeckt was behind this, encouraging an interest in gliding to circumvent Versailles. Thus Germany had no shortage of air-minded youngsters eager to aspire to powered flight – and who already had air experience. Although the Paris Air Agreement of 1926 considerably restricted the number of service personnel permitted to fly, von Seeckt succeeded in creating a secret cadre of trained aircrew. These men were trained in the schools set up for the commercial airline *Deutsche Lufthansa*, and in a top secret military flying training school at Lipetz in Russia. When Adolf Hitler and the Nazis came to power in Germany in January 1933, no time was lost in creating the new *Luftwaffe*.

Wilhelm Deist rightly argued that 'Between 1933 and 1939 Germany's neighbouring states regarded the build-up of the *Luftwaffe* as the most dangerous existing threat to their security. The aeroplane even more than the tank was viewed as the offensive weapon of the future, its potential effects seeming to embody both the totality and the brutality of modern warfare'.[2] Indeed, air power was certainly seen as fundamental to the achievement of Hitler's expansionist aims in foreign policy. At first Hitler intended to achieve *Lebensraum* in the east. Britain, he thought, would either ally itself with him or at least not intervene. It soon became clear, however, that Britain was trying to prevent this. From that point on Hitler had to consider a major war against Britain and mobilise German resources rapidly.[3] Initially, therefore, the *Luftwaffe* was conceived as a comparatively short-range force in anticipation of war with Germany's Polish neighbour to the east and French to the west. Nonetheless it was the people of Britain who feared German air attack more than any other nation. This concern was increased when Nazi Germany withdrew from the League of Nations and the disarmament conference in 1933. The following year Baldwin, who had famously endorsed the view that 'the bomber would always get through', told the House of Commons that Germany's progress in military aviation meant that the aerial defence of Britain no longer began at the White Cliffs of Dover but at the Rhine.[4] In 1935 Hitler was sufficiently confident to blatantly contravene Versailles and reveal his new *Luftwaffe* to a disbelieving world.

Hitler's deputy, *Reichsmarschall* Herman Göring, a Great War fighter ace, was made head of the new Nazi air force. This was a turning point, as with the Deputy *Führer's* political influence the *Luftwaffe's* status increased in terms of rearmament. At its inception this new independent air service's strength stood at 1,888 aircraft of all types, and 20,000 personnel, supported by between thirty and forty airframe and engine manufacturers.[5] The *Luftwaffe* immediately began improving its aircraft and testing them in competitions all over Europe and in large-scale air exercises at home. Influenced by the same factors as British aircraft designers, the emphasis on German aircraft development in the mid-1930s revolved around the monoplane. By 1935 the prototypes of many German aircraft which would become so familiar in the Second World War began appearing. In 1920 Professor Hugo Junkers had opened a factory in Dessau; in 1922 Ernest Heinkel built at aircraft factory at Warnemuende; Claude Dornier began production in Friedrichshafen; in 1924 Heinrich Focke and George Wulf founded the Focke-Wulf aircraft company at Bremen. Whilst all of these would produce bombers and fighters providing the mainstay of the *Luftwaffe* throughout 1939-45, most important to our analysis is the fact that Professor Willy Messerschmitt took over the *Bayerische Flugzeugwerke* (BFW) at Augsburg and began producing sporting aeroplanes. By 1934, Messerschmitt had designed a monoplane, the Me 108 *Taifun*, as an entrant in an international aviation contest, the *Challenge International de Tourisme*, held in Poland. Although the 108 came fifth, sixth and tenth, its 'overall performance', wrote Uwe Feist, 'was impressive'.[6] Already, though, Messerschmitt was working on a new monoplane fighter incorporating the features found in his *Taifun*. As Townsend commented, 'from Me 108 to Me 109 would be a short step'.[7]

During 1933, the technical department of the *Reichsluftministerium* (RLM), known as C-*Amt*, reported on the conclusions of their research into the application of modern technology to air combat. C-*Amt* considered that to meet future needs of German air power, four types of military aircraft were needed: a multi-seat medium bomber, a tactical bomber, a single-seat fighter and a two-seater fighter. The single-seater, which would replace the existing He 51 and Ar 68 biplane fighters, was required to have a top speed of at least 250 mph at 19,690 feet, achieving that height in seventeen minutes with a maximum operational ceiling of 30,000 feet. Thus far the German requirement was almost identical to the RAF specifications F.36/34 and F.37/34. Submissions were made by Arado, Focke-Wulf, Heinkel and BFW. Designs by the first two companies were immediately rejected, leaving Heinkel's He 112 and Messerschmitt's Me 109. Messerschmitt's new fighter first flew in May 1935 – six months before the Hawker Hurricane and nearly a year before the Supermarine Spitfire. Although the He 112 compared favourably to the Me 109, according to Hough and Richards 'a combination of superior salesmanship and swifter development won the day for the Augsburg company'.[8]

Messerschmitt's new monoplane fighter was based entirely upon the principal of producing the smallest and therefore lightest airframe around the most powerful engine – initially a Rolls-Royce Kestrel. The so-called 'Augsburg Eagle' featured a metal-alloy framework, flush-riveted stressed metal covering, leading-edge wing slots in conjunction with slotted trailing-edge flaps which increased the wing area upon demand, retractable main undercarriage, and an enclosed cockpit with a jettisonable canopy – another farsighted consideration. As there was no requirement for wing mounted armament, the 109's wing was extremely thin, the main spar being situated at the mid-chord point. In fact, it became necessary to strengthen the join of the wings and fuselage. Torque also caused landing problems, exacerbated by the narrow track undercarriage. Nonetheless Bungay considered these teething troubles to be 'trivial'.[9] The 109 was initially armed with two nose-mounted 7.92 mm machine-guns and, like the first Hurricanes and Spitfires, a wooden fixed pitch propeller. After extensive testing at Travemünde the 109 was officially declared the winning design and awarded a production contract. According to Mason, 'no authentic figures have ever been traced relating to the performance of the prototype 109s, it is unlikely that the Kestrel-powered 109V-1 exceeded 280 mph'.[10] The first production model, the B-1, however, was powered by the Junkers Jumo 210D, achieved 292 mph at 13,100 feet, reaching 19,700 feet in 9.8 minutes. In April 1937, *Jagdgeschwader Richthofen* became the first unit to replace their obsolete He 51s with the new 109. Messerschmitt's fighter therefore entered operational service before both its British contemporaries.

The development of other German monoplanes used in the forthcoming Battle of Britain must also be examined. The spring of 1937 saw the Ju 87 *Stuka*, a single-engined crank-winged monoplane dive-bomber, enter service. With a crew of two, sitting back-to-back, the *Stuka's* top speed was only 232 mph – slower than any of the *Luftwaffe's* medium bombers. Classified as a short-range moderate performance machine, the Ju 87's virtues had nothing to do with its speed, range, or bomb load but everything to do with the accuracy of bombing made possible by its unique design. The other enemy aircraft were all twin-engined. In 1935, the Heinkel He 111 medium bomber first flew and was in service by 1937 with a top speed of 255 mph. The Dornier Do 17, another medium bomber, also made its maiden flight in 1935. At an international flying event held at Zurich in 1937, the so-called 'Flying Pencil' outpaced all interceptors present at 265 mph. The best German medium bomber, the Junkers Ju 88, did not fly until December 1936, and when war broke out remained at the pre-production development stage. Rapidly pressed into service, the 88's top speed was 286 mph. These were all comparatively fast and modern warplanes. In what proved a massive advantage when the Second World War began, Hitler was able to test some of these designs in actual combat conditions during the Spanish Civil War. The experience gained was immense, putting the enemy air force far ahead of the RAF which was only able to tactically evaluate its new fighters in totally inadequate and artificial air exercises.

German intervention in the Spanish Civil War began in August 1936 when twenty Ju 52 transport aircraft and six He 51 fighters were despatched to assist General Franco's fascist forces. More fighters followed, with pilots to fly them. It soon became clear, though, that such a small number of German fighters could make no impression on the conflict's outcome, not least because the He 51 was inferior to the Russian- and American-built fighters flown by the Republicans. The decision was therefore reached to send a powerful German force – the *Condor Legion* – to Franco's aid. According to James W. Corum, 'The Spanish Civil War was, by any reckoning, the most important single military air power event in the period between the world wars'.[11] In this 'event' the *Wehrmacht* tested new weapons and tactics. For the *Luftwaffe* Spain became an essential proving ground for the new monoplanes. These did not arrive in Spain until the early summer of 1937. Air superiority, however, was soon achieved and maintained, thus providing an early indication of the monoplane's ascendancy. As *Condor Legion* veteran and expert German fighter pilot Adolf Galland wrote, the Me 109s 'were mainly intended to combat the numerous Curtiss and Rata fighters, either as lone wolves or when escorting bomber formations. The Me 109 was definitely superior to them and shot down a great number, the record for "kills" being held by *Leutnant* Harder, until eventually Mölders topped his figure'.[12] Upon arrival in Spain, Werner Mölders succeeded Galland in command of 3/ JG 88, which was converting to Me 109s. With a full complement of 109s Mölders was instrumental in working out the mechanics of combat tactics with the new monoplane fighter. He was uniquely placed to do so, achieving fourteen personal victories over Spain in the process.

Mölders rapidly realised that fighter combat was fast and furious, a cut and thrust affair often lasting but a matter of minutes. Given the high speed and manoeuvrability of the new monoplane fighters, it was quickly realised that inflexible formation attacks – such as those being practised and rigidly enforced by Fighter Command – were totally inappropriate. Fluency and fluidity was required. Pilots needed to keep a sharp lookout – because enemy fighters could appear and attack in a very short time – and be able to break and respond to any given tactical situation, be that from a perspective of defence or attack. What was required now, Mölders discovered, was a combat formation based upon the fighting pair, not a squadron of twelve aircraft flying cohesively in sections of three and in close formation. The pair, or *Rotte*, comprised a leader and wingman. Before battle was joined the *Rotte* operated as part of a *Schwarm* of two *Rotten*. This section of four cruised in line abreast, each aircraft some 200 yards apart, slightly stepped up, permitting pilots the freedom to search for the enemy instead of concentrating on avoiding collision with their neighbour. When battle commenced the *Schwarm* broke into two *Rotten*. The leader's job was to shoot down the enemy whilst his tail was protected by his wingman, or *Katschmarek*. Air Vice-Marshal Johnnie Johnson, officially the top scoring RAF fighter pilot of the Second World War, commented on the *Schwarm*: 'We used to see the 109s flying this loose, flexible, formation, alert, like the four fingers of an outstretched hand. I always thought that they looked aggressive, ready for anything, like a pack of hunting dogs'.[13] Much later, after bitter experience, the RAF copied the *Schwarm*, calling it the 'Finger Four' or 'Crossover Four'. Those days were a long way off, however. Mölders' new tactics allowed the *Condor Legion* to achieve air superiority in 1937 which it never lost. The balance sheet indicated seventy-two German combat losses against 327 Republican aircraft destroyed.[14] Upon return from Spain, Mölders wrote a new manual of fighter tactics for the monoplane which became standard operating procedure throughout the *Luftwaffe* – earning for himself the nickname *Vati* – father – of the German *Jagdwaffe*.

Spain was also important to the Germans because it was there they developed close-support tactics between the air force and army. According to the official British history, the

Rise and Fall of the German Air Force 1933-45, this development was the 'only revolutionary' conclusion drawn from the Germans' experience in Spain. Although tactical air-to-ground co-operation would become an essential feature of Germany's new *Blitzkrieg* tactics, this cannot be considered correct. Mölders' work with the new monoplane fighters was equally, if not more, 'revolutionary' – so much so that over seventy years later his ideas remain the basis of fighter combat. Given that today's fighters are highly sophisticated and computerised fast jets achieving speeds unimaginable in 1937, this can only be considered remarkable. The understanding of fighter tactics gained in Spain would be a huge advantage to the *Luftwaffe* in the early stages of the Second World War. Interestingly, however, Spain led to the *Luftwaffe* over-estimating the abilities of their new monoplane bombers. The new He 111 had encountered only slight opposition, inclining the Germans to believe that they could be operated with only light fighter protection. Moreover, the Germans believed that the fast medium bomber could 'lay waste any country without the fighter defences even having an opportunity to interfere'.[15] If RAF fighter tactics would soon be found wanting, the *Luftwaffe's* inaccurate perception of its medium bombers would likewise ultimately be shot down in flames. Nonetheless, the bomber emerged from Spain confirmed as the most feared weapon so far created by man. This was because of one word: Guernica.

Guernica was a Basque village with a population of around 5,000. Standing between Franco's forces and the capture of Bilbao, it became crucial to the war in northern Spain. The town had no anti-aircraft guns and defensive sorties by Republican aircraft were not a consideration, due to recent heavy losses. The target was of military importance: the road network and bridge in the suburb of Renteria. The raid was a combined operation between the Germans and Italians, involving twenty-three aircraft carrying twenty-two tons of bombs. After the bombing, Me 109s and He 51s strafed the roads around the target. The attack failed to confine itself to the intended, legitimate, military target and destroyed most of the defenceless village. At the time civilian casualties were reported as 1,654, although more recent research indicates a death toll of up to 400. Nonetheless the raid was perceived as a deliberate terror attack aimed entirely at a defenceless civilian population and confirmed the fear of air power prevalent throughout the 1930s. The world's media became virtually hysterical and Guernica's suffering was immortalised in Piccasso's stark and emotive rendition of the tortured souls who suffered and died in this unprecedented air attack. German air doctrine did not, in reality, revolve around terror bombing, however. In fact the indiscriminate bombing of cities was regarded as largely wasted effort and potentially counter-productive. The Italian fascist dictator Benito Mussolini also sent troops to Spain and in March 1938 his *Regia Aeronautica* unleashed heavy attacks on Barcelona lasting several days. As Corum commented, 'The target was Barcelona's civilian populace and Italian air theorist Giulio Douhet's theory of aerial warfare was finally to be given a true test'.[16] The attack caused 1,300 casualties. Although initially the shocked survivors were demoralised, once they recovered the main emotion was anger and defiance. The Germans realised, therefore, that such bombing could actually increase the enemy's will to resist. Consequently *Luftwaffe* doctrine concentrated on supporting land operations. Nonetheless in Spain the bomber had, indeed, always got through and the global fear of it appeared completely justified. So far as Dowding was concerned in England, events in Spain only served to convince him that a strong fighter force was an absolute priority.

So far as the development of the Me 109 was concerned, the unique opportunity to evaluate and improve the new fighter in actual combat conditions was an immeasurable bonus. Moreover, the superiority of the 109 over the He 51, which, according to Corum, 'proved a real dud',[17] was immediately apparent. The 109 was so clearly the best fighter in Spanish skies that production of it was accelerated so that it replaced the He 51 well ahead of schedule.[18] Already, in July and August 1937, the Germans had shown off the 109 to the aeronautical world at the Fourth International Flying Meeting held at Zurich. Five 109s were entered by the German team, billed by the Nazi propagandists as basic production machines already widely in service with the *Luftwaffe*. Although neither statement was entirely true, the fact remains that the 109s out performed the competition. Indeed, Carl Francke set a new speed record of 254 mph. On 11 November 1937 an Me 109 V-13 set a new land speed record at 379.38 mph. This unprecedented speed was made possible because of a new engine: the Daimler-Benz 601, which would become to the German fighter what the Rolls-Royce Merlin was to both the Hurricane and Spitfire. By the end of that year production problems concerning the new engine had been overcome so that it could from then onwards be fitted to production 109s. So was born the Me 109E variant, known affectionately as the *Emil*, and which entered service in early 1939. It was this aircraft, in fact, which equipped the *Jagdwaffe* during the battles of 1940. Another significant milestone had been reached.

Spitfires and Hurricanes during the Battle of Britain period were powered by the Merlin III, the maximum power of which – 1,310 hp – was achieved at 9,000 feet.[19] The DB 601A's maximum power was 1,036 hp at 5,250 feet.[20] The Merlin III, in fact, was a more powerful engine at all altitudes. The DB 601A enjoyed one great advantage over the Merlin, though: it was fuel injected. This meant that the fuel supply was unaffected by gravity – unlike the Merlin's float-type carburettor that was affected by negative-g. Consequently it would be discovered that fuel injection permitted the 109 to always outpace a Spitfire or Hurricane in the dive, because, unlike the RAF fighters, its engine did not momentarily cut out. The DB 601A also had the advantage in fuel consumption.

Another improvement to the early 109s was that the original fixed pitch propeller was soon replaced by the three-bladed VDM 'controllable-pitch' airscrew. This was the equivalent of the British CS propeller, permitting rotation of the blades through 360° and therefore enabling the pilot to select optimum pitch for any situation. The British fighters, as explained, were first updated to the two-pitch propeller, which although better than the original fixed-pitch design was but a half-way house. Although the CS propeller was ultimately fitted as standard to production aircraft, during the Battle of Britain the conversion from two-pitch to CS airscrews was actually undertaken on the fighter stations by de Havilland engineers. This work was not completed on both Hurricanes and Spitfires until 16 August 1940.[21] The new propeller increased the Spitfire's rate of climb by 730 feet per minute. This is another indication that British aircraft designers were actually behind their German counterparts – who, like the air and ground crews involved, learned many lessons from the Spanish Civil War.

The matter of the Me 109's armament is an interesting one. The armament required by a new monoplane fighter is a matter in which the German planners were initially behind the British. In 1932, Wing Commander Arthur Thomson suggested that in future fighters should have eight guns capable of firing 1,000 rounds per minute. Thomson's thoughts

revolved entirely around the rifle-calibre machine-guns that had been used in the Great
War – in which he had flown as a flight commander in Dowding's 16 Squadron. An
armament expert, Squadron Leader Ralph Sorley, endorsed this view in 1934, claiming
that multiple machine-guns would be necessary to destroy modern bombers – which
were now made of metal and enjoyed the benefits of armour plate. Dowding agreed and
included the requirement for eight machine-guns in his specification for the RAF's new
fighters. Hitherto fighters' machine-guns had been mounted in front of the pilot, but it
was impossible to so locate eight guns. The only feature capable of accommodating so
many guns, therefore, was the wings.[22] German designers, however, were naturally unaware
of this and so the first 109s were designed with two engine-cowl mounted 7.92 mm
machine-guns. Another MG 17 was engine-mounted, to fire through the propeller hub,
but this was unsuccessful. The news that the British were using eight machine-guns led
to a rapid re-think. The problem was that the 109's wings were so thin that they were not
strong enough to carry more than two guns, the additional hitting power of which was
inconsequential when offset against the technical difficulties involved with fitting them.
The answer was not to use machine-guns in the wings but cannon – one in each wing,
in addition to the nose-mounted machine-guns. The weapon chosen was the MG-FF
20 mm cannon made by Oerlikon. The cannon's muzzle velocity was much lower than
a machine-gun, however: eight rounds per second offset against seventeen respectively.
Consequently it was a weapon better suited to an above average shot – the 'spread' of
fire from a battery of fast-firing machine-guns being more forgiving and similar to the
effect of a shotgun. Nonetheless the cannon's destructive power was supreme – just one
strike from an explosive 20 mm round could be fatal. The Oerlikon carried sixty rounds
per cannon, the ammunition drum being accommodated by way of blisters on both wing
surfaces. In the fighting ahead cannon would provide the 109E with another advantage: the
German fighter, having both rapid firing machine-guns and the slower but heavier cannon,
enjoyed the best of both worlds. The generally accepted view, however, is that the 109 was
cannon-armed because the German designers recognised the great benefits of this weapon
whereas the British did not. This is not true. The fitting of cannon arose simply because
the Germans underestimated the number of machine-guns that the British would use and,
being unable to wing mount a sufficient number of extra rifle-calibre guns, compromised
by using cannon. It was arguably a reactive compromise – but one that would prove a happy
one for the *jagdfliegern*.

Cannon also featured in the armament of another fighter produced by Messerschmitt
– the twin-engined Me 110 *Zerstörer*. With a crew of two sitting back-to-back, the 110 was
intended as an invincible long-range escort fighter able to clear the path ahead for bomber
formations. Although first flown in 1936, like the Ju 88 it did not enter production until
1939, and was not, therefore, tested in Spain. It was heavily armed, with four forward-firing
machine-guns in addition to two 20 mm cannon, and a rearwards firing machine-gun for
defence. Capable of 350 mph at 23,000 feet, it was faster than the Hurricane but slower than
the Spitfire. Ultimately, however, the 110 proved unsuccessful in its intended role because it
was not manoeuvrable enough to deal with the British single-engined fighters. Britain, of
course, had produced a similar machine, the Bristol Blenheim, but quickly recognised that

the design was a non-starter as a day-fighter. Instead the Blenheim became the mainstay of Britain's nocturnal defences until the arrival of the Bristol Beaufighter. Had the Blenheim been used by day it would have been as dismal a failure as the 110. As Bungay wrote, the 110 'could no more dog-fight than the Blenheim'.[23] The British also made a mistake with the Boulton-Paul Defiant, a single-engine fighter with a pilot and gunner – the latter housed in a turret armed with four Browning machine-guns. Powered by the same Merlin engine as the Hurricane and Spitfire, the extra weight imposed by the Defiant's turret markedly reduced performance (top speed 304 mph). Moreover, the lack of forward-firing armament meant that the pilot and gunner team lacked the split-second hand-to-eye co-ordination required in fast-moving day-fighter combat. Dowding immediately recognised the Defiant's failings but the Air Ministry ignored him and insisted that two of his squadrons were Defiant equipped.[24] They would be tragically massacred in the Battle of Britain ahead. In addition to the success stories of the Hurricane, Spitfire and Me 109, therefore, both sides also made mistakes – in the Germans' case even in spite of their Spanish experience.

As the 1930s began drawing to a close, the *Luftwaffe's* expansion gathered in momentum. In 1937 the *Luftwaffe's* front-line strength was between 2,000-2,500 aircraft of all types. By August 1938 it had increased to 2,900.[25] That year Germany produced 5,235 military aircraft – 8,295 in 1939. Britain's figures for the same years were 2,827 and 7,940 respectively.[26] On the eve of war, at the end of August 1939, *Luftwaffe* strength stood at 3,750, of which 850 were Me 109s.[27] According to Air Ministry Pamphlet 248, 'the German conception of the employment of fighter aircraft was not in a very developed stage on the eve of war. The majority of the fighter force was intended for deployment over the battle area … In support of ground units one of the main functions of the single-engined fighter units was to prevent or hinder activities by enemy reconnaissance aircraft. In addition, single-engined fighter units were intended to protect and escort bomber and dive-bomber formations operating against enemy ground targets'.[28] From this it is clear that the *Luftwaffe* had not considered the kind of protracted, strategic, offensive air operations that became necessary during the summer of 1940. The intention was to fight a series of short, sharp, wars using fast-moving ground forces supported by flying artillery – *Blitzkrieg*. German air policy concentrated upon attack, based upon Douhet. This is evident by the fact that at the outbreak of war forty per cent of *Luftwaffe* units were bomber or dive-bomber units whilst only twenty-five per cent were fighters. So although much has rightly been made of the opportunity provided by Spain, not even the Germans had got air power doctrine right as yet. Even though the *Luftwaffe* had the most up-to-date combat experience and overall was equipped with excellent aircraft, it was not a flawless foe. Still, from a perspective of day-fighter warfare, regardless of the confusion as to how best to employ fighters generally, in the event of contact with enemy fighters the German pilots had a huge edge: Mölders had re-written the book of fighter tactics, based upon his experience in Spain, and these tactics were now standard operating procedure throughout the *Jagdwaffe*. Moreover, as the British Air Ministry observed, 'There is no doubt that in 1939 the Me 109 was superior to any Allied fighter except the Spitfire which, however, was then only available to the RAF in small numbers'.[29]

On 1 September 1939 Hitler invaded Poland. The years of waiting and preparation were over – for both sides.

8

The Battle of France

At 11.15 a.m. on Sunday 3 September 1939 the British Prime Minister, Neville Chamberlain, spoke to the nation:

> This morning the British Ambassador in Berlin handed the German Government a final note stating that unless we heard from them by 11.00 a.m. that they were prepared at once to withdraw their troops from Poland, a state of war would exist between us. I have to tell you that no such undertaking has been received, and that consequently this country is at war with Germany.

For Chamberlain this was the bitterest of personal blows: his work for peace had failed. Appeasement had, however, bought time for Britain to rearm, and for the RAF in particular to expand. According to Calder, 'After the strain of the last few days, this announcement brought relief to many'.[1] Fred Roberts was a young armourer on 19 Squadron at Duxford and spent the beginning of September humping ammunition from trains at Whittlesford. Trains passed the airmen full of children being evacuated from centres of population to the country – to protect them from the threat of Nazi air attack.[2] Such was the fear involved that between the end of June and the first week of September some 3,750,000 people were evacuated, such movements in September alone affecting up to a third of Britain's population.[3] It was fully expected that Germany would immediately attempt to deliver the much talked about and dreaded 'knockout blow' – Londoners believed that Armageddon had arrived when the sirens wailed at 11.27 a.m. that Sunday morning. It was a false alarm, the first of many, caused by an unannounced French aircraft.[4] Duxford's Spitfire squadrons reacted to this perceived threat, as Fred Roberts remembered: 'Shortly after the declaration of war the local air raid sirens were screaming and from the station yard we saw 19 and 66 Squadron aircraft scramble, circle round then land. I remember one of the lads saying "I don't know what good they can do except ram any Germans – there's no ammo in them Spitfires, we have it all here!"'[5] There would be no attempt that year, in fact, at a 'knockout blow' by either side. The truth was that in reality neither was in a position to deliver one, and both sides were anxious not to be the one to unleash unrestricted air warfare. Even after Guernica, the true extent of devastation possible by unrestricted air attacks remained an unknown quantity, discouraging, as Overy wrote, 'adventurism in using aircraft'.[6] The simple truth was that Germany was not in a position to launch a strategic air offensive against Britain.

Meanwhile, Poland suffered. On the first day of the campaign, the *Luftwaffe* destroyed much of the Polish Air Force on the ground in surprise attacks. A day later the Germans achieved total air superiority. From then on the *Luftwaffe* was able to concentrate on supporting the army and destroying Polish ground forces. On 25 September 1939 Warsaw became the latest Guernica. For two days the *Luftwaffe* bombed the Polish capital – long after the military objectives of the mission were achieved. Casualties among Polish civilians were 'huge', according to Mason, who charged that 'they occurred in flagrant violation of all written and unwritten conventions of international conduct and they are forever inexcusable'.[7] Whereas the destruction wrought beyond military targets in Guernica was arguably largely accidental, there was no question that Warsaw's agony was entirely intentional. The exercise served only to further increase and confirm the fear of air attack in Britain. On 28 September – after just four weeks – Poland surrendered. The gallant Polish Air Force had lost a staggering ninety per cent of its operational aircraft and seventy per cent of its aircrews during the brief campaign; the *Luftwaffe* lost no more than twenty per cent of its force.[8] Overwhelming though Göring's victory was, the Poles were determined to fight on and believed that they would ultimately prevail:

> They had fought the Germans with inferior equipment in every respect, but they had learned that the enemy was not a nation of supermen. He could be defeated in individual combat, and if opposed by forces strong in number and fighting spirit he could be defeated in entirety. For the Polish Air Force, at any rate, the campaign of September 1939 dispelled the legend of invincibility; a strong hope remained, which was before long to be realised, that the fight would be taken up again and, this time, with very different results.[9]

Many of the surviving Polish airmen escaped to France, to fight, in due course, with the *Armée de l'Air*. They brought with them a fighting spirit and, more importantly, current combat experience. In 1940 the Poles would prove a most valuable reinforcement for Fighter Command when most needed.

Although the anticipated *Luftwaffe* attack on Britain failed to materialise in September 1939, Fighter Command nonetheless suffered its first casualties in a tragedy called the 'Battle of Barking Creek'. At 6.15 a.m. on 6 September 1939, searchlight batteries reported aircraft passing over West Mersea in Essex at high altitude. In anticipation of the long-feared 'knockout blow' on London, the Hurricanes of 56 and 151 Squadrons were scrambled from North Weald, followed by the Spitfires of 74 Squadron at Hornchurch. The Controller, in a fatal error of misidentification, then vectored the two British forces towards each other. As 151 Squadron cruised up the Thames Estuary the CO, Squadron Leader 'Teddy' Donaldson sighted bandits ahead, but cautioned his pilots not to fire unless they were positively identified as enemy aircraft. Simultaneously the Hurricanes were sighted by 74 Squadron. Climbing beneath the main formation of North Weald fighters were two more Hurricanes, which had taken off late. These the Spitfire pilots mistook to be Me 109 fighter escorts. A section of the Hornchurch Squadron's 'A' Flight then broke away and attacked the hapless pair of Hurricanes. Flying Officer Byrne and Pilot Officer Freeborn opened fire, despatching their targets. Pilot Officer Montagu Hulton-Harrop was hit and killed instantly, his head unprotected by the armour plate that would later be fitted to British fighters upon Dowding's insistence. Pilot Officer Frank Rose was more fortunate, safely crash-landing his damaged aircraft at Hintlesham.[10] This was an early indication that in a heightened state of anxiety and excitement, mistakes could easily occur – both in the air and on the plotting table. It was undoubtedly a sobering experience for Fighter Command and one indicating the extent of expectation of a German massed attack upon the outbreak of war.

The lack of an early effort at delivering a 'knockout blow', however, made it, as Flight Lieutenant Brian Lane, a Spitfire pilot with 19 Squadron, wrote, 'a queer war. Everybody said so … The *Luftwaffe's* expected blows on this island did not fall. Goring contended himself instead with raids by single aircraft against the convoys round the coasts. So for month after month we patrolled the shipping, no doubt frightening many Huns but never so much as catching sight of one'.[11] Spitfires did, however, 'catch sight' of two raiders on 16 October 1939. On that day thirty Ju 88s of I/KG 30 attacked shipping in the Firth of Forth, damaging several ships of the RN. It was the first air attack on Britain during the Second World War. The Germans would also suffer their first losses to the guns of Spitfire pilots: at 2.45 p.m. Flight Lieutenant George Pinkerton of 602 Squadron shot down a Ju 88 that crashed into the sea off Crail, and at 3.30 p.m. Red Section of 603 Squadron sent another raider crashing into the 'drink' near Port Seton. Other Spitfires of the same squadron damaged another Ju 88, but this aircraft was more fortunate and returned safely to Westerland. From that point onwards similar attacks on the RN at their Scottish bases continued, as did Spitfire victories. The following day Gladiators of 607 Squadron destroyed a Do 18 reconnaissance machine. On 21 October, the Hurricane scored its first kill in the defence of Britain when three mine-laying He 115 seaplanes were sent plunging into the sea off Yorkshire by 46 Squadron. This was hardly an august feat, however. On 30 October Pilot Officer P. W. 'Boy' Mould of 1 Squadron scored the Hurricane's first kill over France, a Do 17 destroyed near Toul. On 6 November, though, Pilot Officer Peter Ayerst was the first RAF Hurricane pilot to come face-to-face with the Me 109:

It was a bit of a long story. I was doing what we call "Aerodrome Defence". We used to take it in turns. You sat in the aircraft already strapped in, and waited for an early warning that there was an aircraft approaching. Our early warning system was produced by some French soldiers in a big ditch down the side of our grass airfield. A place called Rouve, between Verdun and Metz, South of Luxembourg. And I was sitting there in my Hurricane. The chaps in the flight office, which was a 12 foot ridge tent, shouted excitedly "THE RED FLAG'S WAVING! THE RED FLAG'S WAVING!" The French soldiers had a powerful pair of binoculars, looking to the East. And if they saw an aircraft, which they couldn't identify, or they could identify as being German, then they would wave a red flag. And that was the early warning system! And as it so happened, this particular day of 6 November 1939, there was lots of blue sky, no clouds. And I could see an aircraft at about 25,000 feet over our airfield. He was obviously doing some overhead photography. So I took off. Of course, being on these two-bladed airscrews, the climbing performance wasn't very great, even at full throttle. So I was only gradually getting up. I'd been chasing in an Easterly direction for a long time trying to get him. And he was way ahead. And we had no radio aids. No navigational assistance from the ground whatsoever. We had inter-communication between aircraft but we didn't have communication with the ground in France for navigational assistance. Nothing like that. We used to patrol up and down the French/German border, 25,000 feet for an hour at a time. Three of us used to go, but we didn't fly bunched up, in fact. Then another three would come up, and we'd go back. And this, weather permitting, went on all day. Various of the Squadron go up. It was quite busy. After I'd been flying far longer than I'd realised, we were going down and I saw the Me 109. I'd never have got closer than two miles, but I could see him because it was good visibility that day. And he went down in some cloud, lower level over Germany. And he went down into that and I lost him. Didn't even get a shot at him. So I said "Oh well ... time for me to get back". I'd been airborne a long time so I thought I'd better start finding somewhere to land. I just slowly carried on in a Westerly direction and saw some aircraft circling. So I thought "Ah! There must be an airfield there." So I went over and there was. And I landed there. It was Nancy. That particular day, our Squadron and 1 Squadron were going to put up the first offensive fighter patrol of the war. And as I was sort of turning round, coming back towards France, underneath me I saw nine aircraft in line astern, turning inside me, one behind the other. And I thought "Here come our boys !" I hadn't been in the air all that long so thought I might as well join on to this formation. So I tacked on the end.

Then I saw bloody great black crosses! So I pulled up and gave a quick squirt at the end one and went down. Unbeknown to me, there were another eighteen of them – twenty-seven all together! Also unbeknown to me as I was crossing Germany back into France, there was a French fighter patrol up of nine aircraft. And the Germans were so concentrating on me, twenty-seven of the bastards, can't think why, they weren't taking any notice of their own backs. They must have thought "We've got superiority and everything here!" And the French waded into them – Shot nine of them down! It was classified as the first big air battle of the war. I was thereafter dubbed "Decoy"! [12]

Then, on 29 November, Squadron Leader Harry Broadhurst, the CO of 111 Squadron, destroyed a lone He 111 off the Northumbrian coast. Fighter Command was not to claim its first 109s, however, until 26 March 1940. On that day, 73 Squadron's Hurricanes engaged enemy fighters over Saarlautern and Trier, claiming four destroyed and two unconfirmed. And so Brian Lane's 'queer war' continued, with still no sign of the 'knockout blow'.

After the defeat of Poland, the *Wehrmacht* rested and prepared for its next campaign: the securing of Germany's northern flank by the invasion of Denmark and Norway. This operation required harmonious co-operation between the German navy, air force and army. It was the first combined operation of its kind of the Second World War and successfully executed. The invasion began on 9 April 1940. Britain sent a task force to Narvik, but the campaign highlighted the problems ahead caused by the lack of a long-range fighter. Flying from aircraft carriers, air cover was provided by a handful of obsolete Gladiator biplanes and one squadron of Hurricanes. The small Norwegian air force was shocked and rapidly defeated. By 10 June it was all over. Once again the superiority of the *Wehrmacht* had been demonstrated to great effect. One matter that particularly vexed Dowding afterwards was the navy's failure to prevent the German seaborne invasion of Norway. Dowding's fear was that if Fighter Command was defeated in the crucial battle for survival he knew lay ahead, would the RN be any more successful in preventing an amphibious invasion of Britain? [13] The historiographers currently pedalling the view that the RN was a greater deterrent to the enemy in 1940 than Fighter Command would do well to consider that fact.

On 2 May 1940, a section of 1 Squadron Hurricanes flew to Orléans. The unit's CO, Squadron Leader 'Bull' Halahan, subsequently reported that:

... a trial took place to discover the fighting qualities of the Me 109 as compared with the Hurricane.

2. Owing to the absence of oxygen apparatus in the Me 109 the trial was carried out between 10,000 and 15,000 feet.

3. The comparison consisted of (a) take-off and climb to 15,000 feet, (b) a dog-fight, and (c) line astern formation.

4. Both aircraft took off together. Both the take-off and initial climb of the Me 109 was better than that of the Hurricane, in spite of the fact that the Hurricane was fitted with a Constant Speed airscrew, and full-throttle and revs were used.

5. At 15,000 feet the aircraft separated and approached one another head-on for the dog-fight. The Hurricane did a quick stall turn followed by a quick vertical turn and found himself on the 109's tail. The pilot of the 109 was unable to prevent this manoeuvre succeeding. From that point the Hurricane pilot had no difficulty in remaining on the tail of the Me 109. The pilot of the Me 109 tried all possible manoeuvres and finally the one most usually employed by the German pilots, namely a half-roll and vertical dive. The Hurricane followed this manoeuvre, but the Me drew away at the commencement of the dive, and it was felt that had the pilot continued this dive he might have got away. However, in the pull-out the pilot of the Me 109 found that it was all he could do to pull the machine out of the dive at all, as fore and aft it became very heavy. In fact the pilot was of the opinion that had he not used the tail adjusting gear, which itself was extremely heavy, he would not have got out of the dive at all. The pilot of the Hurricane found that he had no difficulty in pulling out of his dive inside the 109, but that he had a tendency to black-out, which was not experienced by the pilot of the 109. This tendency to black-out in the Hurricane when pulling out of high speed dives is in my opinion largely due to the rather vertical position in which the pilot sits. It is very noticeable that in the 109 the position of the pilot is reclining, with his legs well up in front of him. It has been noticed that German pilots do not pull their aircraft out of dives at very high speeds, and as I think the position in which the pilot sits is the main reason that black out is avoided, I feel that this is a point which should be duly considered when in the future a fighter is designed to meet other fighters.

6. After the dog-fight the 109 took position in line astern on the Hurricane and the Hurricane carried out a series of climbing turns and diving turns at high speeds. In the ordinary turns the Hurricane lapped the 109 after four complete circuits, and at no time was the pilot of the 109 able to get his sights on the Hurricane. In the climbing turns, though the 109 could climb faster he could not turn as fast, which enabled the

Hurricane again to get round on his tail. In climbing turns after diving, the weight of the elevators and ailerons of the 109 was so great that the pilot was unable to complete the manoeuvre, and in the diving turns he was unable to follow the Hurricane for the same reason.

7. During these tests one point became abundantly clear, namely that the 109, owing to its better camouflage, was very difficult to spot from underneath than was the Hurricane. This difference gives the 109 a definite tactical advantage, namely when they are below us they can spot us at long distance, which we when below them find most difficult. As in all our combats at the moment initial surprise is the ideal at which we aim, I strongly recommend that the underside of Hurricanes should be painted duck-egg blue, the roundels remaining the same, as it is the contrast between black and white only which is so noticeable from below.

8. The Me 109 is faster than the Hurricane by some 30 to 40 mph on the straight and level. It can out-climb and initially out-dive the Hurricane. On the other hand it has not the manoeuvrability of the Hurricane, which can turn inside without difficulty. After this clear-cut demonstration of superior manoeuvrability there is no doubt in my mind that provided Hurricanes are not surprised by 109s that the odds are more than two-to-one, and that if pilots use their heads, the balance will always be in favour of our aircraft, once the 109s have committed themselves to combat.

9. In this connection, judging by the tactics at present being employed by the 109s, namely sitting above us when they can surprise a straggler, and then only completing a dive attack then climb away, I am fairly certain that the conclusion of the German pilots is the same as our own, and I cannot help feeling that until all Hurricane aircraft have Constant Speed airscrews, to enable them to get up to the height at present adopted by the 109s, we shall have few further chances of combat with this particular type of German aircraft.[14]

Halahan's report is as illuminating in certain respects as it is naïve. Firstly, the Me 109 concerned was an E-3 of 1/JG 76, that forced-landed in France on 22 November 1939 and was captured. The comparison trials with 1 Squadron's operational Hurricanes were not flown until nearly six months later. It is hard to understand why more urgency was not attached to this. Secondly, already the German tactical experience was apparent. The 109 pilots had recognised the crucial importance of height, and how to use their machine in manoeuvres best suited to its performance – most notably high speed dives to both attack and evade. Indeed, many years later Wing Commander David Cox, recalling the fighter combats over France in 1941, described the 109 pilots attacking from high above with what he called 'Dirty darts'.[15] This is an early indication that the 'Dirty dart' – a quick 'in and out' hit – had long been practised by pilots who had probably flown in Poland, if not Spain. The only real advantage enjoyed by the Hurricane was its tighter turning circle. The statement 'providing Hurricanes are not surprised by 109s … the balance will always be in favour of our aircraft, once the 109s had committed themselves to combat' almost beggars belief. By Halahan's own admission the 109 pilots' tactics already relied upon height as pre-requisite, a height unachievable by Hurricanes without CS propellers – which at that time they did not have. Halahan would soon be rudely awoken: the enemy pilots would do everything possible to 'surprise' Hurricanes. In just three days time they would begin doing so – many times.

Abruptly, on 10 May 1940 the great storm finally broke when Hitler invaded Belgium, Holland, Luxembourg and France. Two days later Liege fell, and *panzers* crossed the Meuse at Dinant and Sedan. Hitherto, in the naïve hope of remaining neutral, the Belgians had refused Lord Gort's British Expeditionary Force (BEF) permission to fortify their border with Germany. Now the Belgian King called for help, the BEF pivoting forward from its prepared defences on the Belgian-French border. The British advanced for sixty miles over unfamiliar ground expecting to meet the German *Schwerpunkt* – point of main effort – which was expected to follow the same route as in the Great War. It did not. Holland was certainly attacked – the Dutch Air Force being wiped out on the first day – but the main enemy thrust was cleverly disguised. As Allied eyes were firmly focussed on the Belgian-Dutch border, *Panzergruppe* von Kleist achieved the supposedly impossible and successfully negotiated the Ardennes, much further south. German armour then poured out of the forest, by-passing the Maginot Line, rendering its concrete forts useless. The *panzers* then punched upwards, towards the Channel coast – ten days later the Germans had reached Laon, Cambrai, Arras, Amiens and even Abbeville. Indeed, Erwin Rommel's Seventh *Panzer* covered ground so quickly that it became known as the 'Ghost Division'. The effect on the Allies was virtual paralysis, so shocking was the assault, unprecedented in speed and fury. Civilians in Britain were equally shocked – not least after the bombing of Rotterdam on 14 May reportedly caused 30,000 civilian fatalities (although post-war estimates put the death toll at nearer 3,000).[16] Hard on the heels of Guernica and Warsaw, Rotterdam's fate was terrifying news indeed.

The British Advanced Air Striking Force (AASF) had flown to France on 2 September 1939.[17] Fairey Battle light-bombers went first, followed by Blenheims and Hurricanes – but no Spitfires. And Dowding only spared Hurricanes for two reasons: firstly, due to political pressure, he had no choice but to support the French by providing a certain amount of his precious fighters; secondly, that being so, he wisely decided only to send Hurricanes, which he knew were inferior to the Spitfire. Moreover, there were precious few Spitfires available in any case – certainly insufficient to send to France, thereby weakening Britain's defences for – as Dowding would later see it – no good purpose. On 10 May 1940, though, there were six squadrons of Hurricanes in France. One week later the equivalent of six more had crossed the Channel, and another four were operating from bases on the south-east coast of England, hopping over the Channel on a daily basis but returning to England – if they could – at the end of each day. Losses in France rapidly stacked up. The Air Ministry acted as though these casualties were a complete surprise. Dowding's sharp riposte was 'What do you expect? When you get into a war you have to lose things, including precious aircraft. That's exactly what I've been warning you about!'[18] His fears regarding the wastage of fighters were now being realised. The crux of the problem was that the more fighters Dowding sent to France, the further he weakened Britain's defences. Already Dowding had insisted that the minimum strength required to guarantee Britain's safety was fifty-two squadrons, and yet soon he was arguing a case to retain just thirty-six. Although Churchill later wrote that Dowding agreed with him the figure of twenty-five, the latter dismissed this statement as 'absurd'.[19] With the French constantly clamouring for more fighters, and putting Churchill's War Cabinet under increasing pressure, things came to a head on 15 May.

On that day, Dowding joined Newall, the CAS, at a Cabinet meeting. Both men spoke out against sending more fighters across the Channel. These could not, however, be entirely denied as elements of the BEF were poised to attack enemy communications near Brussels.[20] Dowding was dissatisfied and later commented that, 'There had already been serious casualties in France, and they alone had been worrying me a very great deal. I had to know how much longer the drain was going on, and I had to ask for a figure at which they would shut the stable door and say no more squadrons would be sent to France'.[21] Unable to request an interview with the Cabinet every time a new demand for fighters was received, on 16 May Dowding sat and composed the strongest case he could to prevent further fighters being drained away in a battle already lost. The following is extracted from that letter, which Robert Wright described as 'one of the most important documents of the early part of the Second World War'.[22]

> I must therefore request that as a matter of paramount urgency the Air Ministry will consider and decide what level of strength is to be left to the Fighter Command for the defence of this country, and will assure me that when this level has been reached not one fighter will be sent across the Channel however urgent and insistent appeals for help may be.
>
> I believe that, if an adequate fighter force is kept in this country, if the fleets remain in being, and if the Home Forces are suitably organized to resist invasion, we should be able to carry on the war single-handed for some time, if not indefinitely. But, if the Home Defence force is drained away in desperate attempts to remedy the situation in France, defeat in France will involve the final, complete and irremediable defeat of this country.[23]

On the very day that Dowding began his stance to stem the flow of British fighters to France, the Air Ministry required that a further eight half-squadrons be sent across the Channel. Worse, Churchill himself then flew to France, subsequently requesting a further six squadrons and a night attack by heavy bombers. This was ridiculous. Taking aside the problem of fighter strength, Britain had no heavy bombers at that time. As Orange argued, 'This was the pay-off for years of talk and little action'.[24] By 19 May the situation on the continent had deteriorated further still. On that day the War Office and Admiralty began facing the possibility of evacuating the BEF from France, and Churchill finally saw sense. The Prime Minister's decision was recorded in a minute: 'No more squadrons of fighters will leave the country whatever the need of France'.[25] By the following day, only three of Dowding's squadrons remained in France. He considered that this 'converted a desperate into a serious situation',[26] or, as Wright put it, he was now 'able to mend some fences'.[27] The importance of this change in policy cannot be overlooked. Yet again the defence of Britain had occasion to thank 'Stuffy' Dowding.

Interestingly, however, there was one occasion when Spitfires had been used on what could only be described as a foolhardy sortie unconnected with home defence. Operating from Martlesham Heath on the east coast, shortly after first light on Easter Monday, 13 May 1940, six Defiants of 264 Squadron took off, escorted by six Spitfires of 66 Squadron's 'A' Flight, bound for the Dutch coast. Whilst patrolling off The Hague a formation of 12/LG 1 *Stukas* dive-bombing a railroad was attacked. Unfortunately the Ju 87s had fighter escort: Me 109s of 5/JG 26. In the subsequent action *five* of the six Defiants were destroyed by the German fighters.[28] A Spitfire, N3027, was also despatched. The pilot, Pilot Officer George Brown, crash-landed but somehow returned safely home. The German pilots claimed seven Spitfires and just one Defiant, when the reverse was closer to reality. Unfortunately, therefore, it is impossible to identify which German pilot shot down Pilot Officer Brown – the first Spitfire pilot to fall to the 109's guns. In response the Spitfire pilots claimed seven Ju 87s, one Ju 88 and Flight Lieutenant Ken Gillies a 109.[29] Only claims for five *Stukas* were allowed, however, which is exactly how many 12/LG 1 lost in the engagement. Leutnant Karl Borris's 109 was also shot down, reportedly by a Defiant, but given the confusion over aircraft identification in this battle it is questionable as to whether Borris did not fall victim to Gillies. The fact of the matter, however, is that this was a pointless sortie which cost the lives of good men. It was also one which did not fit with Dowding's policy. Both squadrons concerned belonged to 12 Group, the commander of which, Air Vice-Marshal Leigh-Mallory, had opposing tactical ideas to Dowding and Park and which later erupted during the Battle of Britain. This appears to be an early indication of just how wrong Leigh-Mallory could get it in his determination to get 12 Group involved. On 18 May, in fact, as Dowding agonised over the Battle for France bleeding away his precious fighters, Leigh-Mallory visited 19 Squadron at Duxford, making arrangements for the Squadron's move to France.[30] Again, this is an early indicator of how out of touch this group commander was with the greater strategy and what was actually going on around him. Fortunately there was no repetition of either the suicidal sortie to Holland or any attempt to send 12 Group Spitfire squadrons to France.

It was clearly over Northern France, however, that the battle proper was being fought. Squadron Leader 'Teddy' Donaldson was among the Hurricane pilots embroiled and remembered that:

> The French bolted, including their air force. I have never seen so many people running so fast anywhere, as long as it were west. The British Tommies were marvellous, however, and fought their way to the sand dunes of Dunkirk. I was in command of 151 Squadron, and our Hurricanes were sent to reinforce the AASF, flying from Manston to France on a daily basis.
>
> In some respects the Germans were grossly over confident in the air, and so didn't have it all their own way. But every day we had damaged Hurricanes and no ground crews to mend them, dictating that we had to return to Manston every evening. In any event, our airfields in France were being heavily bombed, so had we stayed, although pilots could have got off the airfield to sleep, our aircraft would have taking a beating. 151 Squadron would fly up to seven sorties a day, against overwhelming odds, and on one occasion even stayed on patrol after expending our ammunition so as to prevent the *Luftwaffe* attacking defenceless British troops on the ground.[31]

Among Donaldson's pilots was Pilot Officer Jack Hamar, from Knighton in Radnorshire, who, before joining the RAF before the war, had worked in the family business, a hardware and general store. On 18 May he found himself not behind the counter but on patrol in a Hurricane, three miles north-west of Vitry:

I climbed to 7,000 feet and attacked two Me 110s, succeeding in getting onto the tail of one enemy aircraft (E/A). I opened fire at 300 yards with a burst of five seconds. Whilst closing in I noticed tracer passing over my head, from behind, and looking around discovered the other E/A on my tail. I immediately half-rolled away and noticed two Hurricanes chasing another E/A, which was diving to ground level. I followed down after the Hurricanes, and, as they broke away, I continued the chase, hedge-hopping, but did not seem to gain on the E/A. I got within 500 yards and put in a five second burst. I saw my tracer entering both wings, but did not observe any damage. As my windscreen was by this time covered in oil from my own airscrew, making sighting impossible, I broke away and returned to Vitry.[32]

Hamar's combat report is interesting. A Spitfire, with a top speed of 355 mph, would have caught that Me 110.

Flight Lieutenant Gerry Edge:

During the Fall of France I flew Hurricanes over there with 605 Squadron. After the German offensive began, the roads below were full of columns of civilians and soldiers, all progressing westwards. Once we came upon a *Stuka* that was strafing a column of refugees. It was plain to anyone, especially from that low altitude, that this was a civilian, as opposed to a military column. I am pleased to say that I shot this Boche down. There were no survivors. Does that concern me? Not at all. Of all the enemy aircraft I shot down, that one gave me great pleasure.[33]

Flight Lieutenant Peter Brothers:

Whilst operating over France as a flight commander in 32 Squadron, I naturally took our latest replacement under my wing to fly as my Number Two. Suddenly I had that feeling we all experience at some time that I was being watched. Glancing in my rear-view mirror I was startled to see, immediately behind me and between my Number Two and me, the biggest and fattest Me 109 – ever! As I instantly took evasive action his front end lit up as he fired. I escaped unscathed, the 109 climbed and vanished as I did a tight turn, looking for my Number Two. There he was, good man, cutting the corner to get back in position, as I thought, until he opened fire on me! Suggesting on the radio that his action was unpopular, as there were no other aircraft in sight we wended our way home. Not only had he not warned me of the 109's presence or fired at it, he had had such an easy shot but missed. I dealt a blow to his jauntiness by removing him from operations for two days' intensive gunnery training; sadly it did not help him survive.[34]

John Terraine made clear the importance of fighters to German air operations during the Battle of France. He also argued that a powerful Allied fighter force could have prevented the Germans achieving aerial supremacy over the battlefield and with it devastating results on the ground. The fact of the matter, though, was that the Allies did not have 'a powerful fighter force'. As Terraine stated, whilst on paper, for example, the French fielded 790 operational fighters, the truth was that nineteen out of the twenty-six French fighter squadrons were equipped with the woefully obsolete Morane-Saulnier 406 – which was no match for the 109. Only 'Hurricane pilots', wrote Terraine, 'had the satisfaction of meeting the enemy with adequate equipment and the ability to use it'.[35] Those few Hurricanes were insufficient to stem the tide, however. Terraine continued:

> The German fighters – over 1,200 of them, but above all the Me 109s – ruled the sky, and in doing so they achieved, for the first time against a major enemy, the saturation of a battle area by air power, and that is what won the Battle of France. It was, in fact, won in six days ... The Allies had lost the battle ... to the achievement of complete air superiority by the German Air Force, enabling the *Stukas* to perform, the *panzers* to roam where they willed; this was an achievement above all of the fighter arm, in particular the Messerschmitt 109.[36]

By 26 May it was clear that the Battle for France was lost. On that day the decision was taken for the BEF to retire upon, and be evacuated from, Dunkirk. From then on the whole nature of air operations over northern France changed. The RAF now had to provide a protective umbrella for the retreating BEF in addition to covering the actual evacuation in due course. It was now that Dowding committed his Spitfire force to battle over the French coast for the first time.

9

Dunkirk:
Operation DYNAMO

On 30 May 1940 the evacuation of the BEF from Dunkirk began. The *Luftwaffe's* focus became the prevention of this desperate endeavour. Consequently it was, as Dean wrote, 'a fight at odds'.[1] The contest, however, would be far from one-sided on this occasion. According to *The Luftwaffe War Diaries*:

> The *Luftwaffe* was having to operate at an ever-increasing distance from most of its bases. The *Stukas* of VIII Air Corps were now based on airfields east of St Quentin, but even from there the Channel coast – Boulogne, Calais, Dunkirk – represented the limits of their range … Two weeks of gruelling operations had sapped much of the *Luftwaffe's* strength. Many of the bomber *gruppen* could only put some fifteen aircraft out of thirty into the air. But they went in, raining down bombs of the quays and sheds of Dunkirk harbour. Around noon on the 26 May the great oil tanks on the western edge of the town went up in flames. In a precision raid Stukas destroyed the lock gates leading to the inner harbour. Bombs tore up the tracks of the marshalling yard; ships were set on fire; a freighter sank slowly to the bed of the battered harbour basin.[2]

Dowding's intervention, preventing further fighters being sent to France, was a matter he barely had time upon which to reflect when this new challenge immediately arose. Most importantly, the air operation required to cover the forthcoming Dunkirk evacuation – codenamed Operation DYNAMO – meant that Spitfires could no longer be preserved exclusively for home-defence. So hard-pressed had the Hurricane squadrons been of late that it was now necessary to commit the Spitfire to battle, *en masse*, for the first time. The problem was that Dunkirk lay fifty miles from 11 Group's closest airfield at Manston. This flight was over the sea, and contact would be over the French coastline. The inherent dangers were obvious and hardly conducive to preserving the Spitfire force. Providing continuous fighter patrols from dawn to dusk was impossible, as this would have required every single one of Dowding's precious fighters – leaving Britain itself vulnerable to attack. Another hugely significant factor in the fighting over Dunkirk would be that the British fighters were unassisted by radar. The System only provided a radar network for the defence of Britain, its stations incapable of gathering data from as far away as Dunkirk and beyond. This is why Dowding knew that the battle ahead would be so exhausting for his pilots: as they could not predict or have early warning of an enemy attack, it would be necessary to fly as many standing patrols as possible. Even so,

Dowding knew that given the size of the force he was able to make available – sixteen squadrons – there would be times, howsoever brief, that cover would be unavailable. The man entrusted with Fighter Command's contribution to this operation was the commander of 11 Group: Air Vice-Marshal Park. For what he was about to do, there was no precedent whatsoever.

At this time, however, Fighter Command's pilots were given a performance advantage with the introduction of 100 octane fuel. Of this development, Jeffrey Quill wrote that:

> It had the effect of increasing the combat rating of the Merlin from 3,000 rpm at 6½ lb or 9 lbs boost to 3,000 rpm at 12 lbs boost. This, of course, had a significant effect on the rate of climb.[3]

The Merlin III's capacity for a maximum emergency boost of +12 lbs per square inch was useful for increasing speed for a short-time span. Boost was obtained by pushing a knob on the throttle quadrant, called 'going through the gate', or 'Buster' in correct radio parlance – meaning 'make all haste'. Although the improvements of 12 lbs of extra boost were really only evident up to 15,000 feet, it was another step towards achieving an edge over the 109. Emergency boost, though, could only be used for a few minutes at a time, so as not to damage the engine, and any use of it, in fact, had to be recorded by the pilot in the engine's log. Pilots would use this facility to catch up and intercept an enemy aircraft or, indeed, to escape from a tactically disadvantageous situation. Pilots fighting over Dunkirk would soon find occasion to be thankful of this extra power.

On 21 May, Spitfires were in action off Dunkirk and Calais, 54 and 74 Squadrons claiming a number of enemy bombers. Two Spitfires were lost, both of 74 Squadron. One pilot returned to England but the other was captured. The following day saw 65 and 74 Squadrons claiming more bombers but without loss. On 23 May the first big air battle between the opposing fighters took place over Calais. Spitfires of 54 Squadron claimed three 109s destroyed, whilst 92 claimed two in addition to seven Me 110s shot down.[4] Both squadrons claimed various enemy aircraft as probably destroyed or damage. I/JG 27, however, lost four 109s whilst no 110s are recorded as having been destroyed or damaged that day.[5] The balance sheet was not favourable to Fighter Command: 74 Squadron lost two Spitfires, 92 Squadron five.[6] The total of sorties flown by 11 Group on that day was 250; ten pilots were lost.[7] Already the inexperience of the RAF pilots was beginning to show.

The action was even greater on 24 May, 54, 65, 74 and 92 Squadrons all being engaged, these being Spitfire squadrons of 11 Group based at Hornchurch and Biggin Hill. At this time Park's squadrons were patrolling singly. The *Luftwaffe* fighters, however, were sweeping the Channel coast in *gruppe* strength – some thirty-six aircraft.[8] II/JG 26 pounced on 74 Squadron, giving Pilot Officer John Freeborn reason to be thankful for his Merlin's extra boost:

> As I broke away two Me 109s got onto my tail. I dived steeply with the two e/a following me, one was on my tail the other on my port quarter. As I dived to ground level I throttled back slightly and the e/a on my tail overshot me and I was able to get a three seconds burst at a range of about fifty to 100 yards. He seemed to break away slowly to the right as though he was badly hit and I think he crashed. The second Me 109 then got on my tail but I got away from it using the boost cut-out.[9]

Only 54 Squadron's Spitfires made claims the following day. Pilot Officer Colin Gray, a New Zealander, destroyed a 109 but his own aircraft was damaged. Again, emergency boost got him out of trouble:

> I decided the best course of action was to set off for home as speedily as possible. I pressed the emergency tit, which poured on the fuel, but was only for use in dire emergency as it could overstress the engine. I considered this was justifiable under the circumstances, since I was still inside France and could not see anyone coming to my assistance.[10]

Three other pilots of the same squadron were not so lucky, being shot down;[11] in response, 54 claimed four 110s destroyed in addition to Gray's 109.[12] The positive effect of extra boost in combat was becoming obvious.

On the evening of 25 May, 12 Group's 19 Squadron moved from Duxford in 12 Group to Hornchurch in 11 Group, still north of the Thames Estuary but closer to the French coast. What Flight Lieutenant Brian Lane had previously considered to be a 'queer war' was about to come to an end.[13] As he later wrote, 'the shadow of Dunkirk had fallen across our path … to-morrow it would become reality'.[14] The following day, 26 May, the decision was formally made to retire upon, and evacuate from, Dunkirk. Air Vice-Marshal Park had already decided upon his tactics, which he explained to 11 Group's controllers. Squadrons, like 19, had been brought south to make up the sixteen squadrons he had been assigned for the task. These would operate from airfields near the coast, such as Hornchurch, Biggin Hill, and Manston. After their first patrol, however, they would land at forward stations such as Hawkinge and Lympne, where the fighters would be quickly re-armed and re-fuelled before returning to their patrol lines. The force would be divided so that half worked mornings, the other half afternoons. After the day's second patrol, unless, as Orange wrote, 'the crisis was great', the squadrons were permitted to return to their home or adopted home base as appropriate.[15]

Pilot Officer Michael Lyne remembered arriving at Hornchurch and the following day's events:

> To us the Mess had a new atmosphere, people clearing kit from the rooms belonging to casualties and the Station Commander insisting on closing the bar and sending us to bed early to be ready for the battles awaiting us.
>
> On 26 May we were called upon to patrol over the beaches as a single squadron. I will always remember heading off to the east and seeing the columns of black smoke from the Dunkirk oil storage tanks. We patrolled for some time without seeing any aircraft. We received no information from British radar. We had received excellent VHF radios shortly before, but they were only of use between ourselves, we could not communicate with other squadrons should the need arise.
>
> Suddenly we saw ahead, going towards Calais where the Rifle Brigade was holding out, about forty German aircraft. We were twelve. Squadron Leader Geoffrey Stephenson aligned us for an attack in sections of three on the formations of Ju 87s. As a former CFS A1 Flying Instructor he was a precise flier and obedient to the book, which stipulated an

overtaking speed of 30 mph. What the book never foresaw was that we would attack Ju 87s at just 130 mph. The CO led his Section, Pilot Officer Watson No. 2 and me No. 3, straight up behind the *Stukas* which looked very relaxed. They thought we were their fighter escort, but the leader had been very clever and had pulled his formation away towards England, so that when they turned in towards Calais he would protect their rear. Alas for him we were coming, by sheer chance, from Dunkirk rather than Ramsgate.

Meanwhile Stephenson realised that we were closing far too fast. I remember his call "Number 19 Squadron! Prepare to attack!" then to us "Red Section, throttling back, throttling back." We were virtually formatting on the last section of Ju 87s – at an incredibly dangerous speed in the presence of enemy fighters – and behind us the rest of 19 Squadron staggered along at a similar speed. Of course the Ju 87s could not imagine that we were a threat. Then Stephenson told us to take a target each and fire. As far as I know we got the last three, we could hardly have done otherwise, then we broke away and saw nothing of the work by the rest of the Squadron – but it must have been dodgy as the 109s started to come round. As I was looking round for friends after the break I came under fire from the rear for the first time – and did not at first know it. The first signs were mysterious little corkscrews of smoke passing my starboard wing. Then I heard a slow "thump, thump", and realised that I was being attacked by a 109 firing machine-guns with tracer and its cannon banging away. I broke away sharpish – and lost him.

I made a wide sweep and came back to the Calais area to find about five *Stukas* going around in a tight defensive circle. The German fighters had disappeared so I flew to take the circle at the head-on position and gave it a long squirt. It must have been at this stage that I was hit by return fire, for when I got back to Hornchurch I found bullet holes in the wings which had punctured a tyre.

Alas my friend Watson was never seen again. Stephenson forced-landed on the beach and was taken prisoner.[16]

Flight Lieutenant Lane's report of the action described what happened when the 109s bounced the hapless Spitfires and shot down Pilot Officer Watson:

> … I was forced to break away … I looked round and observed an Me 109 attacking a Spitfire which was almost immediately hit forward of the cockpit by a shell from the e/a. The Spitfire went into a steep dive and I subsequently saw a parachute in the sea about half a mile off Calais.
>
> A dogfight now ensued and I fired bursts at several e/a, mostly deflection shots. Three e/a attached themselves to my tail, two doing stern attacks, whilst the third attacked from the beam. I managed to turn towards this e/a and fired a good burst in a front quarter deflection attack. The e/a then disappeared and was probably shot down. By this time I was down to sea level and made for the English coast, taking violent evasive action. I gradually drew away from the e/a's using 12 lb boost which gave me an air speed of 300 mph.[17]

Clearly the German fighter pilots involved in this action were experienced and knew exactly what they were about. Once more, 12 lbs boost saved the day for a Spitfire pilot.

The 109 Lane considered 'probably shot down' may well not have been: it could have been simply relying upon the benefits of its fuel-injected DB 601A to dive away and escape.

Crushing a blow though losing two pilots – one of which was the CO – was, 19 Squadron was patrolling the French coast again that afternoon. Pilot Officer Michael Lyne:

In the afternoon Brian Lane led us on our second patrol over the evacuation beaches. Suddenly we were attacked by a squadron of 109s. As before we were flying in the inflexible and outdated formation of "Vics of three". Later the basic unit became the pair, or two pairs in what became known as the "Finger Four". Such a formation, as the Germans were already using, could turn very quickly, with each aircraft turning on its own, but the formation automatically re-formed in full contact at the end of the manoeuvre.

Because of our formation we quickly lost contact with each other after the 109s attacked. I found myself alone, but with a pair of 109s circling above me left-handed whilst I was going right-handed. The leader dropped his nose as I pulled up mine and fired. He hit me in the engine, knee, radio and rear fuselage. I was in a spin and was streaming glycol. He must have thought I was gone for good. So did I. But for a short time the engine kept going as I straightened out and dived into cloud, setting compass course shortly before the cockpit filled with white smoke which blotted out everything. In a few seconds the engine seized and I became an efficient glider. On breaking cloud I saw Deal some way off, but remembered the advice to hold an efficient speed. So with 200 feet to spare I crossed the surf and crash-landed on the beach. That adventure ended my flying until 19 February 1941.[18]

It had not been a good start for 19 Squadron. Flight Sergeant George Unwin:

The tacticians who wrote the book really believed that in the event of war it would be fighter versus bomber only. Our tight formations were all very well for the Hendon Air Pageant but useless in combat. Geoffrey Stephenson was a prime example: without modern combat experience he flew exactly by the book – and was in effect shot down by it.[19]

According to Orange, it was 'only after urgent and repeated requests that Park secured Dowding's permission to employ squadrons two at a time and abandon continuous coverage'.[20] Hitherto Dowding had insisted on patrolling singly so as to extend the length of coverage provided. Losses had been high, because the German fighters patrolled in greater strength. A compromise had therefore been reached. On 28 May Park's Spitfire squadrons flew in pairs for the first time. Squadron Leader H. W. 'Tubby' Mermagen, the CO of 222 Squadron, remembered that: 'On 28 May 1940 I led the Squadron in a wing on its first patrol over the Dunkirk beaches, at 6.30 a.m. The sortie lasted two hours and forty-five minutes, a long flight in a Spitfire.'[21]

The commander of 'A' Flight in Mermagen's 222 Squadron was none other than the irrepressible Flight Lieutenant Douglas Bader, who in spite of pranging Spitfires on 19 Squadron had been promoted. On 1 June Bader saw action for the first time, subsequently claiming an Me 109 destroyed and an Me 110 damaged. Squadron Leader Mermagen:

When we landed Douglas stomped over to me and enthused "I got five for certain, Tubby old boy!" Now this was the first time that we had met Me 109s, which were damn good aeroplanes, and everything happened very quickly indeed. To be certain of destroying five enemy aircraft in such confused circumstances was impossible. I said "You're a bloody liar, Bader!" We credited him with one destroyed.[22]

Mermagen was right: fighter combat moved so quickly that it was indeed confusing, the speed involved frequently deceiving the human eye. For this reason both sides inevitably over estimated their kills. Moreover, the more fighters were engaged, the higher became the over-claiming ratio.

From 29 May Park employed his squadrons in wings of four. The loss ratio was not reduced, however, as fresh squadrons arrived, without any combat experience of this kind, and suffered accordingly. On that day three out of five raids were intercepted, but those that got through caused great execution among the soldiers queuing on the beaches below. Combat claims by the Spitfire wings were, Orange wrote, 'exaggerated' and he rightly argued that 'pairs of squadrons would have done as well and also permitted more frequent patrols'.[23] Poor flying weather hindered both sides on 30 May but heavy German attacks over the next two days ensured that the beleaguered troops suffered accordingly. The army asked, 'Where was the RAF?' Those being bombed on the beaches were unable to see that Park's fighters were engaged above the low cloud and attempting to prevent enemy bombers reaching Dunkirk. The RAF personnel involved were working hard; armourer Fred Roberts:

> We worked long days, 5 a.m. until perhaps 8 p.m. It was very tiring, even if we were only waiting around for the Spitfires to take-off or return. After the final stand-down I had to strip the guns in QV-H and give them a thorough cleaning, but no boiling, checking everything, testing the air lines and solenoids, checking the ammo boxes, testing the gunsight. This was the regular evening clean ready for the next morning's early start throughout the whole time we were at Hornchurch.[24]

In spite of Fighter Command's best efforts, the beaches were so badly hit that on 2 June evacuation was switched to night-time. Two days later it was all over. The Fall of France itself was, without question, an unmitigated disaster of immeasurable proportions. The BEF had left behind 68,000 men including 40,000 prisoners of war, and all its armour and artillery. A total of 200 ships had been sunk during the operation, which began hoping to evacuate up to 45,000 troops. The total actually rescued was 340,000, from which the British could take heart.[25] In spite of recent revisionist attempts, this can only be considered a victory within the circumstance of an overall catastrophic defeat. *The Luftwaffe War Diaries* commented thus:

> For the British these were days of hell. Having resolved to evacuate their army … for this purpose they put in everything they had – even their home based fighters, hitherto held carefully in reserve, including the Spitfire Mk IIA, whose performance matched that of the ME 109E. These fighters had one considerable advantage: Dunkirk and the whole battle zone lay well within the operating range of their fighters.

The German account is incorrect, however: no Spitfire Mk IIAs fought over Dunkirk. Indeed, the first of these improved machines did not reach the squadrons until 22 August 1940.[26] The Spitfire that 'matched' the Me 109E was the Mk IA, fitted with the two-pitch propeller. It is noteworthy, however, that the enemy account considered the Spitfire on equal terms to its own single-seat fighter. The New Zealander Alan Deere flew Spitfires over Dunkirk and later wrote:

> In my written report on the combat I stated that in my opinion the Spitfire was superior overall to the Me 109, except in the initial climb and dive; however this was an opinion contrary to the belief of the so-called experts. Their judgement was of course based on intelligence assessments and the performance of the 109 in combat with the Hurricane in France. In fact, the Hurricane, though vastly more manoeuvrable than either the Spitfire or the Me 109, was so sadly lacking in speed and rate of climb, that its too-short combat experience against the 109 was not a valid yardstick for comparison. The Spitfire, however, possessed these two attributes to such a degree that, coupled with a better rate of turn than the Me 109, it had the edge overall in combat. There may have been scepticism by some about my claim for the Spitfire, but I had no doubts on the score; nor did my fellow pilots in 54 Squadron. Later events, particularly in the Battle of Britain, were to prove me right.[27]

The Spitfire had undoubtedly acquitted itself well in this first test against the 109. At the end of the campaign, however, Dowding only had 331 operational Hurricanes and Spitfires. 106 fighters had been destroyed over Dunkirk and eighty of their pilots were lost. The Germans had lost 130 aircraft during the bitter combats over the beaches.[28] According to Peach, over Dunkirk 'the balance in the air shifted to the RAF and its Spitfires … Air Vice-Marshal Keith Park, in his combat assessment reported "total ascendancy" over the German bombers … the balance of advantage lay with the *Luftwaffe* only on 27 May and 1 June. The RAF had established local (albeit impermanent) air superiority'.[29] He added that the Spitfire had performed 'very well at Dunkirk. More importantly the RAF's tactical doctrine, techniques and procedures had been found wanting and many of them were changed – just in time for the Battle of Britain'.[30]

In England replacements for the losses suffered by Fighter Command in France and during the Dunkirk evacuation were hurriedly being trained. Pilot Officer David Scott-Malden, a Cambridge Classics graduate with First Class Honours, was learning how to fly Spitfires at Aston Down, near Stroud in Gloucestershire. In his diary he wrote:

> *Wednesday, June 12th, 1940*: Had a test on a Harvard and passed successfully into Spitfire flight. First solo an indescribable thrill. Felt a pretty king man.
> *Friday, June 14th, 1940*: Paris falls. Astonishing to think of it in the hands of the Germans. Reynaud declares "We will fight on, even if driven out of France". Marvellous days doing aerobatics in Spitfires.
> *Monday, June 17th, 1940*: The French give up hostilities. Cannot yet conceive the enormity of it all. I suppose it will not be long before we are defending England in earnest.[31]

10

The Lull

France formally surrendered on 22 June 1940. Hitler had already been sight-seeing in Paris. Mere words simply cannot convey the enormity of this disaster for the Allies. Although there were those in Churchill's cabinet, namely Halifax and Chamberlain, who urged the Prime Minister to consider a negotiated peace with Nazi Germany, he made the future clear to the House of Commons one day after the Dunkirk evacuation concluded:

> We shall go on to the end, we shall fight on in France, we shall fight on the seas and the oceans, we shall fight with growing confidence and growing strength in the air, we shall defend our island, whatever the cost may be, we shall fight on the beaches, we shall fight on the landing grounds, we shall fight in the fields and in the streets, we shall fight in the hills; we shall never surrender.[1]

On 18 June the last of Dowding's battered squadrons had returned home from France. According to the official history:

> There was, in sum, a gain of eleven squadrons, there being fifty-eight squadrons in Fighter Command on 20 June, compared to forty-seven on 10 May. But this was largely a nominal gain that had yet to be made into a real one; for no less than twelve of these squadrons were unfit for battle and few of the rest had escaped without serious losses. Altogether, 396 Hurricanes and 67 Spitfires were lost outright during the French campaign: and over the same period nearly 280 fighter pilots were killed, missing or made prisoner, and sixty wounded. The result is reflected in the returns of operational strength in Hurricanes and Spitfires at the close of the campaign. On 24 June, for example, nineteen Spitfire squadrons, with an establishment of sixteen initial equipment aircraft and twenty-two pilots each, reported an average operational strength of thirteen aircraft; eighteen Hurricane squadrons, with the same establishment, reported an average of twelve aircraft. The non-operational Hurricane and Spitfire squadrons were in an even worse case. It was to be well into July before all the Command's squadrons were reckoned fit for operations; and even then there was still a deficiency of pilots reckoned fit for operations; and even then there was still a deficiency of pilots amounting to nearly twenty per cent of establishment.[2]

As the foregoing narrative concluded, 'the price paid for intervention had thus been high'.[3]

At a time when the British should have been enjoying their annual summer holidays at such south-east Victorian coastal resorts as Brighton, Eastbourne and Hove, they braced themselves for a German seaborne invasion. At London's railway stations lists appeared of hundreds of coastal locations that could no longer be visited for 'holiday, recreation or pleasure'. Large tracts of the coastline became 'Defence Areas', entry forbidden to those without special permits. Sea-front hotels were requisitioned, beaches were criss-crossed by barbed wire, and machine-guns sprouted from pill boxes everywhere. A curfew was imposed.[4] The great British novelist and broadcaster J. B. Priestley visited Margate and wrote that 'The few signs of life only made the place seem more unreal and spectral'.[5] The British were in no mood, perhaps, for holidays.

In less than a year the map of democratic Europe had been re-drawn by a totalitarian dictator bent upon aggressive territorial expansion. The process had provided graphic and terrifying examples of destruction wrought by aerial bombing. The fear of the bomber that had gathered in intensity throughout the 1930s was confirmed. Having read with horror of the fate of Guernica, Warsaw and Rotterdam, the British people braced themselves for their turn. Hitler had swept aside all challengers and now stood just twenty-two miles from Britain. There was no doubt as to what lay ahead. Churchill's speeches made that clear enough. The *Luftwaffe* was undoubtedly supreme, the undefeated master of the skies over Spain, Poland, Norway, Denmark, Holland, Belgium, Luxembourg and even France. So the nation braced itself and awaited the arrival of German bombers to deliver that long awaited and inevitable 'knock-out blow'. But the attitude was not defeatist. It was defiant. There was no question of capitulation.

Whatever lay ahead, the vast majority of Britons had no doubt that the war against Germany should continue – no matter how hopeless that appeared at that time. Overy dismissed the notion that Britain was 'alone', however, rightly pointing out that this disregarded the 'vital and substantial support of Canada, South Africa, Australia, New Zealand, India and the colonial empire'.[6] Nonetheless none of those nations actually stood within sight of Dunkirk's blazing oil tanks or, indeed, within range of German bombers. Calder talked of the Battle of Britain as being nothing more than a 'myth'.[7] Certainly the facts support persuasive arguments that the *Wehrmacht* had no experience of such a huge amphibious combined operation as the proposed seaborne invasion of England involved; that in reality Germany also lacked the resources necessary for such a great undertaking; that the opportunity was an unexpected one for which there had been insufficient combined planning, and that the *Luftwaffe*, lacking both heavy bombers and a long-range escort fighter, was not actually equipped to achieve the aerial superiority required for an invasion. All of these things are true. But the essential point is that the British people did not know this. At that time the Nazi war machine appeared invincible. But the Britons did not falter or fail in facing the prospect of devastating air attacks that had been feared for so long. They were prepared to weather the storm to preserve their chosen way of life and territory. This is not 'myth'. It is fact. So the crucial thing is that, taking aside arguments as to whether or not Hitler's proposed invasion could have succeeded, the spirit of the British people was supremely defiant and courageous. To save them, the people looked to the pilots of Fighter Command. And the RAF pilots, they knew, had the Spitfire.

After Dunkirk there was a lull in the fighting as both sides retired to repair and take stock. The campaigns fought thus far had proved that an air force with superiority and possessed of the initiative could give powerful and decisive support to rapid armoured thrusts – by preparing the way ahead with concentrated bombing, and then protecting the flanks of friendly forces from enemy counter-attack. The effectiveness of airborne troops, either conveyed by glider or parachute – providing aerial superiority had already been achieved – had also been proven. In France the Germans had met the Hurricane, which had fought well but in hopeless circumstances. Over Dunkirk the Spitfire had earned the enemy's respect. Even so, this was only a 'foretaste of effective fighter opposition'.[8] Supremely confident, Göring had not yet recognised its implications. His *Luftwaffe* now had bases in Northern France, vastly extending the range of its bombers and, most importantly, putting even London within range of the Me 109. That changed everything. The tacticians who had written Fighter Command's Air Fighting Manual could never have been expected to predict Hitler's unprecedented advance to the Channel coast making this possible. Göring, however, did not necessarily support the proposal for a seaborne invasion. Rightly he recognised that 'the planned operation can only be considered under conditions of absolute air superiority'. He believed that a landing under fire was unnecessary because the war against Britain had 'already taken on a victorious course'. The essential condition was destruction of the RAF. As Townsend wrote, 'Without air defences Britain would be impotent … Invasion would then be unnecessary'.[9] This, then, was the task that Göring set-to: annihilation of Fighter Command. After the Fall of France, therefore, the *Luftwaffe* prepared for a new assault.

On 10 June 1940, during the lull between the Fall of France and the Battle of Britain, the A&AEE at Farnborough tested Me 109E-3, *Werk-Nummer* 1304 – the same aircraft that had previously been used for comparison trials with 1 Squadron's Hurricanes at Orléans on 7 May. Trials were flown with Spitfire Mk IA, K9791, fitted with a Rotol CS airscrew. The resulting report is reproduced verbatim:

1. The trial commenced with the two aircraft taking off together, with the Spitfire slightly behind and using +6¼lbs boost and 3,000 r.p.m.
2. When fully airborne the pilot of the Spitfire reduced his revolutions to 2,650 rpm and was then able to overtake and out-climb the Me 109. At 4,000 feet the Spitfire pilot was 1,000 feet above the Me 109, from which position he was able to get on its tail, and remain there within effective range despite all efforts of the pilot of the Me 109 to shake him off.
3. The Spitfire then allowed the Me 109 to get on his tail and attempted the shake him off. This he found quite easy owing to the superior manoeuvrability of his aircraft, particularly in the looping plane and at low speeds between 100 and 140 mph. By executing a steep turn just above stalling speed, he ultimately got back into a position on the tail of the Me 109.
4. Another effective form of evasion with the Spitfire was found to be a steep, climbing spiral at 120 mph, using +6¼lbs boost and 2,650 rpm; in this manoeuvre the Spitfire gained rapidly on the Me 109, eventually allowing the pilot to execute a half-roll on the tail of his opponent.

1. It nearly happened: pilots of 32 Squadron run towards their Gloster Gauntlet fighters, scrambling during the 1937 Air Exercise. Biplanes still equipped most squadrons of Fighter Command at the time of Munich in 1938: had Britain gone to war then – and fought the comparatively lethal Me 109 – the outcome would have been disastrous.

2. Fortunately in October 1938, 32 Squadron received the new Hawker Hurricane Mk I. These are those very machines, on show at Biggin Hill. Note the fixed-pitch wooden Watts propeller – by this time the Me 109 was already equipped with the VDM Constant Speed propeller, which greatly increased performance.

3. Fitters of 56 Squadron maintaining the Merlin engine of a Hurricane during trials with the new aircraft. *Courtesy Paul Weaver.*

4. The original Hurricane Mk Is of 56 Squadron in formation for the cameraman. *Courtesy Paul Weaver.*

5. A pilot of 56 Squadron aloft from North Weald in a Hurricane, L1599, from the first production batch during 1938. The wings and fuselage of these aircraft, like biplanes, were fabric covered. *Courtesy Paul Weaver*.

6. A Hurricane Mk I, N2409, of the first production batch built by Hawkers at Brooklands. Snapped at Gravesend in March 1940 by Flight Lieutenant Peter Brothers, this machine saw action during the forthcoming Battle of France. These aircraft were powered by the improved Merlin III and were fitted with the three bladed de Havilland two-pitch propeller, but lacked both an armoured glass windscreen and a rear-view mirror.

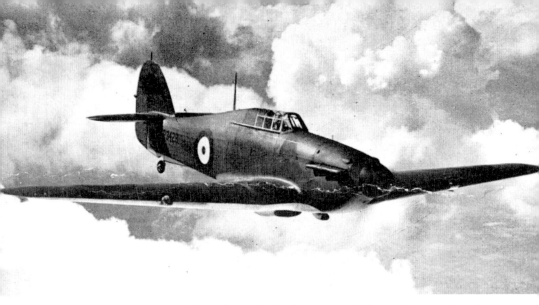

7. Hurricane P3428, of the third production batch, fitted with an armoured glass windscreen and metal-stressed wings.

8. The Chief Designer and a Director of The Supermarine Aviation Works (Vickers) Limited, Reginald Joseph Mitchell, whose visionary monoplane seaplane designs won the Schneider Trophy for Britain, and who subsequently designed the Spitfire. Tragically, Mitchell died of rectal cancer aged forty-two on 11 June 1937, and thus had no knowledge of the immense contribution his fighter made to the fight against Nazi Germany. Due to a deficiency in the current honours system, which fails to recognise achievement posthumously, Mitchell has never received any formal honour for creating the Spitfire. His son, Gordon, campaigned tirelessly to resolve this until his own death in 2009 – but without success.

9. Mitchell's Schneider Trophy-winning design, the S.6B. This was a major step forward in both technology and in the monoplane achieving ascendance over the biplane.

10. Mitchell, centre, pictured at Eastleigh after K5054's successful maiden flight, 5 March 1936. Also pictured is Captain 'Mutt' Summers (extreme left), who had just made that historic flight, and Supermarine Test Pilot Jeffrey Quill (extreme right) who undertook much of the new aircraft's testing and volunteered to fly the fighter in combat during the Battle of Britain – so as to gain first-hand knowledge of its performance in action.

11. Head-on views of the aircraft which formed the development lineage of the Supermarine Spitfire. Top left, top right and middle left: the S.4, S.5 and S.6 Schneider Trophy racing seaplanes; middle right: Mitchell's first and unsuccessful attempt at a monoplane fighter, the Type 224, and bottom: the eight-gun Supermarine Spitfire Mk IA.

12. The prototype Spitfire, K5054.

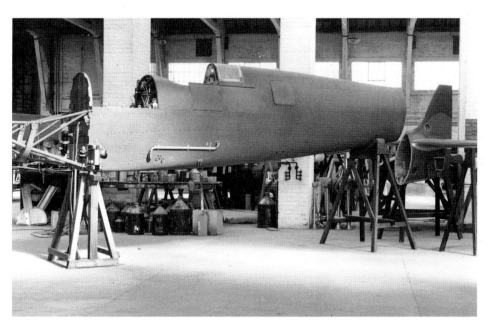

13. One of the first production Spitfire Mk Is being assembled at Supermarine's factory at Woolston, Southampton. This comparatively small factory, however, was unable to cope with mass-producing the Spitfire. A huge 'Shadow Factory' was therefore opened at Castle Bromwich, Birmingham. Although production was initially both slow and problematic, ultimately the majority of the 22,000 Spitfires built were built in Birmingham.

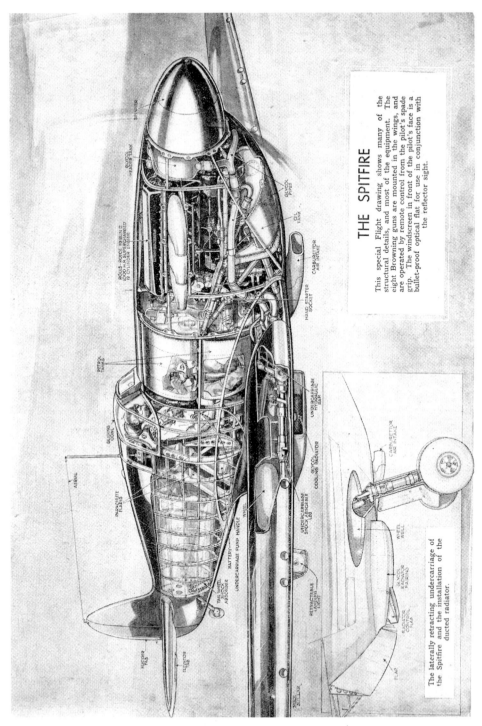

14. A cut-away drawing of the new Spitfire published in *Flight* magazine during 1940. The armoured glass windscreen can clearly be seen, but the aerial mast remained basic. The petrol tanks situated directly in front of the pilot can also be seen.

15. The first squadron to receive the Spitfire was 19 Squadron at Duxford, in August 1938. These aircraft were snapped by armourer Fred Roberts later that year. Like the first Hurricanes, these Spitfires had a fixed-pitch Watts propeller, but, unlike the Hurricane, were covered in a stressed-metal skin.

16. Three 19 Squadron Spitfires flying in Vic formation. Developed pre-war for attacking bombers, the tacticians did not anticipate fighter-to-fighter combat on the basis of a lack of range and, indeed, that the high speeds and 'g' forces involved would make such combat impossible.

17. A squadron of Spitfire Mk Is in the standard Vic formation. Pilots flew in close formation, concentrating too much on keeping station rather than searching for the enemy, and the formation was found too inflexible for high speed fighter combat – which became reality in 1940.

18. A flight of 310 Squadron's Hurricanes in Vic formation.

19. A *Schwarm* of II/J.G. 27 Me 109Es during the Battle of Britain. In reality each aircraft would be spread out, able to search for the enemy, and in action the four machines broke into two pairs – the *Rotte* – each comprising leader and wingman. *Peter Taghon Collection.*

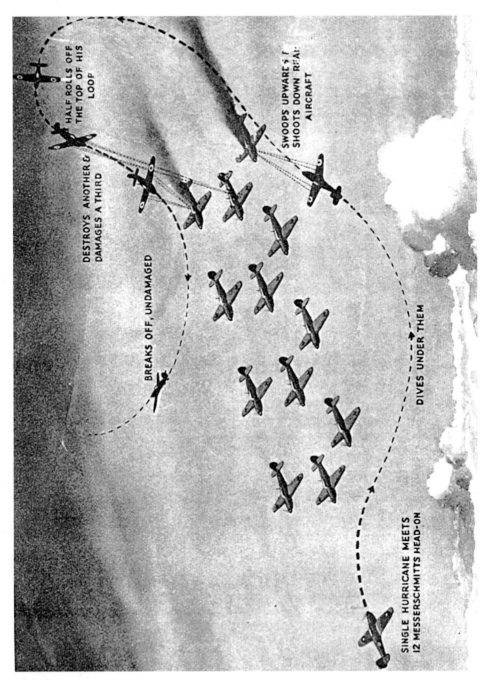

HALF ROLLS OFF THE TOP OF HIS LOOP

DESTROYS ANOTHER & DAMAGES A THIRD

BREAKS OFF, UNDAMAGED

SWOOPS UPWARDS & SHOOTS DOWN REAR AIRCRAFT

DIVES UNDER THEM

SINGLE HURRICANE MEETS 12 MESSERSCHMITTS HEAD-ON

20. Wishful thinking: a spurious tactical diagram published in the Air Ministry's morale-raising account of the Battle of Britain, published in 1941. If anyone believed that Me 109s either flew in the same suicidal formation as the RAF, or would take no evasive action upon sighting an enemy aircraft and, indeed, coming under fire, they were much mistaken.

21. The Spitfire Mk IA of Flight Lieutenant Brian Lane of 19 Squadron, pictured at Duxford in September 1939. This aircraft has the two-pitch de Havilland propeller, armoured windscreen and a reflector – as opposed to the original, simple, ring and bead gunsight. The Squadron's code letters were originally 'WZ', but this was changed to 'QV'. The individual code letter of Lane's personal Spitfire was always 'K'. *Courtesy Henry Fargus.*

Top: 22. Over Dunkirk Fighter Command attempted to put into practise the months of training using completely useless formations and tactics. On 26 May 1940, Squadron Leader Geoffrey Stephenson led 19 Squadron into attack, in vics line astern, throttled right back in an attempt to match the speed of their intended targets – the much slower *Stuka*. Bounced by 109s, 19 Squadron paid the price for its combat inexperience: Stephenson was shot down and captured, and Pilot Officer Watson was killed. This is Stephenson's Spitfire being inspected by a German soldier on the beach at Coquelles, near Calais. Unusually it lacks an individual code letter. The devastating effect of 20 mm cannon fire on the aircraft's tail is evident.

Bottom: 23. Brian Lane, pictured as a Pilot Officer flying Gloster Gauntlets before the Second World War. Although a comparatively reserved intellectual, Lane was a compelling leader, described as 'unflappable' by Flight Sergeant George Unwin. Lane led 19 Squadron during the Dunkirk fighting, after Stephenson's capture, for which he received the DFC. After the death in action of Stephenson's successor on 5 September 1942, Lane became CO himself. Officially rated as an 'Exceptional Fighter Pilot', Lane destroyed at least eight enemy aircraft before his own death in action on 13 December 1942. He remains 'missing' but left behind a superb first-hand account entitled *Spitfire!* (see Bibliography). *Courtesy Henry Fargus.*

24. The Spitfire was preserved for Home Defence and not wasted in a lost battle in France. The Spitfire force, however, provided the majority of air cover to the Dunkirk evacuation – operating temporarily from airfields close to the south-east coast. Here Pilot Officer David Crook of 609 Squadron awaits the call to start up and taxi around the perimeter track for take-off at Northolt during Operation DYNAMO.

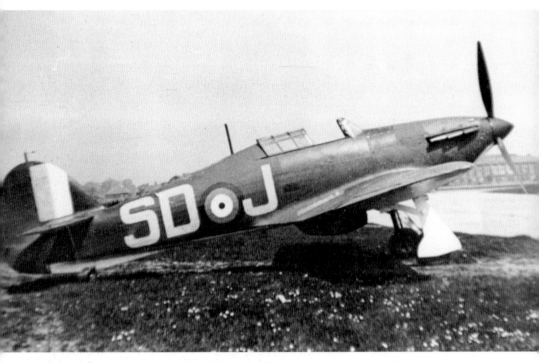

25. A Hawker Hurricane Mk I of 501 Squadron at Tangmere in early May 1940. Later that month this machine fought with the unit during the Battle of France.

26. A Hurricane Mk I of the Czech 310 Squadron has its guns harmonised in the butts at Duxford during the Battle of Britain. By now a rear-view mirror, reflector gunsight and fared aerial had been added. The Hurricane's machine-guns were wing-mounted in batteries of four, closely spaced and near the wing-root, firing just beyond the propeller arc. This made the Hurricane a very steady gun platform.

27. Another 310 Squadron Hurricane Mk I, P3148, at Duxford during the Battle of Britain. An aircraft from the first production batch built by Gloster Aircraft at Brockworth, these machines were fitted with either the de Havilland two-pitch propeller or the Rotol Constant Speed propeller as standard. The latter was superior, however, and a similar airscrew was already fitted to the Me 109. Consequently Constant Speed propellers were fitted to all operational Spitfires and Hurricanes on the fighter stations in August 1940. This aircraft has the Rotol propeller.

28. A rather war-weary Hurricane, also fitted with the Rotol propeller. Sergeant Laurence 'Rubber' Thorogood poses in an 87 Squadron machine during the Battle of Britain at Bibury in Gloucestershire.

29. Pilot Officer 'Crasher' White and his 504 Squadron Hurricane at Fiton during the Battle of Britain.

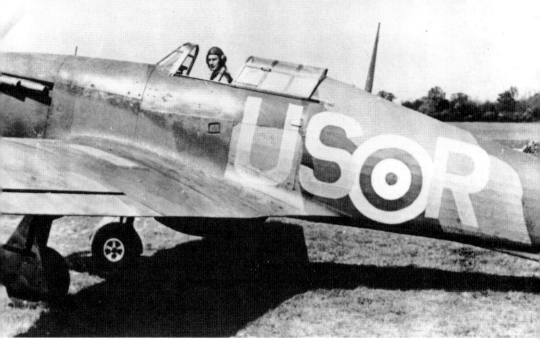

30. Another Hurricane from Hawker's first production batch. Pilot Officer Peter Down of 56 Squadron scrambles from North Weald in August 1940.

31. Hurricanes from the initial production batch were modified to maintain them as operationally capable. This is one such machine, L2012 of 605 Squadron, snapped at Croydon during September 1940. Close to London, the Croydon fighters were heavily engaged, and the airfield was repeatedly bombed – as evidenced by the groundcrews' steel helmets. On 15 September 1940 – Battle of Britain Day – Pilot Officer Tom Cooper-Slipper rammed a Do 17 of 5/KG 3 over Marden. The pilot safely baled out.

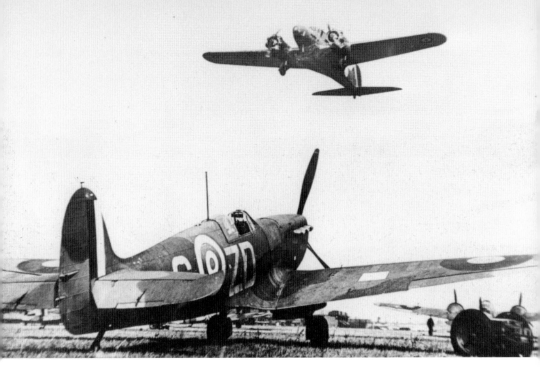

32. An Avro Anson over-flies a Spitfire Mk IA of 222 Squadron at 222 Squadron during the Battle of Britain. Note the yellow square patch painted on the port wing, which changed colour to give warning of gas attack. Again, the starter trolley is plugged in – ready for a rapid take-off.

33. A Spitfire Mk IA of 602 Squadron awaits the call to scramble at Drem in Scotland. The aircraft has the de Havilland two-pitch propeller and its starter trolley plugged in. So far north, Spitfire pilots largely engaged lone or small sections of German bombers. When they flew south to relieve squadrons in 11 Group during the Battle of Britain, the change in the tempo of combat – due to the Me 109 – was often traumatic.

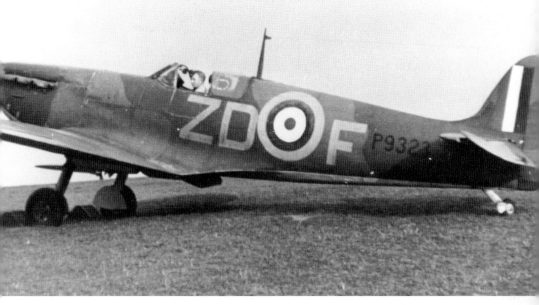

34. Spitfire Mk IA, P9323, of 222 Squadron pictured at Hornchurch during the Battle of Britain. After the Dunkirk fighting, 222 retired to Kirton before re-deployment to Hornchurch, in 11 Group. On 30 August 1940 the unit saw its first day of fighting from its new and heavily beleaguered base. That day, 222 Squadron lost four Spitfires destroyed, one pilot killed, and a further four damaged. Sergeant A. W. Spears was shot down in P9323 and baled out over the Isle of Sheppey.

35. A Spitfire Mk IA of 602 Squadron at Westhampnett, the Tangmere satellite near Chichester and now famous as the Goodwood racing circuit. The way in which the aircraft's eight machine-guns were spread out in the wings can clearly be seen. The wavy camouflage demarcation line along the leading edge is unusual.

36. Few individual pilots achieved high personal scores. This, however, is one that did: Pilot Officer Eric 'Sawn-off' Lock, pictured with his 41 Squadron Spitfire Mk IA at Catterick before the Squadron's deployment to Hornchurch during the Battle of Britain. Between 15 August and 1 October 1940, Lock achieved nine victories, for which he received the DFC and bar. Lock was shot down and killed over the Channel on 3 August 1941 by *Oberleutnant* Johann Schmid of JG 26's *Geschwaderstab* – his final score was 26 destroyed and eight probables. Lock remains 'missing'.

37. The Czech Pilot Officer Frantisek Hradil with a 19 Squadron Spitfire Mk IIA at Fowlmere towards the Battle of Britain's end. In addition to the more powerful Merlin XII and a Rotol CS propeller, this improved Spitfire also had an automatic Coffman engine starter. Hradil was shot down in flames over Southend on 5 November 1940.

38. Sergeant Terry Healey of 41 Squadron confers with his armourer, Corporal Nunn, at Hornchurch in September 1940. Due to a lack of time and foresight, Spitfires and Hurricanes – unlike both the Me 109 and Me 110 – were not armed with cannon but eight .303 machine-guns.

39. This is the only known photograph of an operational Spitfire Mk IB, pictured at Fowlmere, 19 Squadron's base near Duxford. Because the cannons were side-mounted, due to the thin cross-section of the Spitfire's wing, 'g' forces meant that the weapon frequently jammed in combat. Without back-up armament from machine-guns, pilots lost all confidence in the type which was withdrawn. The 'B' wing was subsequently developed with the combined firepower of two cannon and four machine-guns, successfully providing cannon to subsequent Spitfire variants.

40. 19 Squadron's Spitfire Mk IBs were withdrawn in early September 1940 and exchanged with machine-gun armed Mk IAs from a training unit. Although these aircraft were somewhat tired and worn, 19 Squadron was nonetheless pleased to have them. This is the Mk IA of the CO, Squadron Leader Brian Lane DFC.

41. An armourer displays a Hispano-Suiza 20 mm cannon at Biggin Hill after the Battle of Britain, by which time problems with the weapon had been overcome. The British fighters needed this weapon in 1940, however.

42. On 26 September 1940 the He 111s of KG 55 executed a successful attack on the Supermarine factory at Woolston, Southampton. Thirty-six workers were killed and sixty injured. Spitfire production at the plant was temporarily halted, but the raid came too late to have any effect on the Battle of Britain's outcome.

43. On 5 September 1940, Pilot Officer Eric Burgoyne of 19 Squadron was attacked by an Me 109 over Hornchurch. Although he returned safely to Fowlmere, his Spitfire shows evidence of being hit by a 20 mm cannon round. It is often written that the Spitfire was a comparatively delicate machine, unable to withstand battle damage; this, and many other pictures like it, suggests otherwise. Unusually, the aircraft's serial number, P9391, appears in small characters on the fin-flash, instead of on the rear fuselage.

44. The Me 109E was a dangerous adversary indeed. These are machines of 9/JG 26 operating from a cornfield at Caffiers in the Pas-de-Calais during the Battle of Britain.

45. Another camouflaged Me 109E of 9/JG 26, showing the wing-mounted 20 mm Oerlikon cannon.

 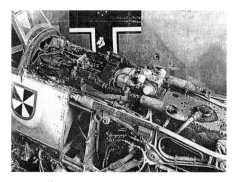

Above left: 46. The Me 109E of JG 3's Oberleutnant Franz von Werra, who forced-landed at Marden in Kent on 5 September 1940, having been shot down by Spitfire pilot Pilot Officer Basil 'Stapme' Stapleton of 603 Squadron. In the foreground can be seen the machine-guns' ammunition box. The Oerlikon cannons can also be seen protruding from each wing.

Above right: 47. The twin engine-mounted 7.92 mm machine-guns of von Werra's 109. Similar to fighters in the First World War, these guns, sited directly in front of the pilot, were easily aimed and fired through the propeller arc via a synchronised interrupter gear.

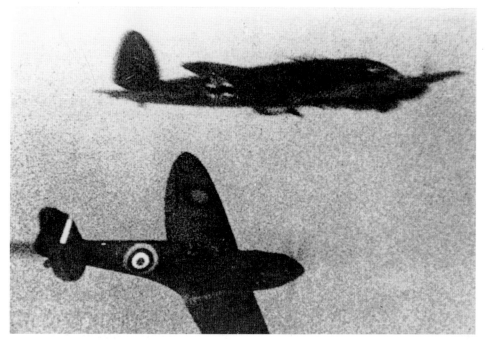

48. Although this photograph was staged by the Germans, it is nonetheless thought-provoking: a Spitfire trailing black smoke breaks off its attack on a He 111.

49. 'How I did it' 1: Flying Officer L. A. Haines of 19 Squadron describes how he turned inside an Me 109 to the New Zealander Flying Officer Frank Brinsden (left) and American Pilot Officer 'Uncle Sam' Leckrone at Fowlmere in September 1940.

50. 'Did he do it?': The Polish Sergeant Anton Glowacki makes out his report to 501 Squadron's Intelligence Officer at Kenley in September 1940. Fighter combat was often confusing, generating a natural over-claiming factor given that the high speed involved could deceive the human eye.

51. 'How I did it' 2: *Oberstleutnant* Adolf Galland, *Kommodore* of JG 26, describes how he shot down two Spitfires en route to General Theo Osterkamp's birthday party at Le Touquet, 15 April 1941. Galland considered the Spitfire superior in defence to the Me 109, due to its better manoeuvrability, and infamously requested that Göring equip his units with Spitfires. *Oberstleutnant* Werner Mölders, *Kommodore* of JG 51, flew a Spitfire and a Hurricane at Rechlin in September 1940. He considered both types inferior to the 109, although the Spitfire was 'one class better' than the Hurricane

'IF YOU DON'T BELIEVE ME, HERE ARE THEIR PROPELLORS"

This "People's War"

"It's the stuck-up woman she is since Lord Beaverbrook brought down 2 Dorniers with her frying-pan."

Left: 52. After an engagement it was frequently difficult, or indeed impossible, to corroborate pilots' combat claims, vexing pilots, intelligence officers and, indeed, historians many years after the event! This cartoon sums up the situation so far as the pilots themselves were concerned, and was discovered pasted into the log book of a Battle of Britain Spitfire pilot.

Right: 53 The Spitfire was unique in that its contribution was not just in the war-torn skies over England in 1940. So much did the iconic fighter capture inspire the nation that it became the focus of a spontaneous outbreak of popular support for both the decision to fight on alone and Fighter Command: The Spitfire Fund. Cities, towns, corporations and the rich all patriotically clamoured to donate £5,000 to Lord Beaverbrook and pay for a Spitfire. Indeed, housewives all over Britain happily donated their aluminium cooking utensils to the Ministry of Aircraft Production's 'Saucepans to Spitfires' campaign. This classic Low cartoon perfectly epitomises the intense rivalry involved and support for The Spitfire Fund. Although a comparatively small number of other aircraft types were donated, this enterprise largely revolved around the Spitfire – which became the very symbol of freedom and defiance.

54. An Me 109E taking hits from Spitfire pilot Pilot Officer David Crook of 609 Squadron during the Battle of Britain.

55. Proof of the pudding: groundcrew of Tangmere's 145 Squadron pose with the fin of a He III destroyed by the unit's Hurricanes on 11 July 1940. Damage from multiple machine-gun bullet hits can clearly be seen. This is incomparable, however, to the effect of an explosive 20 mm cannon shell – as evidenced by the foregoing photos of two 19 Squadron Spitfires hit by such a heavy round.

5. Comparative speed trials were then carried out, and the Spitfire proved to be considerably the faster of the two, both in acceleration and straight and level flight, without having to make use of the emergency +12 lbs boost. During diving trials, the Spitfire pilot found that, by engaging fully coarse pitch and using -2lbs boost, his aircraft was superior to the Me 109.

In general flying qualities the aeroplane is inferior to the Spitfire and the Hurricane at all speeds and in all conditions of flight. It is much inferior at speeds in excess of 250 mph and at 400 mph recovery from a dive is difficult because of the heaviness of the elevator. This heaviness of the elevator makes all manoeuvres in the looping plane above 250 mph difficult including steep climbing turns. No difference was experienced between climbing turns to the right and left. It does not possess the control which allows of good quality flying and this is particularly noticeable in aerobatics.[10]

The content of this report can only be considered surprising. The same 109 had performed extremely well when compared to 1 Squadron's Hurricanes two months before. Having previously been subjected to a forced-landing, however, it is fair to question whether the machine's performance remained at its peak. This is especially important when considering that the RAF aircraft used in the trial was the latest Spitfire and fitted with a CS propeller. Nonetheless, the report would certainly have been morale boosting to Fighter Command's Spitfire pilots.

The previous day, Wing Commander George Stainforth – of Schneider Trophy fame – flew the 109 in a series of comparative trials concerning the turning circles of the 109, Spitfire and Hurricane. Stainforth's subsequent report concluded that the Hurricane out-turned the 109 'within about one complete turn', and that 'The Messerschmitt appears to be only slightly faster than the Hurricane'. The Spitfire, he continued, 'out-turned the Messerschmitt almost as easily as the Hurricane'. The 109, however, was considered to have a 'large turning circle' and be 'generally extremely unmanouevrable'. Finally, 'the pilot of the Spitfire reports that he had no difficulty in sitting on the Messerschmitt's tail, and could, in fact, have tightened up his turn quite a lot more and got well on the inside. He was at +5 boost – almost full throttle'.[11] Stainforth's report clearly erred on the side of the Spitfire as to which of the three was overall best performer.

In Germany similar trials had also been undertaken and reported upon accordingly:

In the following performance and air combat comparison that has been performed at the *E-Stelle Rechlin* between Me 109E and Me 110C and the captured enemy fighters Spitfire, Hurricane and Curtiss, shall be brought to notice. The results of the comparison are to be announced immediately to all *Jagd* and *Zestörer* units, to guarantee appropriate air combat behaviour in the engagements on the basis of technical conditions.

The Me 109E type clearly out-performs all foreign aircraft.

Speed: the Spitfire is at 0 m by ca. 20 km/h, at 4 m by ca. 10 km/h. Hurricane and Curtiss at 0 and 4 km altitude by ca. 60 km/h. A similar superiority of the Me 109E exists in climb performance too. Climb times to 4 km: Me 109E – 4.4 minutes, Spitfire 5 minutes, Hurricane 5.6 minutes, Curtiss 5.2 minutes.

The Me 110C is inferior speed-wise to the Spitfire, superior to the Curtiss and Hurricane. Regarding the climb performance the Curtiss is equal at ground-level, up to 4 km superior then inferior. Hurricane is inferior up to an altitude of 2 km, then superior up to 6.5 km. The Spitfire is equal at ground level but otherwise superior.

The best climb for Me 109E and Me 110C is achieved with shallow climb angle and higher speeds than the enemy fighters. It is wrong to climb away steeply or climb behind an enemy fighter with the same angle.

Before turning fights with the Me 109E, it must be noted that in every case, that all three foreign planes have significantly smaller turning circles and turning times. An attack on the opponent as well as disengagement can only be accomplished on the basis of existing superiority in performance.

The following suggestions are made:
The Spitfire and Hurricane have two-pitch propellers. Climbing away with the Me 109 and Me 110 must be done with the best climbing speed or even higher speeds of about 280 – 300 km/h. On aircraft with two-pitch propellers with low blade angle the engine will experience a very high over-revolution, and on the hand with a high blade angle high boost pressure – therefore, in other words, performance loss.

On a sudden push forward on the stick to dive, the carburettor of the enemy fighters cuts out due to negative acceleration. This evasive measure, diving, is also recommended.

The rolling ability of the enemy fighters at high speeds is worse than that of the Me 109. Quick changes of the trajectory along the vertical axis cause, especially with the Spitfire, load changes around the cranial axis, coming from high longtitudinal thrust momentum, and significantly disturb aiming.

In summary, it can be said that all three enemy aircraft types are inferior to the German planes regarding flying qualities. The Spitfire has bad elevator and rudder stability on the target approach. In addition, wing-mounted weapons have known shooting-technique disadvantages.[12]

Those trials provided an opportunity for none other than Major *Vati* Mölders to fly and evaluate three of the enemy aircraft types he had been shooting down:

It was very interesting to carry out the flight trials at Rechlin with the Spitfire and Hurricane. Both types are very simple to fly compared to our aircraft, and childishly easy to take-off and land. The Hurricane is good natured and turns well, but its performance is decidedly inferior to that of the Me 109. It has strong stick forces and is "lazy" on the ailerons. The Spitfire is one class better. It handles well, is light on the controls, faultless in the turn and has a performance approaching that of the Me 109. As a fighting aircraft, however, it is miserable. A sudden push on the stick will cause the engine to cut, and because the propeller has only two pitch settings (take-off and cruise), in a rapidly changing air combat situation the engine is either over-speeding or else is not being used to the full.[13]

This assessment is remarkably fair, in fact.

Although CS propellers were on the way to Spitfire and Hurricane squadrons, the Merlin's lack of fuel injection could not be addressed and was something the RAF pilots had to cope with. The experience of the fighting thus far also led to certain improvements being absorbed into the 109 programme, leading to the Me 109E-4. This variant had seat and head armour to protect the pilot, and the fuel tank, upon which the pilot effectively sat, and which had been found vulnerable from an astern attack, was also armoured. The canopy was re-designed, offering better visibility, and armament was finally standardised at two wing-mounted Oerlikon cannons and twin engine-cowl mounted machine-guns. A certain amount of aircraft, designated Me 109E-4B, were modified to carry a single *Sprengbombe Cylindrisch* (SC) 50 kilo bomb, enabling the 109 to be used in a *Jagdbomber* role. The Me 109E-7, produced in August 1940, had a 300 litre auxiliary fuel tank in an attempt to improve range, or alternatively could carry an SC 250 kilo bomb. The Me 109E was now ready to fight the Battle of Britain and challenge the RAF for aerial superiority. It was a circumstance that Professor Willy Messerschmitt could never have imagined when he drew the first pencil lines on his Augsburg drawing board back in 1934.

On the night of 18/19 June 1940 the lull broke and Spitfires made their first nocturnal kills. Neither the Hurricane or Spitfire had been designed or intended as night-fighters, but Britain's nocturnal defences were in such a state of unpreparedness that the experiment appeared justified. At 12.30 a.m. that night, Flight Lieutenant A. G. 'Sailor' Malan of Biggin Hill's 74 Squadron destroyed a He 111 over Chelmsford, followed by another forty-five minutes later. Fifteen minutes before Malan's second kill, Flying Officer John Petre of 19 Squadron shot down an He 111 of 4/KG 4 over Cambridgeshire. A Blenheim of 23 Squadron was also present, forcing Petre to make a quarter attack and during which, after watching his tracer ammunition set the raider's engine alight, his Spitfire 'literally blew up in his face' causing 'terribly disfiguring burns'.[14] The unfortunate pilot's Spitfire had been hit in the petrol tank by the He 111's rear gunner. At 2.15 a.m. Flying Officer Eric Ball, also of 19 Squadron, destroyed another 4/KG 4 machine over Margate. Such successes were rare, however, although that month 19 Squadron flew twenty nocturnal patrols.[15] This was a reaction to the fact that virtually all *Luftwaffe* sorties over England that month occurred during the hours of darkness.[16] Strangely the Hurricane was not used at night at this time, probably because of the pressure many of these squadrons had recently been under, or perhaps because the Spitfire was already considered superior. Later, when the Spitfire began replacing the Hurricane completely as Fighter Command's frontline fighter, Hurricane Mk IIs gave great service as first a stop-gap night-fighter, then a successful offensive night intruder. Nonetheless, the Hurricane did not make its first kill at night until some time after the Battle of Britain, when the night *Blitz* on British cities was in full swing.

At this time the Air Ministry was trying to resolve the issue of day-fighter armament, which was a reaction to two things: anticipation of the Germans fitting armour plate to protect their bombers' engines, and secondly the proven destructive power of the 109's Oerlikon. Interestingly, although the Hurricane's wing was thicker – and arguably therefore stronger – trials around achieving a cannon-armed fighter featured almost entirely around the Spitfire. This can only be because the Air Ministry were already looking ahead and recognised that the Spitfire had much potential for development, whereas the Hurricane did not. Moreover, the cannon, weighing ninety-six pounds each, increased weight-loading. The Spitfire's superior margin in performance was more able to absorb this than the Hurricane, which already lagged behind both the Spitfire and, more importantly, the Me 109. Confusion, however, existed over the best armament configuration and combination. Initially it was thought that just two cannons, one in each wing and without any machine-guns, would suffice.

On 27 June 1940 the first cannon-armed Spitfire, R6761, was delivered to 19 Squadron at Fowlmere. Soon the Squadron was entirely equipped with the cannon-armed Spitfire Mk IB. Only one comparable Hurricane existed. This was also fitted with two Hispano-Suiza cannons, but unlike the Spitfire, the wings of which accommodated the cannon internally, the Hurricane's were fitted in two under-wing exterior pods. During the Battle of Britain, this machine saw action, flown by Flight Lieutenant Dick Smith of 151 Squadron, who later described the aircraft as 'a heavy old cow'.[17] Indeed, in battle that day, Smith was 'frustrated by the poor performance' of this aircraft.[18] Hawker also produced a four cannon one-off, but although this too was delivered to 151 Squadron it saw no combat. Ultimately, however, the Hurricane Mk IIC would be armed with four cannons, but, because of impaired performance, this was employed not as an interceptor day-fighter but as a successful ground-attack and night intruder aircraft.

Flying Officer Frank Brinsden remembered that he and his fellow pilots of 19 Squadron were 'chuffed' to learn that they were to be the first cannon-equipped Spitfire squadron.[19] The CO, Squadron Leader Philip Pinkham, lectured his pilots on 1 July regarding the advantages and disadvantages of their new weapon. The disadvantages he listed as:

1. Stoppages too frequent. Stoppages of one cannon makes it very difficult to keep a steady sight with the other.
2. Fire period restricted to six seconds, making defence against other fighter aircraft very difficult.
3. Lack of "spread".

The advantages, Pinkham explained were:

1. Terrific destructive power.
2. High muzzle velocity decreasing amount of deflection necessary in deflection shooting.
3. Increased range and accuracy.[20]

Pinkham also began exploring new tactical formations so as to maximise his cannon-armed Spitfires' potential. On 4 July the Squadron flew to practice his new ideas. Instead of flying in the usual 'vics', 'A' Flight's sections dived in echelon from 2,000 feet above and to the side of three target aircraft from dead astern. They closed rapidly and gained steady sighting at high speed before breaking away downwards and to one side. The new formation was then posted up at dispersal in diagramatic form.[21] This was forward thinking indeed – for which Pinkham has not previously been appropriately accredited. This new formation relied upon two sections of two flying in line astern and was highly manoeuvrable – similar, in fact, to the *Schwarm*. The only difference and continued drawback was that the Spitfires remained too close together. Still, this was very much a step in the right direction. What was not, ironically, was the cannon's unreliability. Flying Officer Frank Brinsden:

> Our initial pleasure at receiving the Mk IBs soon turned to disappointment when they did not function well in practice. I personally got into several scraps when both jammed after firing only a few rounds. Distortion somewhere, under "G" forces, was suspected and I proved this on several practice sorties over the Wash when both cannons jammed when "G" forces similar to those applied in combat built up.[22]

Armourer Fred Roberts remembered that:

> We took a lot of stick from the pilots over these stoppages. For a while they wanted to blame the armourers and then, when a full magazine of ammunition was expended, the pilots complained that they only had six seconds of firing time against the eighteen seconds of the Browning machine-guns. We had little help and no encouragement from the armament staff at Duxford … Even the "experts" who came from RAF Northolt to help could only listen and learn from us!
>
> Most of the trouble stemmed from the cannons being mounted on their sides, the empty shell cases therefore being ejected sideways from the breech and deflected back into it. The nose of the shell dropping slightly and striking the breech end of the barrel, buckling the shell case at the neck caused another kind of stoppage. We fitted various kinds of deflector plates. We altered the angle of the plates, fitted rubber pads to dampen the force of the spent shell case, but none of these experiments worked. We also had magazine feed trouble, caused by it lying on its side whilst mounted on the cannon. To counter this we tried varying the tension applied to the magazine spring but that was unsuccessful.[23]

So important was this matter that Dowding himself was involved. In a letter to the Air Minister, Sir Archibald Sinclair, he nailed the problem: 'These guns were designed to operate on their bellies but have been mounted on their sides. This has led to technical difficulties'.[24] It was crucial that these 'technical difficulties' were resolved, but for the present 19 Squadron's frustrations would continue.

On 2 July 1940 day-fighting resumed between the opposing fighter forces when the Germans began attacking Channel-bound convoys and south coastal ports. These attacks were frequent. On 2 July Fighter Command flew ninety-one sorties, 282 the following day and 399 on 8 July.[25] Dowding reacted by moving a number of Spitfire and Hurricane squadrons to the coastal airfields of Hawkinge, Manston, and Warmwell. The problem Fighter Command faced was that these combat took place over the sea, inevitably leading to many pilots being reported 'missing'. It was clear, however, that the *Luftwaffe* had re-grouped and had now turned its attention to Britain. Flying Officer Frank Brinsden summed up the mood in Fighter Command:

At squadron level I don't think that we were fully aware of what was going on. We were just keen to have a crack at the Germans, and the prevalent attitude was that we couldn't wait for them to come. Given that the French and Belgians had proved of little use during the defence of their homelands we were glad that we were on our own. We were absolutely confident that we were better than the enemy, and wanted an opportunity to bloody Hitler's nose.[26]

Flight Sergeant George Unwin added simply that, 'We never considered being beaten. It was just not possible in our eyes'.[27] If Göring wanted a fight, Fighter Command was clearly happy to oblige.

As ever, the Prime Minister perfectly captured the mood in typical Churchillian style:

The Battle of France is over. I expect that the Battle of Britain is about to begin ... The whole fury and might of the enemy must very soon be turned on us. Hitler knows that he will have to break us in this island or lose the war. If we can stand up to him, all Europe may be free and the life of the world may move forward into broad sunlit uplands. But if we fail, then the whole world, including the United States, including all that we have known and cared for, will sink into the abyss of a new Dark Age made more sinister, and perhaps more protracted by the lights of perverted science. Let us therefore brace ourselves to our duties, and so bear ourselves that if the British Empire and its Commonwealth last a thousand years, men will still say "*This* was their Finest Hour".

11

The Battle of Britain

The Battle of Britain began on 10 July 1940 – although in truth there had been fighting over shipping in the Channel for the previous fortnight. Nonetheless on 14 July it was recorded that Dowding had a total of twenty-five operational Hurricane squadrons at his disposal, and nineteen of Spitfires.[1] By 1 September there would be eight more Hurricane squadrons, and another still by 28 October.[2] 1 September would see one less Spitfire squadron, but twenty on 28 October.[3] This does not mean, however, that all of these fighters were either operational or deployed to airfields in south-east England to meet the *Luftwaffe's* main assault. For example, on 6 July, Fighter Command's strength was 871 fighters – but only 644 of them were operational; on 7 September Dowding's strength peaked during the Battle of Britain at 1,161 fighters – of which but 746 were operational.[4] Throughout the battle, Dowding's squadrons were spread throughout his four fighter groups covering the entire British Isles – not concentrated purely in the principal combat zone of south-east England as the enemy both desired and believed. Due to the presence of *Luftflotte* Five in Norway, Dowding could never discount the possibility of a major raid against the industrial area of north-east England and so retained operational fighters in 13 Group – which proved a wise precaution. There was also merit in not concentrating fighter forces so as to prevent their destruction on the ground. Because there were squadrons distributed throughout the country, therefore, it must be understood that the entire force available to Dowding was never pitched into battle simultaneously. There was always a substantial reserve upon which Air Vice-Marshal Park could call from neighbouring groups – in theory at least – in the event of his 11 Group force being either fully engaged or even overwhelmed. Within 11 Group, Park's tactics were in perfect accord with Dowding's strategy, his intention being to preserve his fighters as best he could and not commit them to a war of attrition against the high-flying 109s.

When war had broken out the British aircraft factories were all twenty per cent below their target output, and had fallen behind so much by the time of Dunkirk that manufacturers were collectively 1,000 aircraft behind contract.[5] On 14 May, however, the Ministry of Aircraft Production (MAP) was established under the highly motivated, resourceful and energetic Lord Beaverbrook. By June Beaverbrook had cracked the whip: 446 fighters were produced against 325; 496 in July, 476 in August, 467 in September and 469 in October.[6] This meant that as fighters were lost in battle they were replaced. Of crucial importance is that the production of British fighters massively outstripped German production: between

June–October 1940, Germany's factories churned out a total of 1,870 fighters – Britain's response was 3,958.[7] But there were still not enough of the superior Spitfire. Between 6 July and 1 November, 991 Hurricanes were produced but only 608 Spitfires.[8]

As Overy pointed out, in 1939 the Spitfire took 'two and a half times the man hours to produce a Hurricane'.[9] As already explained, however, this is far too simplistic an explanation as to why there were still many more Hurricanes than Spitfires in 1940. The fact of the matter is that Supermarine's small workforce and premises at Southampton was too small to mass-produce anything. This was formerly a comparatively small factory producing, in the main, biplane flying boats, which suddenly found itself swamped by large orders for Spitfires. The solution was to apply the principals of mass-producing automobiles to Spitfires. Initially, the new factory erected for this purpose at Castle Bromwich in Birmingham was equipped by Morris Motors and run by Lord Nuffield. Unfortunately it proved much more difficult to adapt the automotive industry to the production of aircraft, leading to Lord Beaverbrook taking over control of the operation shortly after taking office – and by which time not one Spitfire had emerged from Nuffield's factory. 'The Beaver' gave control of the Castle Bromwich Aircraft Factory (CBAF) to the aircraft manufacturer Vickers. Things began moving immediately. Experienced workers were brought to Birmingham from Supermarine at Southampton, and the more complex parts of the machine were produced at the latter factory. In June Beaverbrook's target of just ten Spitfires was miraculously achieved; twenty-three followed in July, thirty-seven in August and fifty-six during September.[10]

The important thing is that all of these Spitfires produced by the CBAF were new Mk IIs. This enjoyed several benefits over the Mk IA currently in operational service, and it was naturally important to expedite production and delivery to the squadrons. The Spitfire Mk II was powered by the Merlin XII which produced 1,175 hp as opposed to the Merlin III's 1,030 hp. The Mk II's top speed was 370 mph – 15 mph faster than the Mk IA. Its rate of climb was 2,600 feet a minute, 473 feet a minute more than the Mk IA. The new engine was fitted with a Coffman automatic starter, which reduced starting time, and, most importantly, all of the new Spitfires were fitted with the Rotol CS propeller.[11] Nonetheless, the first Mk IIA was not delivered to 611 Squadron until 22 August 1940. By the end of October 1940, 195 had been delivered to Fighter Command. Concurrently the Hurricane was also being improved. On 4 September Fighter Command received the first deliveries of the Hurricane Mk II. Hawker's improved fighter was powered by the Merlin XX, which produced ten hp more than the Spitfire Mk II's Merlin XII; the Hurricane Mk II was also fitted with the CS propeller as standard. These improvements increased the Hurricane's top speed to 342 mph – but this was twenty-eight mph slower than the new Spitfires, twelve mph slower than the Me 109E-3.[12] It is obvious which British fighter had the greater potential for further development at this stage.

On 16 July, Hitler made clear his intentions towards Great Britain:

As England, despite her hopeless military situation, still shows no sign of willingness to come to terms, I have decided to prepare, and if necessary, to carry out a landing operation against her.

The aim of this operation is to eliminate the English motherland as a base from which war against Germany can be continued, and, if necessary, to occupy the country completely.[13]

The proposed invasion was called 'Operation *Seelöwe*'. By 17 July there were two powerful *Luftflotten*, Two and Three, established in France for the aerial assault on England. This combined force amounted to 2,600 aircraft, of which 760 were Me 109s, and 220 Me 110s. Although it was to play a limited role in the Battle of Britain, *Luftflotte* Five was based in Norway with a further 190 aircraft, including thirty Me 110s.[14] The *Oberkommando der Luftwaffe* (OKL) had been provided with an intelligence appraisal of the RAF. Regarding Fighter Command, the report stated that Dowding had 'fifty fighter squadrons, each having about eighteen aircraft, there are 900 front line fighters available, of which about 675 (seventy-five per cent) may be regarded as serviceable. About forty per cent of the fighters are Spitfires and about sixty per cent are Hurricanes. Of these types the Spitfire is regarded as the better … In view of the combat performance and the fact that they are not yet equipped with cannon guns, both types are inferior to the Me 109, while the Me 110 is inferior to skilfully handled Spitfires … The British aircraft industry produces 180–300 fighters per month … it is believed that production will decrease rather than increase'. Moreover, the *Luftwaffe* was 'in a position to go over to decisive daylight operations owing to the inadequate defences of the island'. In conclusion, the Operations Staff believed that 'The *Luftwaffe* is clearly superior to the RAF as regards equipment, training, command and location of bases. In the event of an intensification of air warfare the *Luftwaffe*, unlike the RAF, will be in a position in every respect to achieve a decisive effect this year if the time for large scale operations is set early enough to allow advantage to be taken of the months with relatively favourable weather conditions (July to the beginning of October)'.[15] In certain respects the report was fairly accurate. In others it was supremely overconfident and inaccurate – as German aircrews would soon discover first-hand.

The Battle of Britain lasted for sixteen weeks of high summer and underwent five distinct phases:

1. 10 July – 12 August: Attacks on Channel convoys and coastal objectives including the south coast's all-important radar stations.
2. 13 August – 18 August: heavier attacks on radar stations and airfields.
3. 19 August – 6 September: heavy attacks concentrated on 11 Group's Sector Stations.
4. 7 September – 30 September: Round-the-clock bombing of London, the start of 'tip and run raids' by high-flying Me 109 Jabos, and attacks on the British aircraft industry.
5. 1 October – 31 October: Continued attacks on aircraft factories, nuisance 'tip and run' raids and high altitude fighter sweeps.

It is not the intention to recount a narration of the Battle of Britain here. For such an account the reader is referred to both *The Battle of Britain* by T. C. G. James, that work being the official narrative prepared by the Air Historical Branch, and this author's *The Few: The Battle of Britain in the Words of the Pilots*, which provides an extensive oral history of the conflict through the personal accounts of 100 pilots. Instead, the battle will be examined through combat reports and other contemporary sources.

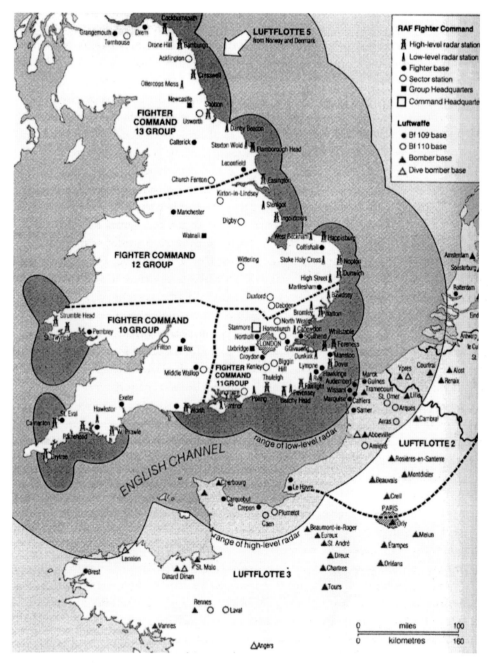

56. Map showing the disposition of Fighter Command groups, sector stations and RDF coverage, and *Luftwaffe* deployment in north-west France during the Battle of Britain. *Courtesy Air Vice-Marshal J. E. Johnson.*

On 14 July 1940 the Channel battles were in full swing. Even though bad weather that day helped protect the nine convoys steaming through Channel waters, Fighter Command still flew a total of 597 sorties. A convoy off Eastbourne attracted the day's only substantial raid: the whole of IV/LG 1's *Stukas*, accompanied by thirty Me 109s of JG 3 (and possibly JG 51). Battle was joined when the raiders were intercepted by the Hurricanes of 615 and 151 Squadrons, and the Spitfires of 610. Among the 151 Squadron pilots engaged was Pilot Officer Jack Hamar, who later reported vividly on the action:

> At 1500 hours the Squadron was ordered off from Rochford to intercept E/As south of Dover. At approximately 1520 hours, when the Squadron was almost over Dover, a bunch of Me 109s were sighted about 5,000 feet above our formation, in which I was flying Red Two. As it looked as though the E/A were about to attack us, the leader ordered our defensive line astern tactics. As we turned sharply to port, two Me 109s were seen diving to attack the last aircraft in our formation. "Milna Leader" attacked the leading Me 109 and I the second. I turned inside the E/A, which had pulled up into a steep left hand climbing turn. I closed rapidly and opened fire at about 250 yards with a 45° deflection shot. The E/A seemed to falter and straightened out into a dive. I placed myself dead astern at about 50 yards. I opened fire, closing to almost no distance. I saw a large explosion just in front of the pilot and a large amount of white smoke poured from the E/A, which by this time was climbing steeply. I was then forced to break away quickly due to fire from the rear, lost sight of the E/A and therefore did not see it crash. This action was also witnessed by Flying Officer Forster.[16]

Hamar's report is of interest for several reasons. 'Milna Leader' was Squadron Leader 'Teddy' Donaldson who had led 151 with distinction throughout the Battle of France. It is interesting that Donaldson had recognised the inferiority of the 'vic', at least in defence, and had adopted his own 'line astern tactics'. In addition to Hamar out-turning his opponent, he opened fire 'from almost no distance' – all successful fighter pilots attacked as close as circumstances permitted. Also, Hamar's target emitted 'a large amount of white smoke'. This was probably coolant, indicating beyond doubt that the enemy machine was badly hit and unlikely to return across the Channel. As previously explained, 109 pilots largely depended upon the advantage provided by their fuel-injected engines to evade pursuing RAF fighters by diving away at full throttle. Inevitably such a sudden exertion would produce a stream of black exhaust smoke from the engine. The sight of an enemy aircraft, albeit possibly hit somewhere, diving vertically at high speed and producing a quantity of black smoke understandably gave the impression that it had been destroyed. For obvious reasons fighter pilots were unable to hang around and watch their victims crash to earth – and in any case most of these combats were fought at high altitude, above cloud. Indeed, Hamar wrote, 'I was then forced to break away quickly due to fire from the rear, lost sight of the E/A and therefore did not see it crash'. Given the fact that Hamar's target emitted a plume of white, as opposed to black, smoke, it is more likely that it was, in fact, destroyed. Indeed, Hamar was credited with having destroyed the 109. Nonetheless, accreditation of a definitely destroyed enemy machine in this case – likely though it was – actually contravened the rules for the registration of combat claims. The criteria set by the Air Ministry for a confirmed kill was specific:

1. The enemy aircraft had to be seen on the ground or in the sea by a member of a crew or formation, or confirmed as destroyed from other sources, e.g. ships at sea, coastguards, the Observer Corps and police.
2. The enemy aircraft had to be seen to descend with flames issuing. It was not sufficient that only smoke was seen.
3. The enemy aircraft must be seen to break up in the air.[17]

The simple truth was, though, the RAF Intelligence Officers became so overworked due to the increasing number of aerial combats that corroborating pilots' claims with evidence from witnesses became an impossible task. Moreover, the speed and confusing nature of such combat naturally generates an over-claiming factor. Several fighter pilots, for example, could simultaneously attack an enemy aircraft, each unaware of the other, and henceforth one German aircraft destroyed could become multiplied on the daily balance sheet. This is why Fighter Command's claims substantially exceeded the actual German losses. So chaotic was the situation, in fact, and the need for accurate information so great, that on 13 August three revised categories were implemented:

1. Destroyed: covering all cases where there was no doubt, although confirmation from a second source was no longer required.
2. Probably Destroyed: to be applied in all cases where the enemy aircraft broke off combat in circumstances in which its loss appeared likely.
3. Damaged: applicable to inconclusive combats wherein the enemy aircraft appeared to have at least been damaged.[18]

The *Luftwaffe* had a different process to confirm kills. In the RAF, for example, kills could be shared between pilots. This was not permitted by the Germans. Moreover, claims were not allowed for 'probables' or damaged aircraft – only those destroyed. Each such claim required a witness and first had to be approved by the *Geschwaderstab* before final confirmation by the *Reichsluftfarhtministerium*. Nevertheless, although Fighter Command grossly over-claimed throughout the battle, the Germans were equally guilty of overestimating their combat success. Indeed, in the period between 12 and 19 August German Intelligence would claim 644 British aircraft destroyed when the true figure was only 141.[19] As Seb Cox wrote, '… the lack of reliable intelligence began to affect German strategy … exaggerated claims of success against Fighter Command deceived some German commanders'.[20] Fighting over enemy territory, however, it was difficult for the Germans to file precise claims – as indeed would be the case for Fighter Command between 1941 and 1944.

One undisputed claim was filed on 28 July by Flight Lieutenant Dillon Kelly:

I was Blue One of 74 Squadron and was flying about 300 yards astern and to port of Red Leader when we saw some Me 109s a little below us (we were at 18,000 feet). Red Section turned and dived down to port. I likewise turned to port but found a formation in Vic of three Me 109s pass about 300 yards across my nose. I took a snap shot at them but noticed no effect. Immediately after this I saw three Me 109s to port diving down very fast. I found it necessary to use boost cut-out and dived down on the leading one whom I managed to get on the tail of by diving steeply and turning left. I closed to 250 yards and opened fire with slight deflection and saw after a few seconds the machine turn left, dive and a tongue of flame appeared on the port side. It then dived down into the sea, burning. Blue Two confirms that he smoke and glycol coming from the enemy aircraft before he broke away to engage a second enemy aircraft.[21]

The Spitfires of 74 Squadron had scrambled from Manston to counter a threat heading towards Dover. Inexplicably the German bombers turned about, however, and a dogfight ensued between the Spitfires, Hurricanes from Hawkinge, and the enemy fighter escort: 109s of I and II/JG 51. The CO of 74 Squadron was the British 'ace' Squadron Leader 'Sailor' Malan, who attacked the leading *Rotte* of 109s – destroying one and damaging the second. The evidence available suggests that the second aircraft attacked by Malan was flown by none other than JG 51's *Kommodore* and the 'Father of German Air Fighting' himself: Major Werner Mölders. *Vati* was wounded and pursued across the Channel by Pilot Officer P. C. F. Stevenson, who in turn was attacked by *Oberleutnant* Leppla of I/JG 51. Both Stevenson and Mölders subsequently crash-landed back at their respective bases. Pilot Officer John Freeborn's Spitfire was also damaged, and Sergeant Tony Mould baled out, wounded. Pilot Officer J. H. R. Young, though, was killed when shot down over the Goodwin Sands. Both Mould and Young had been shot down by the Luftwaffe's other leading *experten* of the day: *Hauptmann* Adolf Galland, *Kommandeur* of III/JG 26. Galland's *Katschmarek*, *Oberleutnant* Joachim Müncheberg, destroyed a Hurricane of 257 Squadron. Kelly's combat report is particularly interesting for several reasons. Firstly it is unusual that the Me 109s were flying in a vics of three. Secondly although the 109s were diving, Kelly caught his target using extra boost – further confirming the value of this improvement. Thirdly there is no question as to the fate of the 109 he attacked, most likely *Unteroffizier* Hemmerling of 6/JG 51, who was killed.

Half an hour later, at 3.00 p.m., 41 Squadron's Spitfires engaged III/JG 53 over Dover. Pilot Officer 'Ben' Bennions hurried to the assistance of Flying Officer Tony Lovell, who had been wounded in the thigh and subsequently crash-landed at Manston, and reported that:

I ordered Yellow Section to carry out a Number One attack on this aircraft. Using the emergency boost I closed right in using full deflection and firing from 200 yards to 100 yards. The enemy turned over on its side and went vertically downwards. I followed using full boost and gave two more bursts of about four seconds each from a position slightly left of astern, and after the second burst the whole of the enemy fuselage was enveloped in black smoke.[22]

Leutnant Below also ended up in the Channel, but was later picked up by a German seaplane. Again, the Spitfire pilot had used 'full boost' to catch the enemy fighter.

On 11 August 1940 19 Squadron took on charge Spitfire X4231. This aircraft was armed not just with two cannon, as were the unit's existing experimental Mk IBs, but also two machine-guns in each wing. Squadron Leader Pinkham test flew the machine for one hour and ten minutes. Although concerned that it may be under-powered, afterwards he recorded in his log book that the Spitfire performed 'Quite normally' and referred to the armament as being 'obviously the right combination'.[23] The Squadron diarist wrote that the

'General opinion is that the new Spitfire is a step in the right direction. Possibly another step in the same direction would be re-equipping with the old eight-gun machines'.[24] Based in 12 Group, 19 Squadron had so far had little opportunity to fire their cannons in anger. That changed on 16 August, as the Squadron's diary relates:

Thirty miles due East of Harwich, 1730 hours. On returning to Coltishall, "A" Flight was asked to investigate. The "investigation" proved to be approximately 150 enemy aircraft consisting of bombers and fighter escort. Enemy aircraft were moving approximately southwards, bombers in front, escort of forty – fifty Me 110s stepped up behind, and a further escort of Me 109s at 1,000 feet – 1,500 feet above and to starboard of main formation. "A" Flight attacked in two sections of three and four aircraft respectively. Three definitely shot down and one probable, all Me 110s. Sergeant Roden's aircraft had several bullet holes but no other damage. The Me 110s, on being attacked, commenced milling in an attempt, which was successful, to keep us from the bombers. Generally speaking the enemy showed little enterprise. As far as could be observed the Me 110s had no rear gunners. Six of the seven Spitfires involved in the engagement had cannon stoppages. Results would have been at least doubled had we been equipped with either cannon and machine-guns, or just eight machine-guns. During the engagement the Me 109s did not attack.[25]

Flight Sergeant George Unwin flew as Red Three in Flight Lieutenant Brian Lane's Red Section:

As we went in to attack the bombers, the Me 110s saw us and attacked. I attacked one of the 110s and gave him a short burst. He half-rolled and went down almost vertically. I could not see what happened to him as I was attacked by another. I out-turned him and found myself with a perfect target at close range. My starboard cannon had a stoppage but I fired the remainder of my port cannon's ammunition into the 110. Bits fell off the enemy aircraft and he went into a steep dive, during which the tail came off. I followed him down and when I came out of cloud saw the end of a splash into the sea which I assumed was him.[26]

Again, this is another combat of interest. Firstly the frustration of 'A' Flight with their unreliable cannon in this, the Squadron's first major action in the Battle of Britain. Unwin destroyed a machine of 2/ZG 26 and damaged another of *Stab*/ZG 26. The only other Spitfire pilot to score was Sergeant Jack Potter, who shot down a 110 of II/ZG 76. Going into a defensive circle was a standard reaction by 110s when attacked by British fighters, the German machine being no match for either the Spitfire or Hurricane. Why the 109s failed to intervene is also puzzling, except to say that fuel considerations may have been critical.
RAF Intelligence reported on the deployment of enemy escort fighters:

Escorting fighters are dispersed in various positions relative to the bomber formations they are protecting. During the early phase of attacks on this country it was usual for the fighter escort to fly behind and several thousand feet above the bomber formation. If our fighters attacked the bombers, the escort would descend and attack them providing that they (the German fighters) were not outnumbered. If our fighters attacked the enemy fighter escort, the latter would usually form a self-defensive circle, thus ceasing to afford protection to the bombers which they were supposedly escorting.

Heavy casualties suffered by the bombers led to a change of tactics involving an increase in escorting fighters with new dispositions relative to the bomber formations. Fighters were encountered ahead and on both flanks as well as above and behind the bombers and usually flying in close proximity to the latter. On occasions the individual bomber units were found to be more spaced out with fighters weaving amongst them. Accompanying formations of fighters have also been observed acting as a remote escort of "freelance" patrols, flying at a great height above and in the vicinity of the bomber formations, but they have rarely taken offensive action.[27]

The tactics used by the German bomber formations is a much neglected subject, which will now be examined as this is also relevant to this analysis – not least because Fighter Command's actual role in the Battle of Britain was to defend the nation against the 'knock out blow'.

The basic cohesive battle formation around which the *Kampfgeschwader* was built was the *Kette* of three aircraft flying in an arrowhead formation, similar to the RAF vic. In daylight *Gruppen* disposed their aircraft in three main formations (see Appendix 4, Figs. 1-3). These were comprehensive and included patterns for cruising and attacking, and could easily be changed during flight upon the leader's command. When more than one *Gruppe* was flying together, the bombers generally flew in *Gruppen* line astern. Each *Gruppe* was 500 feet above the preceding formation and between a quarter and three miles separated them. On occasions the raiders flew in shallow vics, giving the impression of abreast formations in three waves (see Fig. 2). All formations, in both lines astern and abreast, were usually flown 'stepped up'. The enemy bombers tended to operate at heights between 10,000 feet and 20,000 feet, but the favoured optimum height was 13,000 feet to 17,000 feet. RAF Intelligence noted that 'it has been observed that the various units forming the main formation fly very close together and often succeed in maintaining their cohesion when attacked'.[28] When intercepted, the bombers would not adopt independent evasive tactics but rely upon the mutual fire support provided by their close formation flying, and, if present, their fighter escort. This applied to large formations. Small formations, or individual bombers, attempted to shake off intercepting fighters by:

1. Seeking the nearest available cloud cover.
2. Descending at ground or sea level, at high speed, making a 'jinking' low level escape at full throttle.
3. Using dive brakes, when fitted, to enable execution of a steep dive, combined with turns, thus causing attackers to overshoot.

Also, according to the RAF Intelligence Officers, bombers 'sometimes simulated damage by emitting smoke from an apparatus fitted either in the tail or behind engine nacelles'.[29]

Mass formations sometimes split into sub-groups on crossing the English coastline, each bound for different targets. Also, small groups of aircraft sometimes flew independently towards the same objective, but often it was only one group that penetrated to the target with any determination. This led RAF Intelligence to assume that 'the subsequent behaviour of the remaining groups has given the impression that their role has been to confuse our defence and divert our fighters from the main intention. These subsidiary formations have either dropped bombs on what has been an unidentifiable target short of the objective or turned for home without taking any offensive action. These tactics have been successful in that our fighter control has experienced difficulty in anticipating the development of the operation in its early stages and this has sometimes increased the difficulties of bringing about a successful interception'.[30] Also, the raiders frequently approached their targets on a dog-leg course, also intended to confuse the RAF fighter controllers. From the foregoing, it is clear that the interception of enemy bombers was no 'piece of cake' – from any perspective.

At this stage of the battle, the German fighters were also employed on *freie jagd* – 'free hunt' or 'free chase' – fighter sweeps over south-east England. Two or three of these sorties a day was the norm. After take-off from their bases in the Pas-de-Calais, the 109s assembled between 15,000 feet and 18,000 feet, then climbed and crossed the British coast at 21,000 feet to 24,000 feet. Each side would try to out-climb the other, so as to enjoy the immeasurable advantage of height, sun and, therefore, surprise. The 109s took thirty minutes from take-off to passing over the south-east coast, usually over Dover which became known as 'Hellfire Corner'. Allowing sufficient fuel for the return journey left just 20 minutes for operations over enemy territory, representing a penetration of just 125 miles. As Adolf Galland wrote, 'This was the most acute weakness of our offensive. An operating radius was sufficient for local defence but not enough for such tasks as were now demanded of us'.[31] It was not just the RAF that suffered during the Battle of Britain for years of misguided doctrinal thinking. That the Germans even considered that they would be able to achieve air superiority over England when their fighters could only fly as far as London almost beggars belief. Göring, however, believed that Dowding would be faced with no choice but to locate all of his operational fighters in south-east England to meet the main assault. This indicates two things: gross over-confidence and poor intelligence. Nonetheless, whilst engaged on *freie jagd* sorties, cut free of escorting slow bombers, the 109s were able to gain height and operate at a situation of tactical advantage in which their 'dirty dart' tactics ruled supreme. An extraordinary demonstration of this occurred over Canterbury on 18 August 1940 – a day of concentrated attacks on 11 Group's Sector Stations and famously dubbed 'The Hardest Day' by Alfred Price.

On that fateful day, *Oberleutnant* Gerhard Schöpfel, the *Staffelkapitän* of 9/JG 26 led III/JG 26, in Major Galland's absence, on a *freie jagd* with a *gruppe* of Me 109s from JG 3. These forty fighters crossed the British coast high over Dover, twenty-five miles ahead of the main raiding force. To the south-west, the Do 17s of 9/KG 76 flew at low-level towards Beachy Head, sneaking in beneath the British radar screen. By 1.00 p.m., 17, 54, 56, 65 and 601 Squadrons were patrolling the Canterbury-Margate line, intending to parry any thrust at the fighter stations north of the Thames. Four more squadrons climbed to defend Biggin Hill and Kenley, but 11 Group still had reserves, Air Vice-Marshal Park keeping nine further squadrons at readiness.

Certain of the RAF fighters, however, were in a dangerous tactical position as they clawed for height to reach their patrol lines. At 1.30 p.m. over Canterbury, Schöpfel, high up and concealed by the sun, watched the Hurricanes of 501 Squadron climbing in vics of three. It was a situation where one aircraft may achieve surprise and success. Schöpfel alone, therefore, attacked and achieved total surprise: within seconds both 'weavers' were dispatched, their fate unseen by the remaining Hurricanes. Unable to believe his luck, Schöpfel then downed the rearmost aircraft but still 501 Squadron continued climbing in tight formation, completely unaware of their comrades' fate. Schöpfel then pulled behind another Hurricane and it too fell in flames. Worse could have followed but Schöpfel's 109 had been hit by debris from his last victim, so close had his attack been executed. With his windscreen covered in oil, the German dived away as III/JG 26 engaged the remaining Hurricanes in an inconclusive dogfight. Schöpfel, as Price wrote, had 'profited from the failings of the tight-combat formation still in use in many Fighter Command squadrons' enabling him to 'knock down four Hurricanes in two minutes, killing one pilot and wounding three others'.[32] It was an absolutely classic example of the success possible when fighters were allowed to roam, at altitude, seizing any tactical opportunity favourable to them. In sum, as Galland commented, 'The first rule of air combat is to see the opponent first. Like the hunter who stalks his prey and manoeuvres himself unnoticed into the most favourable position for the kill, the fighter in the opening of a dogfight must detect the opponent as quickly as possible in order to attain a superior position for attack'.[33] Schöpfel had done just that, and the German tactics, emphasising the leader as killer, together with incompetent RAF battle formation, did the rest.

By 1.24 p.m. on 18 August, a running battle had developed all the way from Kenley to the coast, tying down many defending fighter squadrons and which gave KG 1 a clear run in to attack Biggin Hill. Most bombs fell on the runway and in a wood to the east of it. Over Cranbrook, five 65 Squadron Spitfires found and shot up a straggling KG 1 He 111. The Spitfires were led by Flying Officer Jeffrey Quill, the Supermarine test pilot who, to his great credit, had volunteered to fly with Fighter Command and gain first-hand combat experience. Flying Officer Jeffrey Quill:

> In 65 Squadron we did not fly the useless formation comprising Vics of three, but instead our four sections flew in line astern. This could be rapidly opened out sideways and, like the German line abreast *Schwarm*, required much less concentration. 18 August, however, was a hectic day and we suffered a fatal casualty, Flying Officer Franek Gruszka. The trouble was that our two Poles, Szulkowski and Gruszka, were inclined to go off chasing the enemy on their own, so determined were they. None of us saw what happened to Gruszka, and back at Hornchurch Szulkowski was very upset that his friend was missing.[34]

Fighter Command's more experienced squadrons, realising that the 'vic' was suicidal, were trying to address this. Most, including Squadron Leader George Denholm of 603 and Squadron Leader 'Sailor' Malan of 74 Squadron, were experimenting with variations of line astern formations. One of the most successful Spitfire squadrons of the period was 603, commanded by Squadron Leader 'Uncle' George Denholm, who remembered: '603 Squadron had to learn quickly. We rapidly determined not to allow ourselves to be bounced. I therefore decided to fly on a reciprocal of the course provided by the ground controller, until at 15,000 feet when the Squadron would turn about, climbing all the time. Flying in this way meant that we usually saw the enemy striking inland beneath us and were therefore better positioned to attack. We also ensured that pilots always flew in pairs, for mutual protection'.[35] Squadrons in 11 Group were learning on the job – but their tactical experience was not passed on to other squadrons within the Command. As Flying Officer Frank Brinsden wrote, 'At the time I thought intelligence briefing was sadly lacking'.[36]

The comparative lull in the fighting after the exertions of 18 August permitted Dowding to rotate some of his squadrons, replacing battle weary units in 11 Group with fresh squadrons from 13 Group. So far as the operational numbers game was concerned this was fine, but the northern squadrons lacked experience in fighting the 109. On 19 August, 616 Squadron moved from Leconfield in Yorkshire, where, as Pilot Officer William Walker remembered, 'only a few minor raids had disrupted our existence',[37] to Kenley in Surrey. There Walker found that there was 'an atmosphere of purpose … and we found ourselves having to respond to a life of far greater activity than at Leconfield'.[38] On 22 August, 616 Squadron patrolled over Dover, inevitably in vics of three, and were bounced by JG 51. The Spitfire of Pilot Officer Hugh 'Cocky' Dundas was hit 'so hard' that he 'assumed a heavy anti-aircraft shell was responsible'.[39] Having baled out with a dislocated shoulder, the following day Dundas 'learned the humiliating truth: I had not been shot down by our own ack ack, as I thought, but by an Me 109 none of us had even seen'.[40] Three days later 616 was bounced again, losing one pilot killed and another missing. Pilot Officer Walker: 'We were very unsure of ourselves at this time. Everything happened so quick, and of course our formations of vics and lines astern were all wrong. There was so little information available to us. Very little was passed on by those squadrons that were relieved as they couldn't wait to get out of the place! Fighting in the south, where the 109s always seemed to have the advantage of height and sun, was very different to chasing after unescorted bombers up North'.[41] Walker would always remember the events of 26 August:

> That day I was allocated Spitfire R6633, and was to fly in Yellow Section, led by Flying Officer Teddy St Aubyn, a former Guards officer. The plane stood within fifty yards of our hut and so I walked over and placed my parachute in the cockpit with the straps spread apart and ready for wearing immediately I jumped in. Two of the groundcrew stood by the plane with the starter battery plugged in. I walked back to the hut as the sun rose and added a little warmth to a chilly start. Pilots sat about either reading or exchanging the usual banter that had become routine. We had spent many months in this way, which was now a way of life. At 8.00 a.m. our second breakfast arrived at dispersal, and was just as fulfilling as our breakfast of four hours earlier: coffee, eggs, bacon, sausages and toast to replenish our undiminished appetites.[42]

Throughout Fighter Command, this was the typical start to a fighter pilot's day. It was not until around 11.30 a.m. that the first big raid was incoming above Dover: forty He 111s and twelve Do 17s, escorted by eighty 109s, all bound for Biggin Hill and Kenley. Air Vice-Marshal Park responded with seventy RAF fighters, among them seven Spitfires of 616 Squadron's 'A' Flight. Walker continued:

> The telephone rang in the dispersal hut and a shout of "Yellow Section, scramble! Patrol Dungeness/Dover Angels Twenty!" sent me running to my plane. I leapt onto the wing and was in the cockpit, parachute strapped on, within seconds. I pressed the starter and the engine fired immediately. The groundcrew removed the plug from the cowling and

pulled the remote starter battery clear. I waved the chocks away and taxied the aircraft, followed by my Section Leader and Sergeant Ridley, to the end of the runway for take-off. Within minutes Yellow Section was airborne. We headed East, climbing quickly and passing through cloud, reaching our patrol course in some fifteen – twenty minutes. We flew in wide formation and had been airborne for about an hour without sighting any enemy aircraft when suddenly several 109s appeared.[43]

Over Dungeness the hapless Spitfires were bounced, having been unfortunate enough to have been espied by Major Werner Mölders, who was leading all three *gruppen* of JG 51 on a *freie jagd*. Flying Officer Teddy St Aubyn's Spitfire was hit in the coolant system, the pilot crash landing at Eastchurch; Flying Officer George Moberley crashed into the sea and was killed, as was Sergeant Marmaduke Ridley who crashed near Dover. St Aubyn was the fifteenth kill of *Oberleutnant* 'Pips' Priller, *Staffelkapitän* of 6/JG 51, whilst Moberley and Ridley are believed to have been killed by *Hauptmann* 'Joschko' Fözö, *Staffelkapitän* of 4/JG 51. Only one of 616 Squadron's pilots brought his guns to bear, Flight Lieutenant Denys 'Kill 'em' Gillam, of Blue Section: 'On arriving at 10,000 feet we were ordered to intercept two forty plus raids. We climbed to 11,000 feet and discovered about 100 Me 109s all around and above us. I ordered line astern and we formed a circle. One Me 109 appeared on Blue Two's tail, so I turned on to it and fired at it down to 4,000 feet. I then followed it through cloud and on coming out saw the aircraft hit the water straight ahead'.[44] Gillam's victim was *Leutnant* Hoffman of 7/JG 51.

Major Mölders himself, as usual attacking from behind and slightly below, aimed at Spitfire R6633 and claimed his twenty-seventh kill. Pilot Officer William Walker:

When the 109s hit us I banked steeply to port, towards a 109, but suddenly my machine was raked with bullets. I never even saw the one that attacked me. The flying controls ceased to respond and a sudden pain in my leg indicated that I had been hit. Baling out seemed to be a sensible option. My two comrades of Yellow Section had both vanished.

I pulled back the hood and tried to stand up but realised that I had not disconnected the radio lead, which was still plugged in, and had to remove my helmet before I was free to jump. The aircraft was still banking to port, so jumping out was easy. I was still at 20,000 feet and pulled the ripcord immediately. A sudden jerk indicated that all was well and that I was on my way down. I looked around but could not see a single aircraft. Below there was 10/10ths cloud. I had no idea where I was. It seemed to take ages to reach the clouds and passing through I realised that I was still over the Channel. Thinking that I would soon land in the sea prompted the thought that I had better remove my heavy flying boots. I did this and let them fall. I watched them spiral down for what seemed like ages and then realised that I was much higher than I thought. I inflated my Mae West and eventually landed in the sea. I easily discarded my parachute and could see the wreck of a ship sticking out of the water a few hundred yards away and swam to it. I reached it and climbed on, sitting there for about half an hour until a fishing boat came alongside and I clambered aboard. I was now extremely cold from my immersion and wet clothes.

The fishermen gave me a cup of tea, well laced with whisky, as we headed for land. When about two miles offshore an RAF launch came alongside and I was transferred to it. By this time the tea concoction had worked quite disastrously on my cold stomach. Fortunately there was a loo aboard to which I retired, with some relief. I was still enthroned when we reached Ramsgate harbour. An aircraftman kept knocking on the door and enquiring whether I was okay. It was some time, however, before I was able to emerge! I was carried up the steps to a waiting ambulance, by which time quite a crowd had gathered and gave me a cheer as I was put in the ambulance. A kind old lady handed me a packet of cigarettes, so I decided that being shot down was perhaps not such a bad thing after all![45]

This patrol had been a catastrophe for 616 Squadron. Since having arrived at Kenley a week previously, seven out of fifteen Spitfires had been lost, four pilots killed and an equal number wounded. The Squadron Clerk, clearly a master of the understatement, recorded the action as 'a most unfortunate engagement'.[46] Moreover, it was yet another demonstration of the advantage of height, sun and surprise.

30 August was another day of heavy and interesting fighting. As a large enemy formation battled its way across Kent towards Biggin Hill and Kenley Sector Stations, the 11 Group Controller called for assistance from neighbouring 12 Group. In accordance with Dowding's strategy, 19 Squadron was scrambled from Fowlmere in the Duxford Sector to patrol Biggin Hill, due to 11 Group's squadrons being engaged further forward. A squadron of Park's own Hurricanes, 253, were vectored from their Maidstone patrol to cover Kenley.[47] At 11.10 a.m., 222 Squadron's Spitfires – fresh to the battle – was scrambled from Hornchurch to patrol Gravesend. Sergeant Iain Hutchinson remembered that: 'It was the first time we had engaged the enemy since our arrival at Hornchurch only the previous day, and was the usual scenario: the 109s were higher and knew exactly what they were doing, whilst we were just learning the ropes. I didn't even see the one that hit me'.[48] Fortunately Sergeant Hutchinson, who was unhurt, managed to crash land his Spitfire near Hornchurch. Sergeant Reg Johnson: 'In our first 48 hours at Hornchurch we lost 18 Spitfires and a number of pilots. We proceeded to go into action in the tight formation we had been trained to use, but consequently our losses were heavy. Eventually we evolved a "Tail End Charlie" Section which weaved about, above, below and to the rear of the Squadron (which was still in tight formation). It helped. I was made a permanent member of Green Section, with Pilot Officer Laurie Whitbread and one other, and we were given that job to do'.[49] According to the 222 Squadron Operations Record Book (ORB), on 30 August 'the Squadron was very positively engaged in operations and flew three patrols during the day. Sergeant J. I. Johnson was killed, and Flight Lieutenant Matheson and Sergeant Edridge were wounded'.[50] During those three sorties, 222 lost a total of six Spitfires destroyed and three damaged in yet another example of a 'green' squadron being roughly handled whilst still adjusting to the completely different tempo of combat.

Another squadron fresh to south-east England was also in action, over Deal: the CO, Squadron Leader 'Uncle' George Denholm, was shot down and baled out, as was Sergeant Sarre later in the day. Further, the Hurricanes of 253 Squadron were new to Kenley, having arrived from Prestwick only the day before, and during the morning's fighting suffered three Hurricanes damaged and three destroyed. Two pilots were killed. That afternoon the Squadron lost another pilot killed and two more aircraft damaged. The 109s also gave the hapless 616 Squadron trouble again: over West Malling, 109s attacked the Squadron head-on, shooting down Pilot Officer Jack Bell, who was killed. As these raids withdrew, fresh waves of enemy fighters and bombers were incoming at twenty minute intervals, provoking further combat. Indeed, the scale of fighting was such that Air Vice-Marshal Leigh-Mallory decided to send the Hurricanes of Squadron Leader Douglas Bader's 242 Squadron to Duxford, where it would remain at readiness to respond to any further requests for assistance from 11 Group.[51]

At 4.00 p.m., 300 plus enemy aircraft were reported over Kent and the Thames Estuary, the raiders splitting up to attack the airfields at Kenley, North Weald, Hornchurch, Debden, Lympne, Detling and Biggin Hill. At 4.20 p.m., sixty He 111s of I/KG 1 and II/KG 53, escorted by Me 110s, crossed the coast north of the Thames. The 11 Group Controller requested reinforcements from 12 Group. At 4.23 p.m., therefore, 242 Squadron was scrambled from Duxford, Squadron Leader Bader leading fourteen Hurricanes off from Duxford with orders to patrol North Weald at 15,000 feet.[52] The enemy formation next showed its true intention, I/KG 1 heading for the Vauxhall Motor Works and aerodrome at Luton, whilst II/KG 53, being the larger of the two raiding parties, began to fight its way to the Handley Page aircraft factory at Radlett. At 4.25 p.m., 56 Squadron was scrambled from North Weald, and 1 Squadron from Northolt. At 4.55 hours, two Spitfires of 222 Squadron were sent up from Hornchurch, whilst Squadron Leader Harry Hogan's 501 Squadron had already taken off from Gravesend. At 4.50 p.m., whilst flying east over Chatham, 501 Squadron tally ho'd a large force of He 111s which sub-divided into *staffeln*, each in an arrowhead pattern.[53] According to the Squadron's combat report:

> The bombers were at 15,000 feet and flying west, south of the Thames Estuary towards London. Stepped up behind them were formations of Me 109s and 110s. The enemy aircraft turned north over Southend, and the Squadron circled around them, attacking the second Vic head-on. This broke up, and one He 111 jettisoned its bombs. Another was pursued by two of our fighters and landed on the water near the *Girdler* lightship. Another crashed in Southend. Our aircraft were not attacked by fighters, which were some distance behind.[54]

Shortly after take-off, 1 Squadron sighted six enemy aircraft 'north of London',[55] which it prepared to attack, but fortunately recognised them as Blenheims before any gun buttons were thumbed. Upon breaking away, Squadron Leader Pemberton's pilots saw the enemy formation: thirty to forty bombers protected by a similar number of fighters and in no standard formation from 12,000 – 25,000 feet. 1 Squadron's subsequent attack was carried out with each pilot acting independently. Sergeant Merchant reported that:

> I was Number Two of Red Section and upon sighting enemy followed my Section Leader in line astern. After attacking a Do 17, which was in company with another E/A, an Me 110 dived on me from astern. Breaking away, I shook him off, and then saw ahead a single He 111K. Climbing and going ahead, I attacked from the beam. On the second attack the port engine stopped. At this moment a Hurricane from another squadron dived on the rear of the He 111 and got in a burst. Again attacking from the front I got in a long burst, and a

man jumped by parachute. A further two parachutists jumped after about one minute, as I put in another burst. The aircraft dived down and crashed in the middle of a road near a cemetery to the east of Southend.[56]

The He III claimed by Sergeant Marchant crashed at Lifstan Way, Southend; it was the same raider claimed by 501 Squadron, so this is a prime example of how one actual enemy loss became two, as it were, and so on.

1 Squadron's Pilot Officer Pat Hancock:

I pursued the main body of enemy aircraft. One He III was lagging behind. I gained height and prepared to attack it. Before doing so, however, a Spitfire did an astern attack of about five seconds duration. I then went in and fired several long bursts at each engine in turn. I observed smoke, oil and flames coming from each engine. I did not follow the aircraft to the ground as a Vic of Me IIos appeared to be attacking me. I evaded them and returned to base.[57]

Again, the He III attacked by Hancock is believed to have been that which came to grief at Lifstan Way. The Spitfire mentioned was no doubt one of the two 222 Squadron machines involved: Flying Officer Cutts and Sergeant Davis also claimed a He III 'probable' in that area.

1 Squadron's Sergeant Clowes also claimed a He III that 'emitted smoke and some flames', reporting that on his second pass the bomber's 'perspex nose exploded',[58] although this too was the Lifstan Way raider. Another shared kill was the 5/KG 53 He III that crashed at Colne Engaine, near Halstead: this bomber was first attacked and damaged by 1 Squadron's Pilot Officer Matthews before being finished off by 56 Squadron's Flight Lieutenant 'Jumbo' Gracie.[59] 1 Squadron's CO, Squadron Leader Pemberton, attacked an Me IIo 'in company with a Hurricane of LE squadron',[60] which was one of two IIos that crashed at Ponders End, to the east of Enfield. 'LE' was the code letters of Squadron Leader Bader's 242 Squadron. The 242 Squadron combat report stated that:

Squadron 242 was ordered at 1623 hours from Duxford to patrol North Weald at 15,000 feet on a vector 190°, just north of North Weald. They received a vector of 340°. Three aircraft were noticed to the right of the formation, so the Squadron Leader detached Blue Section to investigate.

Green Leader then drew attention to a large enemy formation on their left so the rest of the Squadron turned and saw a vast number of aeroplanes flying in an easterly direction. These were recognised to be from seventy – 100 E/A, twin-engined and in tight formation, stepped up at 12,000 feet, after which there was a gap of 1,000 feet, then another swarm of twin-engined machines stepped up from about 15,000 feet to 20,000 feet.

Green Section was ordered to attack the top of the lower formation; Red and Yellow Sections were ordered into line astern. It seemed impossible to order any formation attack. The Squadron Leader dived straight into the middle of the formation closely followed by Red Two and Red Three; the packed formation broke up and a dogfight ensued. Squadron Leader Bader saw three Me IIos do climbing turns to the left and three to the right. Their tactics appeared to be to climb in turns until they were nearly stalling above the tail of

Squadron Leader Bader's aircraft. Squadron Leader Bader fired a short burst into the Me 110 at practically point blank range and the E/A burst into flames and disintegrated almost immediately. Squadron Leader Bader continued his zoom and saw another Me 110 below and so turned in behind it and got a very easy shot at about 100 to 150 yards range. After the E/A had received Squadron Leader Bader's first burst of from two to four seconds, the enemy pilot avoided further action by putting the stick violently forwards and backwards.

Squadron Leader Bader got in another burst and saw pieces of the enemy's starboard wing fly off; then the whole starboard wing went on fire and the E/A went down burning in a spiral dive. Squadron Leader Bader then saw in his mirror another Me 110; he did a quick turn and noticed five or six white streams coming out of forward-firing guns; the E/A immediately put his nose down and was lost, but subsequently seen far below. Squadron Leader Bader saw nothing around him, called Duxford and was told to land.[61]

Red Two, Pilot Officer Willie McKnight, went in to attack with Squadron Leader Bader; he got behind an Me 110 and opened fire at 100 yards, the enemy aircraft bursting into flames and crashing. After a beam attack on a formation of He 111s, Red Two turned the tables on an Me 110, which had attacked him from behind, chasing the enemy machine from 10,000 to 1,000 feet. From just thirty yards, McKnight opened fire; the 110 crashed at Enfield Sewage Farm, Ponders End. After the initial Section attack, Red Three, Pilot Officer Denis Crowley-Milling, damaged an He 111, which Pilot Officer Hart confirmed having seen go down in flames. Yellow One, Flight Lieutenant Ball, emptied a third of his ammunition into an Me 110, which Pilot Officer Stansfield also attacked, the 110 going down with both engines on fire, and so it went on, with many more claims by 242 Squadron's elated pilots.

This was what Squadron Leader Bader and 242 Squadron had been desperately waiting for: an opportunity to engage the enemy in numbers. As indicated by the foregoing, however, there were other squadrons involved in this combat, which also recorded victories. Due to the high numbers of engaging fighters, however, various pilots had independently attacked and claimed the same German aircraft, which became duplicated on the balance sheet. In the heat of the moment, however, the relatively inexperienced 242 Squadron had been oblivious to the presence of other RAF fighters and so believed that 242, and 242 alone, was responsible for this successful interception. In total, 242 Squadron claimed seven Me 110s destroyed and three probables, and five He 111s destroyed.[62] At the time, these claims were accepted unconditionally and without question, prompting various congratulatory signals. Certainly the destruction of twelve enemy aircraft for no loss would have been remarkable – had it been accurate.

Long after the event, Douglas Bader explained:

What happened was we got off a squadron, just 12 of us, and we had everything in our favour, height, I knew where the Germans were, and we had the sun. We shot down a few without any problems whatsoever. When we were writing out our combat reports afterwards, Leigh-Mallory rang me up and said "Congratulations, Bader, on the Squadron's performance today".

I said "Thank you very much, Sir, but if we'd had more aeroplanes then we would have shot down a whole lot more!" He asked what I meant and I explained that with more fighters our results would have been even better. He said "Look, I'd like to talk to you about this", and so I flew over to Hucknall and told him what I thought.[63]

So it was that the seeds were sewn for 12 Group to operate large formations of fighters – contrary to the System and to Dowding's orders. The evidence proves, however, that the whole theory was flawed from the outset: it was not just the twelve Hurricanes of 242 Squadron in action against the Hatfield raiders, as Bader mistakenly assumed, but around fifty RAF fighters in total. Moreover, it is important to note that the Hatfield raid had not been escorted by the lethal 109s, but by the inferior Me 110, which undoubtedly contributed to the interception's success. It is also a prime example of the increased over-claiming factor when many fighters are engaged.

At Fowlmere, 19 Squadron was becoming exasperated after further problems with the cannon. On 1 September, Squadron Leader Pinkham reported accordingly to Duxford's Station Commander, Group Captain Woodhall:

> In all of the engagements so far occurring it is considered that had the unit been equipped with eight gun fighters it would have inflicted far more severe losses on the enemy. Furthermore, Captain Adams from the Ministry of Aircraft Production, who recently visited the unit to report on the guns, has stated that the guns at present installed in the cannon Spitfire would never function satisfactorily until they are mounted up-right, or possibly with a modification to the existing wing. It would take some months before this modification could be completed and it is considered most unfair that pilots should be expected to attack enemy formations of the size encountered at present with unreliable armament. It is most strongly urged that until stoppages at present experienced have been eliminated, this squadron should re-equip with Browning-gun Spitfires. It is suggested that a way of doing this would be to allot the present cannon armed Spitfires to an OTU, and withdraw Browning-gun Spitfires from there for use in this squadron.[64]

Group Captain Woodhall endorsed Pinkham's view to 12 Group HQ, and later wrote that:

> This further failure of 19 Squadron's cannons was unacceptable, so I got on the phone to "L. M." and urgently requested that the Squadron should have its eight-gun Spitfires back. The following afternoon the AOC-in-C, "Stuffy" Dowding himself, landed at Duxford without warning. I greeted him and he gruffly said "I want to talk to the pilots of 19 Squadron", so I drove him over to Fowlmere. There he met Sandy Lane and other pilots. He listened to their complaints almost in silence. Then I drove him back to his aircraft, which he was piloting personally. As he climbed into the aeroplane, he merely said "You'll get your eight-gun Spitfires back." "Stuffy" was a man of few words, but he had listened to us all, asked a few pertinent questions then made his decision. As a result, that evening the instructors from the OTU at Hawarden flew their eight-gun Spitfires to Fowlmere, returning with the cannon Spitfires.[65]

Flight Sergeant George Unwin:

> This was good news. We were absolutely fed up with the cannons. Being in 12 Group and
> playing a supporting role meant that we didn't get into action as often as we would have
> liked, and when we did it was only for the cannons to jam. We were much more confident
> with the machine-gun Spits, but they were clapped out old things from an OTU, although
> we realised that beggars can't be choosers! [66]

By 4 September 19 Squadron's change over back to eight-gun Spitfire Mk IAs was complete.
Ironically Squadron Leader Pinkham was killed in action the following day, when shot
down in one of them over Kent. In the short-term, however, 19 Squadron was once more an
altogether more effective fighting unit. In the long-term the cannon issue was a matter that
Dowding and the MAP had to resolve. Captain Adams' opinion that the Spitfire's wings
should be adapted so as to permit the cannon to be mounted upright, as intended by the
manufacturer, was indeed correct. Ultimately this was made possible by the fitting of blisters to
both wing surfaces which accommodated the originally intended ammunition drum. This fed
and ejected shells as intended by the manufacturer, resolving the problem – although not in
time for the Battle of Britain. In due course the cannon-armed Spitfires would also be armed
with four machine-guns, like the experimental Spitfire Mk IB X4231. This would actually
provide the Spitfire with not just armament equal to the Me 109, but two machine-guns more.
Interestingly, however, the Me 109E engaged during the Battle of Britain already had blisters
fitted to wing surfaces to accommodate the Oerlikon's ammunition drum, enabling correct
mounting of the weapon. This was known to RAF Intelligence from examinations of captured
109s. Like the question of tactical fighter formations, it is difficult to understand, therefore,
why the German method was not simply copied from the outset. So, for the remainder of the
Battle of Britain, the 109 would have the edge so far as firepower was concerned.

On 31 August, 11 Group's Sector Stations were pounded hard. On this day Fighter
Command suffered its heaviest losses: thirty-nine fighters and fourteen pilots killed
against forty-one enemy machines. Elements of 222 Squadron operated from Hornchurch's
forward base at Rochford that day, so as to disperse the Station's Spitfires. At lunchtime 222
was scrambled to patrol Canterbury at 20,000 feet. Over Maidstone an incoming German
raid was sighted, comprising of twenty-four Me 109s escorting a formation of He 111s.
Among the Spitfire pilots engaged was Pilot Officer Laurie Whitbread:

> I manoeuvred until the Me 109 appeared in my sights, the enemy aircraft climbing slowly
> away, not having seen me. I fired from about 400 yards and rapidly closed to within fifty
> yards, when I could see the bullets entering the fuselage from tail to cockpit. The 109 half
> rolled onto its back and remained in that attitude, flying quite slowly with a little white
> smoke issuing from it. It eventually nosed down slowly when I was obliged to lose sight of
> it having noticed an aircraft approaching my tail, which turned out to be a Spitfire. [67]

This enemy fighter was probably one belonging to 1/JG 77, which crashed between
Walderslade and Broxley at 1320 hours. The pilot, *Unteroffizier* Keck, baled out and was

captured. Again there are classic ingredients in this combat report: very close range – fifty yards – and, in the absence of actual flame, the all-important white smoke.

On 2 September, Pilot Officer Richard Hillary of 603 Squadron was in action over his home station of Hornchurch, at 20,000 feet: 'I lost sight of the Squadron and saw four Me 109s in line astern and above me. I climbed up and attacked the rear 109, getting to about 50 feet of him before opening fire. The Me 109 went straight down with thick smoke pouring out and I did not see it again'.[68] Again, the range is impressive – just fifty feet. The Spitfire pilot's bullets clearly found their mark, although he does not state what colour smoke emitted from the enemy aircraft. The 109 concerned was awarded as a 'probable'.

By the beginning of September it was clear to the OKW that the necessary conditions for invasion had still not been achieved. On the night of 24 August, RAF Bomber Command had attacked Berlin. This Hitler seized upon as justification for bombing London.[69] In previous campaigns the Polish and Dutch had surrendered after the bombing of their main centres of population, and the Danes did so at just the threat of it.[70] Hitler hoped, therefore, that the same would be true of Britain. Göring hoped that the round-the-clock bombing of London ordered by Hitler would finally exhaust Fighter Command. Moreover, Göring believed that London was the only target capable of forcing Dowding's hand to commit all his fighters in defence of.[71] Until that point the *Luftwaffe's* concentrated attacks on 11 Group had been producing the required result – albeit slowly. And as the summer wore on, time was running out. According to *The Luftwaffe War Diaries*: 'This alteration in tactical policy is viewed by the British, from Churchill downwards, as a fundamental German mistake that saved the defences from destruction. The fighter bases at last had a breathing space and could now recover from the serious damage they had received'.[72] This, however, is not a view shared by German scholar Horst Boog, who argued that:

> The thesis that the British fighter defences would have broken down had German air attacks on fighter installations been continued for another fourteen days, and that this would have jeopardized the fate of Great Britain, exaggerates the effects of the German bombing attacks and disregards the overall potential available on either side. Fighter Command could have withdrawn its units from airfields in the south-eastern coastal area to bases out of range of German single-engined fighters, or 11 Group's fighters could have been reinforced by those of the other three groups.[73]

The evidence supports Boog's view, but nonetheless 11 Group's sector stations still gained an essential breathing space.

This new phase saw Göring himself take personal command of the *Luftwaffe* effort. By this time the Germans were becoming increasingly frustrated at their failure to achieve the required objective. Surprisingly, it was not the bomber force that came under criticism but the fighters. Galland wrote that the 'unjustified accusations had a most demoralising effect on us fighter pilots, who were already overtaxed by physical and mental strain. We complained of the leadership, the bombers, the *Stukas*, and were dissatisfied with ourselves. We saw one comrade after the other, old and tested brothers in combat, vanish from our ranks. New faces appeared and became familiar, until one day these too would disappear, shot down in the

Battle of Britain'.[74] Tested to the limit, operating at the extremity of their range, the 109 pilots began exhibiting signs of 'chronic stress and acute fatigue', known as *Kanalkrankheit*.[75] Clearly having confidence in the perceived technical superiority in their Me 109E was insufficient to see the *jagdflieger* through such a protracted and difficult aerial campaign. The problem revolved around the requirement for bomber escort, as Galland explained in detail:

> Fighter protection created many problems, which had to be solved in action. As in Spain, the bomber pilots preferred close screening, in which their formation was surrounded by pairs of fighters pursuing a zig-zag course. Obviously the proximity and visible presence of the protective fighters gave the bomber pilots a greater sense of security. However, this was a faulty conclusion because a fighter can only carry out this purely defensive task by taking the initiative in the offensive. He must never wait until he is attacked, because then loses the chance of acting. The fighter must seek battle in the air, must find his opponent, attack him and shoot him down. The bomber must avoid such fights, and he has to act defensively in order to fulfil his task: war from the air. In co-operation between bomber and fighter, these two fundamentally different mentalities obviously clash. The words of Richthofen expressed in the First World War, summarising the task of the fighters, often came to our lips. Fundamentally, they are still valid today: "The fighter pilots have to rove in the area allotted to them in any way they live, and when they spot an enemy they attack and shoot him down; anything else is rubbish".[76]

It was not just the RAF, therefore, that suffered from tactical disagreements. The Germans had an excellent short-range defensive fighter in the 109, which was performing the role of an offensive escort fighter to which it was completely unsuited. Moreover, there were just not enough of them. With double the force, even given the limitations of performance, close escort could have been provided in addition to fighter sweeps in strength. This, however, was not possible given the size of force available. Furthermore, the longer-range Me 110, which did have the range to do the job, proved to be a disappointing failure. Although it was fast, it was simply not manoeuvrable enough to fight the Hurricane or Spitfire. So the Germans too, having suffered from purely offensive doctrinal thinking between the wars, also suffered now for having paid insufficient attention to the fighter force.

In an effort to negate to some extent the inflexibility of Göring's escort orders, the 109 pilots flying top cover pushed altitude higher still. Galland's highest combat occurred at 25,000 feet, but the 109s pounced from even as high as 27,000 feet – close to the lower limits of the stratosphere.[77] From that extreme height the German pilots could see the British fighters clearly as they climbed above the cloud layer. On 7 September, as London was being bombed, 222 Squadron's Spitfires engaged the German fighters at 27,000 feet; Pilot Officer Laurie Whitbread reported that:

> We engaged an enemy formation of Me 109s. I became separated from the rest of the Squadron so I climbed back to my original altitude and flew round looking for a target. I found one in a formation of twenty-five to thirty Do 215s, which appeared to have no fighter escort. Keeping in the sun, I dived down on the last aircraft which was straggling

behind some 100 yards at the rear of the formation and flying at 20,000 feet. I carried out a quarter attack from the port side (formation was flying westwards along south bank of the Thames at Dartford). I opened fire at 300 yards, range closing rapidly. The starboard engine set on fire and I broke away, the return fire from the rear three gunners and my closing range making it advisable.[78]

Although Whitbread had damaged his target, mutual fire support had prevented him pressing home his attack, indicating how dangerous attacking bombers could be.

One of the Spitfire pilots who fought over London during these intense September air battles was Pilot Officer Roger Hall of 10 Group's 152 Squadron. The experience left a profound impression and he later wrote that, 'I recalled for an instant Mr Baldwin's prophecy, not a sanguine one, made to the House of Commons some five years before when he said that the bomber would always get through. Now it was doing just that'.[79]

On 11 September, Air Vice-Marshal Park instructed his fighter controllers that squadrons were to be despatched in 'pairs to engage the first wave of enemy. Spitfires against fighter screen, and Hurricanes against bombers and close escort'.[80] This was because the Spitfire was superior at high altitude whereas the Hurricane's best performance was at heights around 18,000 feet.[81] Air Vice-Marshal Park reported comprehensively on this phase of the battle. Regarding enemy fighter tactics he wrote that:

The favourite tactic was to send a very high fighter screen over Kent from fifteen to forty-five minutes ahead of bomber attacks, presumably to draw up our fighter squadrons and exhaust their petrol before the main attack crossed the coast. At other times the high fighter screen arrived only a few minutes in advance of the bomber formations with close escort. Fighter escorts normally consisted of two parts: (a) a big formation above and to the flank or in rear of the bombers, and (b) smaller formations of fighters formatting with the bombers on the same level or slightly below. The latter formations endeavoured to prevent head-on attacks by our fighters against the incoming bombers.[82]

Of such head-on attacks, Flight Lieutenant Gerry Edge later recalled that, 'They didn't like that head-on attack, you know, but you had to judge the break-away point exactly right. If you left it to the last 100 yards then you were in trouble, due to the fast closing speeds, but once you got the hang of it a head-on attack was a piece of cake. When you opened fire you would kill or badly wound the pilot and second pilot. Then you'd rake the whole line as you broke away. On one attack, the first Heinkel I hit crashed into the next'.[83] Such attacks clearly required both skill and courage.

Park's report also stated that, 'The enemy attempted in this phase to draw our fighter patrols off from his bombers by high altitude diversions … increasingly high fighter screens were sent inland to draw off and contain our fighters, whilst the bomber formations, closely escorted by further fighters, endeavoured to sweep in some 6,000 to 10,000 feet below'. To counter this, 'The general plan adopted was to engage the enemy high fighter screen with pairs of Spitfire squadrons from Hornchurch and Biggin Hill half-way between London and the coast, and so enable Hurricane squadrons from London sectors to attack bomber formations and their close escort before they reached the line of fighter aerodromes East and South of London. The remaining squadrons from London Sectors that could not be despatched in time to intercept the first wave of attack by climbing in pairs formed a third and inner screen by patrolling along the line of aerodromes East and South of London. The fighter squadrons from Debden, Tangmere and Northolt were employed in wings of three or in pairs to form a screen South-East of London to intercept the third wave of the attack coming inland, also to mop up retreating formations of the earlier waves. The Spitfire squadrons were re-disposed so as to concentrate three squadrons at each of Hornchurch and Biggin Hill. The primary role of these squadrons was to engage and drive back the enemy high fighter screen, and so protect the Hurricane squadrons, whose task was to attack close escorts and then the bomber formations, all of which flew at much lower altitude'.[84]

This section of Park's report is of particular interest. Firstly, the commander of 11 Group was clearly not averse to using large formations of fighters, as he had at Dunkirk, when the occasion demanded – but not as a matter of course. Secondly, it is clear that only the Spitfire was able to deal with the high flying escorts and 'protect the Hurricane squadrons' in action at lower altitude. Had Fighter Command only been equipped with Hurricanes, it would have been powerless to counter the threat represented by the high-flying escorts. Nonetheless it was not just Hurricane pilots who shot down German bombers, as indicated by this report by 92 Squadron concerning 11 September: 'Thirteen aircraft of 92 Squadron were ordered off from Biggin Hill at 3.20 p.m. to intercept a raid coming in over the coast by Dungeness. Squadron encountered a large formation of bombers with fighters above. Squadron was split up over Maidstone and all our aircraft carried out individual attacks on a large formation of He 111s and fighters Me 109 and 110. The individual aircraft carried out series of beam, quarter and head-on attacks. Six He 111s were shot down round about Rye and Dungeness and confirmed by the Irish Fusiliers. Further, one Me 109 was seen crashing and the pilots also claim one Me 109 and one Me 110 as a probable'.[85] Again, however, the actual result was less impressive. 92 Squadron's Flight Lieutenant Alan Wright had attacked the same He 111 of 6/KG 1 as had three Spitfire pilots of 66 Squadron. Pilot Officers 'Wimpey' Wade and Denis Williams of 92 Squadron shared the destruction of an He 111 of I/KG 26, but otherwise no other enemy aircraft brought down over England that day can be attributed to 92 Squadron.[86] Be that as it may, Park's report related a telling observation: 'As our successes against these bomber attacks increased, there was a noticeable increase in the ratio of enemy fighters to bombers, the ratio in latter part of the phase being about four fighters to one bomber.'[87]

Across the Channel, there had been further disagreement between the enemy fighter and bomber forces. The fighter pilots remained convinced that the inflexible orders binding them to the bomber formations were preventing them using initiative to attack intercepting British fighters. Also, the bombers flew slowly at 21,000 – 23,000 feet, to avoid anti-aircraft fire. This low speed exacerbated the fighters' problems as the 109s had to constantly weave to and fro, so as to keep station. Weaving occasionally took the fighters too far from the bombers for comfort, leading to the *Kampfflieger* demanding still closer escort. Göring consequently ordered that both the 109s and 110s were to be bound to the bombers until such time as the entire formation was attacked by British fighters. This gave the advantage of surprise, initiative, altitude and speed to Fighter Command. Although the *jagdfliegern* repeatedly argued their case, Göring was unmoved. An official history recorded that '… the spirit of the bomber arm as well as the spirit of the fighter arm – already badly shaken by the superiority of the Spitfire – suffered accordingly'.[88] Famously, Galland recalled a meeting with Göring at which the *Reichsmarschall* admonished the *jagdfliegern*, whom he held responsible for the failure to date:

> I tried to point out that the Me 109 was superior in the attack but not so suitable for purely defensive purposes as the Spitfire, which, although a little slower, was much more manoeuvrable. He rejected my objection. We received many more harsh words. Finally, as his time ran short, he grew more amiable and asked what were the requirements of our squadrons … Göring turned to me. I did not hesitate long. "I should like an outfit of Spitfires for my group". After blurting this out, I had rather a shock, for it was not really meant that way. Of course fundamentally I preferred our Me 109 to the Spitfire, but I was unbelievably vexed at the lack of understanding and the stubbornness with which the command gave us orders we could not execute – or only incompletely – as a result of many shortcomings for which we were not to blame. Such brazen-faced impudence made Göring speechless. He stamped off, growling as he went.[89]

On 15 September came the greatest assault. On this day, the *Luftwaffe*'s bombers and fighter-bombers flew 201 sorties, 109s flying 769 and 110s forty.[90] Although at the end of that day Fighter Command had claimed to have destroyed 185 enemy aircraft,[91] the actual figure was fifty-six, representing five per cent of the total German force.[92] In response, Fighter Command flew 529 sorties against the two major raids on London, and lost twenty-eight aircraft: thirteen destroyed by fighters, six by bombers; the other nine were lost in unknown circumstances.[93] Eight of Fighter Command's losses were Spitfires (four per cent of sorties flown), the other twenty Hurricanes (six per cent of sorties flown). On that basis a Hurricane was more likely to be shot down than a Spitfire by a ratio of one third.[94] According to Alfred Price, 'This was due to the superior performance of the Spitfire, in particular in the climb, and the fact that the fuel system was better protected and less likely to catch fire'.[95]

Earlier, on 7 September, Squadron Leader Bader had lead a wing of three 12 Group squadrons into action over London. On that day it over-claimed by a factor of 5:1. The so-called 'Big Wing' also saw action, twice, on 15 September, claiming a total of 45 enemy aircraft destroyed, five shared, ten probables and one damaged. Given that the total number actually destroyed by Fighter Commanded numbered only fifty-six, the Wing's claims were clearly greatly inflated. Unfortunately, so intense was the fighting that day that it is impossible to state with certainty how many German machines Bader's pilots really did destroy. Nonetheless, it undoubtedly made a massive contribution on 'Battle of Britain Day' to negatively impacting on the enemy's morale. Göring had told the *Luftwaffe* that Fighter Command was 'down to its last fifty fighters'.[96] On 'Battle of Britain Day', Park committed all of his fighters in 11 Group to battle. Substantial reinforcements were also provided by 10 Group, in addition to Big Wing's five squadrons. Pilot Officer Richard Jones flew with 19 Squadron in the Big Wing that day: 'They thought we were finished, but I reckon that when we turned up over London – sixty fighters in formation – it must have put the shits up 'em!' [97] Indeed it did. Demoralised *Luftwaffe* aircrews returned to France describing how they had been met over the target by 'eighty' British fighters. [98]

Unsurprisingly given the respective aircrafts' performance, the Wing had also decided that 'the Spitfires (19 and 611 Squadrons) would attack the fighter escort, the Hurricanes (242, 310 and 302 Squadrons) tackling the bombers'. [99] At 12.10 p.m., during the Wing's first action that day, over Westerham Flight Sergeant Unwin engaged 3/JG 53's *Staffelkapitän*, *Oberleutnant* Haase: 'I was Red Three with Flight Lieutenant Lawson. We sighted the enemy aircraft which were flying in Vics of three. The escorts dived singly onto us and I engaged an Me 109 with a yellow nose. I gave one burst of six seconds and it burst into flames. The pilot baled out and the enemy aircraft crashed between Redhill and Westerham'. [100] Haase was killed as his parachute failed to open. As other Me 109s dived on 19 Squadron, Sergeant David Cox climbed and flew south. A few minutes later he found six 109s of 2/JG 27 flying in the same direction. Simultaneously the Germans saw the Spitfire, and so Green One attacked from astern. Cox's target immediately half-rolled and dived away. Four of the fighters then broke off and continued south, no doubt low on fuel, but the sixth attacked Cox head-on. As his assailant reared up to pass over the fleeting Spitfire, Cox climbed and turned sharply, attacking from below. The 109 dived through cloud, pursued by the Spitfire pilot who, upon emerging, saw his victim's wreckage burning in a field. [101] This was at Lodge Wood, near Uckfield, and the pilot, *Unteroffizier* Walburger, was captured unhurt.

611 Squadron's ORB provides a dramatic account of the action as it affected that Spitfire squadron:

611 Squadron joined Wing of Hurricanes over Duxford at 15,000 feet at 1131 hours then climbed to 27,000 feet to the left and above the Wing which was at 22.000 feet. When SW of London, fifty enemy bombers and thirty Me 109s escorting above were sighted coming from south. The Wing went into attack the bombers and escort turning south-east. 611 Squadron kept beside the Me 109s which were to the west and above. After the Wing attack had broken up bomber formation, the Me 109s did not come down. After waiting for about seven minutes, S/Ldr McComb informed Wing Leader that he was coming down, and gave order echelon port. The Squadron proceeding at the time south-east and up sun of the enemy. The Squadron in line astern, three sections of four aircraft executed a head-on attack down onto a formation of about 10 Do 215s and Do 17s. Then flying at 18,000 feet in a south easterly direction. S/Ldr McComb attacked Do 215 head on, hits observed, no results. Pulling up he made a beam attack on an Me 110 which turned in its back and went down. The Squadron formation then broke up. S/Ldr McComb chased an Me 109 which was in a dogfight with a Hurricane, but could not catch up with them as he was too far behind. He then proceeded to the coast in the hope of attacking homing lame ducks before returning to base. P/O Williams, after making his attack with the Squadron but without any observed results, saw a Do 215 attacked by six fighters crash into a wood near Bishopsbourne, Kent. Two of the crew baling out. P/O Lund dived into initial attack but enemy aircraft passed through his sights before he could fire. P/O O'Neill attacked six or seven times a Do 215 which had fallen behind the enemy formation. Four Hurricanes also attacked at same time. He chased this enemy aircraft as far as Dungeness where three other Spitfires carried on the

attack. He then returned to base, being short of petrol and ammunition. F/Lt Leather carried out a head on attack on three Do 215s. No results observed. He then attacked a Do 215 at rear of large formation using up remainder of his ammunition. The port engine exploded and stopped. A number of other fighters also attacked this enemy aircraft and Red 2 reports seeing two crew bale out and machine crashed near Bishopsbourne, Kent.

P/O Pollard, after firing a short burst in the initial dive attack, chased, in company with one other Spitfire and a Hurricane, a Do 215. Between Rochester and Herne Bay, enemy aircraft lost height, smoke coming from port engine. Crew of two baled out and aircraft crashed on edge of a wood about four miles south of Herne Bay. He landed at Detling at 1305 hours having lost his bearings, later returned to G 1.

Yellow Three, P/O Brown after initial dive attack on pulling out saw no enemy aircraft. After circling for about ten minutes he returned to home base. P/O Walker after initial dive attack on pulling out saw no enemy aircraft. He developed engine trouble and had to force land at West Mailing at 1235 hours. F/Lt Stoddart fired one quick burst in initial dive attack, and then had to take evasive action in order to avoid attack from Me 109s. He circled for some time and then returned to base. F/Sgt Sadler after initial dive saw twelve Do 215s going south east so executed two frontal attacks on leader. Enemy aircraft believed hit but no results were seen. Abandoned chase at Lympne being short of ammunition and petrol. P/O Dewey fired a short burst at a Do 215 but observed no results. After circling for some time returned base. Sgt Levenson broke formation to attack an Me 109 but enemy aircraft got away. He then flew towards large formation of Do 215s flying at 18,000 feet. After sighting one Do 215 by itself at 14,000 feet he rolled over and carried out an old astern attack diving onto the enemy. Got in a long burst and both enemy aircraft motors were smoking when he broke away. Climbing again, he carried out the same attack. He broke away when both engines and both mainplanes immediately behind them were on fire.[102]

Soon, the radar screens indicated further formations moving out from Calais. Between 2.10 and 2.35 p.m., eight or more formations of German bombers and their escorts crossed the English coastline between Rye and Dover, heading for London. As Squadron Leader Brian Lane later wrote, the Wing 'ran into the whole *Luftwaffe* over London. Wave after wave of bombers covered by several hundred fighters'.[103] Unfortunately, the 'whole *Luftwaffe*' was some 4,000 feet above the Wing, however. As the Duxford fighters climbed, the inevitable 109s plunged down. Again the 611 Squadron ORB provides a stirring account of a Spitfire squadron in action:

611 Squadron ran into several formations of bombers before sufficient height could be reached so ignored them, attempting to get height in Westerly direction to keep Me 109s off Wing. The squadron consisted of eight aircraft in three sections flying line astern. It was not possible to out climb the Me 109s and the Wing appeared to be both attacking and being attacked. When at 20,000 feet over West London, the Squadron Leader sighted a formation of 25 Do 17s proceeding South unmolested and being by then separated from the Wing, gave the order Sections Echelon Right. The Squadron dived down on the formation, coming out of the sun. At the end of the general attack, Me 110s came down. S/Ldr McComb attacked rear E/A. Rear gunner ceased firing and smoke appeared

from port engine. He then pulled up into a loop and dived again in inverted position. Guns worked perfectly in this position and E/A went down in flames. Result of attack is confirmed by Yellow Two and Yellow Leader. S/Ldr McComb then blacked out badly and came to in the clouds. After looking around and seeing nothing he returned to base. P/O Williams carried out a No. 3 FC attack on an He 111. A second burst at eighty yards was given but no result observed. E/A returned machine-gun fire. He was unable then to return to Squadron which had now broken up, but observing two enemy formations, he made an astern attack on No. 3 of the last section of the formation of Do 215. The formation turned north but Red 2's target fell out, losing height. He then carried out another attack finishing his ammunition. E/A descended into the clouds, one engine stopped, Red Two following. Cloud was 2,000 feet thick and on emerging no E/A was visible but two minutes later he saw enemy airman descending by parachute. Latter landed on edge of wood corner of Hawkhurst Golf Club about 15 miles North of Hastings.

F/Lt Leather followed Red Leader into attack astern and took machine next to his as his target was already aflame. He fired all ammunition and when broke away the Do 17 was in flames. He then was forced to land at Croydon at 1540 hours and later flew to G l, rejoining the Squadron.

P/O Brown had first to evade enemy fighters and then put one short burst into the Do 215 already attacked by Red Leader which had one engine out of action. Oil or glycol from E/A covered up windscreen and so he had to break away. Then he attacked one E/A which broke away from formation using deflection. E/A went into a steep spiral dive with escape hatch over pilot's seat open. No further results seen as large formation of Me 110s appeared and Yellow Two escaped into cloud.

P/O Lund attacked a Do 215 which was also being attacked by several other aircraft. He saw flashes of fire and smoke coming from E/A. While climbing back to main formation of bombers, one Me 110 came down on him so he fired one short burst before turning away and down. As the E/A passed his port side, black smoke was pouring from engine. No more E/A seen after this so he returned to base.

F/Sgt Sadler after attacking with Squadron, saw a Do 215 break away and begin losing height. He made two attacks on this E/A, his second attack being made at fifty yards. A Hurricane also attacked after him and the E/A apparently badly disabled disappeared below cloud.

P/O D. H. O'Neill lost touch with Blue Leader but after circling for about 6 minutes had to evade 8 Me 110s into cloud. Up again out of cloud saw Me 109s attacking one Hurricane and attacked one of these over Faversham without observing result although E/A took evasive action. After being attacked by another Me 109, he returned to base landing, however, by mistake first at Debden.

Sgt Levenson after attacking without visible result an Me 109 and a crippled Do 215 found himself at 10,000 feet over Brooklands aerodrome. He then saw about fifty Do 215s guarded by two Me 109s overhead. He climbed to 1,000 feet below formation and delivered a quarter frontal attack opening fire first at 100 yards, developing this into normal quarter attack at about 200 yards when all his ammunition was exhausted. He observed ammunition hitting leading E/A and the leading vic of four A/C broke away to port, smoke coming from engines of No.1 and No.2. No further result was seen but he assumed that No.1 was out of action. F/Lt Stoddart and P/O Dewey, owing to refuelling, took off 15 minutes after the squadron. The weather above cloud was perfect with visibility good.[104]

Squadron Leader Brian Lane:

At approximately 1440 hours AA fire was sighted to the south and at the same time a formation of about thirty Do 215s was seen. I climbed up astern of the enemy aircraft to engage the fighter escort which could be seen above the bombers at about 30,000 feet. Three Me 109s dived on our formation and I turned to starboard. A loose dogfight ensued with more Me 109s coming down. I could not get near to any enemy aircraft so I climbed up and engaged a formation of Me 110s without result. I then sighted ten Me 109s just above me and attacked one of them. I got on his tail and fired several bursts of about two seconds. The enemy aircraft was taking violent evasive action and made for cloud level. I managed to get in another burst of about five seconds before it flicked over inverted and entered cloud in a shallow dive, apparently out of control. I then flew south and attacked two further formations of about thirty Do 215s from astern and head-on. The enemy aircraft did not appear to like the head on attack as they jumped about a bit as I passed through. I observed no result from these attacks. Fire from the rear of the enemy aircraft was opened at 1,000 yards. Me 110s opened fire at similar range but appeared lo have no idea of deflection shooting.[105]

Squadron Leader Lane's combat represented the only protracted dogfight between the opposing fighters on this day. Flight Sergeant Unwin was Lane's Red Three, and reported sighting 'thousands of 109s'.[106] When the Wing was attacked, at close range Unwin fired a three second burst at a 109 which half-rolled and dived steeply into the clouds. Although the Spitfire pilot pursued his prey, he lost the 109 at 6,000 feet when his windscreen froze up. Climbing hack up to 25,000 feet, a *Rotte* of 109s appeared above him, flying south. Unwin gave chase and caught both over Lydd. The first consequently burst into flames and went down vertically, and the second crashed into the sea.[107] It is likely that these two 109s were from I/JG 77: *Oberleutnant* Kunze, of the *Geschwaderstabschwarm*, was killed when his aircraft crashed at Lympne; *Unteroffizier* Meixner also lost his life when his 109 crashed into the sea off Dungeness at about 2.55 p.m. This brought Unwin's total of Me 109s definitely destroyed on 15 September to three. It was a rare feat.

After the great raids of between 7 September and 15 September, it was clear that there was no chance of the *Luftwaffe* delivering that all-important and long expected 'knock-out blow'. On 16 September, unable to sustain such heavy losses any further, a furious Göring changed tack once more, ordering that in future daylight raids would be carried out by smaller formations of up to *gruppe* strength but with strong fighter escort; single bombers or fighter-bombers would undertake frequent nuisance raids on London and other industrial targets when cloud was favourable; the main bombing effort, however, was to be made under cover of darkness.[108] Moreover, a greater emphasis was to be placed on targets connected with the British aircraft industry.[109] This latter strategy, however, was too little too late. The season was waning rapidly. In truth the time had already passed for a seaborne invasion. There was no chance that these raids would have a sufficiently negative effect on British aircraft production to influence the outcome of a battle already lost. Indeed, on 17 September Hitler indefinitely 'postponed' Operation *Seelöwe*.[110]

The *Kanaljäger*, however, were still not cut loose to fly the *freie jagd* operations they so craved. Instead, Göring decided to shackle bombs to a *staffel* of 109s in each *gruppe*. The *jagdflieger* were exasperated. Galland:

> We started from the premise that the fighter was apparently unable to give sufficient protection to the bombers. This was true. But instead of accepting the front-line pilots' explanation and if possible eradicating the cause, or, as an alternative, stopping those untenable raids, the following conclusion was drawn: if the fighter arm is unable to protect the bombers, it must deliver the bombs to England on its own account. Political propaganda reasons may also have persuaded our leaders to make such a faulty decision. The raids on England had become a question of prestige, and as day bombing could not be continued and night raids were only in preparation, this gap was to be filled by fighters transformed into fighter-bombers ... Instead of making it possible to achieve the goal of a raiding war on England – for the success of which air superiority was imperative – by a powerful strengthening of the fighter arm, we were weakened by it transforming fighter planes into bomb carriers. The operative value of fighter-bombers cannot be denied, but only pre-supposing a surplus of fighter aircraft. To use a fighter as a fighter-bomber when the strength of the fighter arm is inadequate to achieve air superiority is to put the cart before the horse.[111]

In spite of such objections, this new phase would continue to test Fighter Command.

The first 'Tip n' run' raid, as these attacks widely became known, occurred on 20 September. Twenty-two II/LG 2 Me 109 *Jagdbombers*, or more commonly *Jabos*, protected by numerous fighters, made a sortie to London. Not knowing of the enemy's new plan, the RAF controllers did not at first react, and were therefore surprised when II/LG 2 swooped down and dropped bombs on the capital. The 11 Group Spitfire squadrons from Biggin Hill and Hornchurch were scrambled late, and the enemy fighter escort pounced on them over the Maidstone area. 222 and 603 Squadrons were scrambled from Hornchurch at 10.55 a.m., but as they desperately clawed for height at full throttle over the Thames Estuary, the Me 109s fell on them. The first pilot of Fighter Command to fall that day was 222's Pilot Officer Laurie Whitbread. Sergeant Reg Johnson remembered:

> My vivid memory is that this sortie was a 'B' Flight commitment only, led by Pilot Officer Broadhurst in Blue Section, followed by Pilot Officer Whitbread, myself and another in Green Section. We climbed to the suicidal height of 14,000 feet and stooged around in tight formation with only one pair of eyes available to scan the sky in front, perhaps over 200°. I do not think that we deserved to be jumped upon, but we certainly invited it. We were banking gently to the left, which allowed me at No. 3 to look over the top of No. 1, and I shouted the warning "Bandits, 2 o' clock above –attacking!" I turned over and dived straight down. There is no way that Pilot Officer Whitbread could even have seen the enemy, formating as he

was on the aircraft to his left and with three-quarters of his head and back to the attackers. When I left it was his right side facing the 109s, which were already in firing-range. I can only assume that having received my warning he too rolled to his right, exposing his left side to the enemy and was hit before he could commence his dive. It was a tragedy.[112]

Pilot Officer Whitbread had either been killed by *Oberleutnant* Hans 'Assi' Hahn of ll/JG 2 *Richthofen*, or Major Adolf Galland, Kommodore of JG 26. His loss was caused by a late scramble and continued use of the vic formation.

At 10.45 a.m. Flight Lieutenant Ted Graham of 72 Squadron had led off from Biggin Hill the Spitfires of Pilot Officers Lindsay, Males and Holland. Flight Lieutenant 'Pancho' Villa and Sergeant Rolls also entered the fray a few minutes later. At 11.20 a.m. over Canterbury, twenty-three-year-old 'Dutch' Holland was blasted out of the sky.[113] Although badly wounded he managed to bale out and was admitted to hospital. Pilot Officer Lindsay was also shot up, but although his Spitfire was seriously damaged the pilot was unhurt.

Over Maidstone at 11.30 a.m., *Hauptmann* Johannes Seifert of I/JG 26, and *Oberfeldwebel* Heinrich Gottlob of II/JG 26 each picked off a 253 Squadron Hurricane. Sergeant R. A. Innes safely baled out but Pilot Officer Barton was wounded and later admitted to Ashford Hospital. *Oberleutnant* Erbo Graf von Kageneck of III/JG 27 fired at a Hurricane, possibly P5179 flown by Sergeant Kee. Also at 11.30 a.m., in the south London area, *Gefreiter* Gruber of III/JG 27 attacked and damaged a Hurricane, possibly V6722 flown by Pilot Officer Glowacki of 605 Squadron. The squadron diary related:

A showery day with high winds. It appears that rough seas during the last few days have delayed German invasion plans. The moon is now well in the wane. Squadron did one patrol today and encountered only Me 109s which adopted different tactics to usual by flying alone in twos, threes or fours over a wide area which our pilots found very harassing, never knowing when they would swoop down on them. No losses, but Pilot Officer Glowacki's aircraft damaged Category II from cannon and machine-gun fire.[114]

At 11.35 a.m., *Hauptmann* Seifert struck again when he attacked Pilot Officer Edsall of 222 Squadron, seriously damaging his. At the same time, *Feldwebel* Heckman of II/JG 3 shot down 222 Squadron's Pilot Officer Assheton, who safely abandoned his aircraft high over Kent. At 11.34 and 11.35 a.m., Major Werner Mölders destroyed two Spitfires of 92 Squadron over Dungeness: Pilot Officer Howard Hill, a twenty-year-old New Zealander, was killed and Sergeant P. R. Eyles was never seen again. Flight Lieutenant Alan Wright:

92 Squadron was split in half due to oxygen failure. The first half were surprised by Me 109s. Howard and Eyles, both of Green Section, were lost. I have a vivid picture in my mind of me leading Green Section on that day. After the split, the front two sections, led by the CO, Squadron Leader Sanders, were left flying in a close formation of two Vics in line astern. I happened to glance to my left and was amazed to see a 109 taking the place of the Spitfire that I expected to see there, a glance to the right showed another one! I immediately shouted "BREAK!" and pulled up and around in a tight turn. The others

probably reacted similarly. I noticed that we were immediately above a coastal town. I cannot remember what I did after the break, when flying at 200-300 mph one can, in just a few seconds, find oneself quite alone and unable to re-join the action.

At that time, many squadrons, including ours, would be vectored towards our targets in a close formation of nine, comprising three vics with two weavers criss-crossing overhead and safeguarding the blind area behind the formation. Its advantage was that the 11 aircraft as a whole were very manoeuvrable. The danger was that if anything happened to the weavers and they were unable to use their R/T, the rest of the Squadron would be utterly vulnerable. On this occasion, in the rush to scramble, one or more of the rear pilots could have failed to switch on their oxygen, or it may not have been working properly, so that in the confusion the first half were left unaware that no-one was guarding their tails. No oxygen at the height of Everest could put you to sleep without you even realising it. Very sad, especially about Howard Hill who had flown with our Squadron since the previous October. [115]

92 Squadron's Red Two, Pilot Officer T. S. Wade, attacked an Me 109 at 1145 a.m., 27,000 feet above Folkestone:

Ganic Squadron was split up due to attack by Me 109s. I got on the tail of one and after a short burst the enemy aircraft dived away steeply. At about 4,000 feet it pulled out and started evasive tactics. After two-three minutes it headed south-east at 5,000 feet. I fired a number of short bursts from astern at 100 - 150 yards range but was unable to close any further. After doing evasive medium turns for a short period he pulled up steeply into cloud at 2,000 feet, fifteen miles from the French coast after which I lost him. I had seen my ammunition going into the wings but without the desired effect. [116]

92 Squadron's CO, Squadron Leader P. J. 'Judy' Sanders, also attacked an Me 109 at 11.45 a.m., firing 2,450 rounds at it:

As Squadron Leader patrolling Dungeness I knew that there were enemy aircraft about and was weaving. At 27,000 feet, Blue Section, behind me, was attacked, so I broke quickly to the left and saw an Me 109 also turning left behind me. I gave one short burst about 120 yards from above and from the right. The enemy aircraft at once half rolled to the right and dived steeply for about 10,000 feet. He then pulled up and I got a good deflection shot at him from above and slightly behind. He half rolled again and dived. I fired intermittently at him on the way down and he did not pull out. I came out of the dive at 500 feet and he crashed into the sea about five miles south of Dymchurch and disappeared. I tried to re-group the Squadron and received instructions to return to base and land. [117]

Sanders was also attacked and his Spitfire damaged, possibly by *Leutnant* Altendorf of II/JG 53. He subsequently returned safely to Biggin Hill, although soaked in petrol from a ruptured fuel tank, only to burst into flames when he lit a cigarette shortly after landing. Fortunately he survived but was out of the battle from then on.

At 12.10 p.m., 25-30,000 feet over the Ashford/Canterbury area, Biggin Hill's 72 Squadron Spitfires met fifty Me 109s. Afterwards, Sergeant Rolls submitted the following report:

I was Red Two in a section told to intercept the enemy fighters. We took off at 1040 and after having completed a patrol by ourselves were instructed to rejoin the rest of the Squadron as the leading Section. We did this and met the enemy near Canterbury. We were climbing up towards one batch of Me 109s when we were warned by our rearguard of another lot diving down on us. We kept climbing into the sun and the rest of the Squadron had used evasive action to get rid of the Me 109s. I soon found myself over Ashford and unable to see any of my Squadron near me. I was flying along at 22,000 feet when I saw what appeared to be a Spitfire or Hurricane diving down to 16-18,000 feet and then climbing again. I decided to have a look at it so I got into a position so that I had the sun behind me and could see the machine clearly. As it came up in the climb I saw plainly that it was actually an Me 109 with a yellow nose and fin. I let it climb up again and waited, thinking perhaps it would dive again. It did so and then I dived out of the sun onto its tail and waited for it to start to climb before I pressed the tit to fire. I let it have about three seconds fire and the 109 did a stall turn to starboard and I followed it. I saw a large black piece break away from the side of the cockpit on the port side. I got it in my sights again as it turned and let it have another four seconds burst. This time I saw smoke and what appeared to be oil and water coming from underneath it. It turned to dive and as it did I let him have a final burst when the whole back of the cockpit dropped away and the rest dropped down towards cloud. This was at about 12,000 feet. I flew through the cloud and made for the aerodrome as I had only 10 gallons of petrol left. I watched the spot where the machine went in and it was near Wye, between a wood and lake so far as I could make out from my own position. I landed back with three gallons of petrol and a leaky glycol seal.[118]

Sergeant Rolls had shot down the only Me 109 to crash in England that day, an E-4, 2789, of 9/JG 27, which went in at Ospringe, Kent, killing the pilot, *Unteroffizier* Erich Clauser.

Although the surprise attack of 20 September, 1940 had been successful, the Germans soon found, to their discomfort, that even the Hurricane could run rings around a bomb-laden Me 109. The action had provided Fighter Command with a salutary lesson of how dangerous the 109s still were. Even though their numbers were reduced by the requirement for *Jabos*, the 109s providing escort were more able to act upon their own initiative. Pilot Officer Geoff Wellum: 'I remember that during September and October 1940, Me 109s were always in the Biggin Hill Sector in numbers and caused problems. I recall that they were always above us as we never seemed to be scrambled in time to get enough height. Our climb was always a desperate, full throttle affair, but we never quite got up to them. I did manage to get a crack at two Me 109s on one patrol but although I saw strikes I could only claim them as damaged.' [119]

These raids continued over south-east England until the winter of 1940. As controllers could never be sure that incoming fighter sweeps did not contain *Jabos*, every such threat had to be reacted to. This would make for an exhausting time for Fighter Command's pilots. Nonetheless, on 31 October 1940, the Battle of Britain ended. Neither side had been fought to a standstill, so there was no victory or defeat in the usual sense. But Hitler's aim of invasion had been thwarted, and that, therefore, made the victory Fighter Command's.

Churchill roused the nation and paid homage to the young pilots of Fighter Command in one inspirational sentence: 'Never in the field of human conflict has so much been owed by so many to so few'. In response to the Prime Minister's tribute Squadron Leader Brian Lane wrote, 'I think he was actually referring to our Mess bills, anyway!' [120] Further comment would be superfluous.

12

Spitfire Ascendant

The RAF had learned much during those sixteen weeks of high drama. On 7 November, Air Vice-Marshal Park reported that:

> The following changes in minor tactics have been found necessary:
> 1. The use of sections of four aircraft instead of three aircraft;
> 2. The pilots of a squadron to be trained to work in pairs for defensive fighting instead of working singly;
> 3. Formations patrolling on a wider front, instead of in the old "train" of sub-formations, line astern.
> 4. The adoption of more flexible formations, instead of the old type of rigid formation.
> 5. The general adoption of an above-guard, even when the enemy is attacked from above, instead of all members of a formation going down to engage.[1]

No longer would RAF fighter pilots be committed to battle in the suicidal vic formation. The Commander of 11 Group, which had borne the brunt of the fighting, also reported on the 'Performance of Enemy and Our Own Fighters':

> Below 20,000 feet: during intensive air fighting over the continent in May and June, the superiority in performance and armament of our eight-gun fighters was one of the principal causes of the very high morale of our pilots. Until about the close of September 1940, our fighters had little difficulty in dealing effectively with enemy fighters. Most engagements during this period took place at heights below 20,000 feet, where our Spitfires and Hurricanes, although in the case of the Hurricane not as fast, are more manoeuvrable and effective. At first the Me 110 was looked upon with a certain amount of awe, but after their first engagement with this type, our pilots were of the impression that it was the easiest of the enemy fighters to deal with, and now regard it with a certain amount of contempt.
>
> It is found that up to about 20,000 feet a Spitfire is faster than both the Me 109 and Me 110. A Hurricane with a constant-speed Rotol airscrew is about as fast as a Me 109 at ground level but becomes slower as height increases. Compared to a Me 110, the Hurricane has little difficulty in overtaking this aeroplane at heights up to about 20,000 feet. Above this height the Me 109 is able to easily out-climb the Hurricane fitted with a constant-speed airscrew, but up to heights of about 15,000 feet a Spitfire with a constant-speed

airscrew is just able to out-climb the Me 109. Both Hurricanes and Spitfires are able to out-climb the Me 110.

Above 20,000 feet: All types of enemy fighters are now said to be faster above 20,000 feet. This undoubtedly due to the fact that their engines are fitted with two-stage superchargers. Our fighters, fitted with engines with single-stage superchargers, are most effective between heights of 15,000 feet and 20,000 feet, and above this the power falls off rapidly, with a consequent falling off in performance both in manoeuvrability and speed.

As a result of this our fighters have found themselves at a serious disadvantage in the present stage of the battle, when engagements are taking place at heights above 25,000 feet and sometimes above 30,000 feet. At these heights the performance of enemy fighters is vastly superior to that of ours and it is only as a result of clever tactics that our pilots are making the best of this situation and obtaining a certain amount of hard-earned success.[2]

As the Battle of Britain had worn on and the *Luftwaffe's* experience in fighting aircraft with performance comparable to its Me 109 increased, it had sensibly pushed up the altitude at which the 109 operated – because it was there that the 109 had the edge. Because fighter combat is dictated by height and surprise, the RAF could not simply fly within the height-band at which their aircraft performed best. To do so would have simply invited 109s to bounce them out of the sun and from high above. So the RAF had to respond and take the 109 on at high altitude. The only British fighter capable of doing so was the Spitfire. As Park also wrote of the Hurricane Mk II '… although the engine is designed to operate at 30,000 feet, the aeroplane itself was never meant to operate at this height, and no amount of increase in engine power will have the effect of turning it into a high altitude fighter'.[3] And for all the Hurricane's attributes, that was its failing. Fighter combat was changing, with very high altitude increasingly becoming the decisive factor. As the Hurricane could not compete in that environment, its days as a front-line interceptor were numbered. Park considered that in future fighters should be able to achieve speeds of over 400 mph and heights of 'at least 40,000 feet'.[4] In due course the Spitfire would do just that.

If there was one thing for which the Hurricanes earned respect from its pilots, though, it was its ability to absorb great damage and keep flying. Galland wrote of a Hurricane that refused to go down: 'I had damaged her so badly she was on fire and ought to have been a dead loss. Yet she did not crash, but glided down in gentle curves. My flight companions and I attacked her three times without a final result. As I flew close alongside the wreck, by now thoroughly riddled, with smoke belching from her, from a distance of a few yards I saw the dead pilot sitting in his shattered cockpit, while his aircraft spiralled slowly to the ground as though piloted by a ghostly hand'.[5] Douglas Bader also enthused about the Hurricane: 'Best of all it was a marvellous gun platform. The sloping nose gave you a splendid view, while the eight guns were set in blocks of four in each wing, close to the fuselage. The aeroplane remained rock steady when you fired. Unlike the Spitfire with its lovely elliptical wing which sloped upwards to the tip, the Hurricane's wing was thicker and straight. The Spitfire was less steady when the guns were firing because, I have always thought, they were spread further along the wing and the recoil effect was noticeable'.[6]

Other pilots remembered the Hurricane:

Pilot Officer John Greenwood, 253 Squadron:

We thought they were wonderful to fly after Battles. We thought they were great. But of course they weren't really. When we went into battle with them we found that the Hurricane was far, far inferior to the Me 109.[7]

Sergeant Charles Palliser flew Hurricanes with 17, 43 and 249 Squadrons:

If you offered me two Spitfires and one Hurricane, I'd take one Hurricane. Because they were TOUGH! They were like a cruiser, not a destroyer. And you could really fly. I had one of them where I had nearly no control … my rudder was hanging on by a thread and one of my ailerons was shot off, and the fuselage was damaged. But I was still flying! The engines, of course, were the same as a Spitfire, but the Hurricane flew at about twenty-five miles mph less than a Spitfire. I reckon I flew Spitfires for a week. I thought "Gee whiz, I'd like to take it home". You know, the controls and what it could do. It was really faster than the Hurricane, was much smaller than the Hurricane. Anyway I went back to my Hurricane and said "This is for me!" And that was that. The Hurricane always got me home.[8]

Sergeant Leonard Bartlett flew Hurricanes with 17 Squadron:

The Hurricane was a follow on from biplanes. It had a metal wing but it was of fabric construction aft of the cockpit. It was immensely strong, had a wide undercarriage, and you could do anything with it. It would get you out of trouble. Flying – it was immensely strong and a very good aeroplane. The Spitfire was different. You got into a Hurricane, but somehow, a Spitfire tended to fit more around you. It had a much narrower undercarriage. Airborne it was fine. Once airborne both were great. But I think landing separated them. On runways you had to be very careful with a Spitfire, or you were in real trouble.[9]

Sergeant Tony Pickering was with 501 Squadron at Kenley and Gravesend:

One day I came across a lone Ju 88 somewhere over Kent, heading back to sea. I thought that it would be no problem to catch up the Hun, press the gun button and that would be it. Suddenly he just pulled away from me, just left me standing, had at least an extra fifty mph on me, and that was the last I saw of him. The Hurricane just wasn't fast enough. We even used to bend the throttle levers in flight, trying to squeeze a bit more boost out of the Merlin. A Spitfire would have caught that Ju 88. In the Hurricane's favour was that it could take a terrific amount of punishment but still keep flying, whereas the Spitfire couldn't take quite as much.[10]

Although the Hurricane was later used in ground-attack roles, carrying both bombs and sometimes armed with four cannons made possible by its strong wing, its performance limitations dictated its complete replacement by the Spitfire – its cannon problems resolved – as the RAF's front-line day fighter in 1941. No-one could argue, however, that the Hurricane and its pilots had not done sterling work when it mattered most, however – and that was during the dark days of 1940.

The fighting in 1940 had shown that good though the Me 109 was – unlike the Me 110 which was found fundamentally wanting as a day-fighter – it was not perfect. In September 1940, the RAE at Farnborough comprehensively reported on 'Messerschmitt 109. Handling and Manoeuvrability Tests'. The aircraft's 'most serious defect', the report concluded, was the 109's 'inability to roll fast in a high speed dive because of its heavy ailerons', although the Spitfire, it said, was 'about as bad'.[11] In Germany, it had already been decided that the Me 109E had come to the end of its useful development and a replacement, the *Franz*, had been produced. The new Me 109F was curvaceous, whereas the Me 109E was angular in appearance. Tellingly, it had elliptical wings – like a Spitfire. Redesigned radiators, flaps, a symmetrical engine cowling, removal of tail struts, new supercharger intake and a smaller rudder completed the airframe package.[12] The fighter was also powered by a new and improved engine, the DB 601E. In the battles of 1941 and 1942, the Me 109F would prove a tough adversary, until, of course, the FW 190 appeared and, in the words of the top scoring RAF fighter pilot of the Second World War, Air Vice-Marshal Johnnie Johnson, 'saw us all off'[13]. And so fighter development went on, with both sides effectively locked into an arms race that would soon involve the Americans – who were able to produce the long-range offensive fighter that both sides needed so badly in 1940: the North American P-51 Mustang. The American designers, though, had the benefit of the RAF's early wartime experience and the P-51 only became far and away the best fighter of the Second World War once it was powered by a Rolls-Royce Merlin engine. So in terms of long-term Allied fighter design and development, the British experience in producing the Hurricane and Spitfire was essential.

Conclusion

As Horst Boog argued, 'It was fighter strength that won the Battle of Britain'.[1] Although imperfect, the Me 109 had proved a tough adversary. But which of the two principal British single-engined fighter types made the greatest contribution to winning the Battle of Britain? As ever, this remains an emotive issue, guaranteed to provoke lively debate.

Officially, one of the main reasons for the *Luftwaffe's* defeat in the Battle of Britain was its '… failure to take sufficient account of the fighting qualities of the Spitfire and Hurricane, which had first become evident in France and over Dunkirk. The single and twin-engined fighter force employed in the Battle of Britain – which was thought to be ample in strength – was consequently outclassed by those very fighting qualities in combination with the British system of plotting and fighter control'.[2] Indeed, the German bomber and fighter crews' morale was 'badly shaken by the superiority of the Spitfire',[3] so there is no doubt regarding which of the British machines was feared most. Nonetheless, to Battle of Britain Hurricane pilot and squadron commander Peter Townsend it rankled that the 109 pilots treated Hurricanes with 'contempt'.[4] He countered that, 'We thought they were great and we would prove it by shooting down around 1,000 *Luftwaffe* aircraft in the Battle. The *Luftwaffe* airmen often mistook Hurricanes for Spitfires. There was the crew of their famous *Heinkel* which "landed in the sea" on Wick airfield, who swore a Spitfire had downed them. During the Battle of France, Theo Osterkamp seemed to see Spitfires everywhere. There were no Spitfires in France, only Hurricanes. Even General Kesselring said "Only the Spitfires bothered us". The *Luftwaffe* seemed to be suffering from Spitfire snobbery'.[5] Be that as it may, the following statement by *Leutnant* Heinz Knocke of 1/JG 52 is telling: 'The Supermarine Spitfire, because of its manoeuvrability and technical performance, has given the German formations plenty of trouble. "*Achtung* Spitfire!" German pilots have learned to pay particular attention when they hear this warning shouted in their earphones. We consider shooting down a Spitfire to be an outstanding achievement, which it most certainly is'.[6] There was clearly more prestige attached to destroying a Spitfire than a Hurricane, therefore. This is clear when analysing German combat claims: an impossibly high proportion of Spitfires when the actual size of the Spitfire force in action over southern England is considered.

Townsend also highlights the problem of aircraft misidentification. In the heat of battle, with everything moving at high speed and pilots in a high state of excitement and anxiety, mistakes were bound to happen. One particularly interesting piece of combat footage preserved by the Imperial War Museum, for example, shows Sergeant Alan Fearey, a Spitfire pilot later killed in action with 609 Squadron, making a determined and protracted – but fortunately inconclusive – attack on a Hurricane. Throughout the Battle of Britain and during the period of skirmishing which followed until February 1941, RAF pilots frequently reported combat with and the destruction of 'He 113s'. Although this fighter was produced, it never entered service with the *Luftwaffe* and did not, therefore, see any action whatsoever. It was not inexperienced pilots who wrongly identified enemy aircraft types. On 5 November 1940, for example, 19 Squadron's Flight Sergeant George Unwin – one of Dowding's most aggressive and successful Spitfire pilots in the Battle of Britain – claimed the destruction of a He 113 in a big fighter clash between the Duxford Wing and JG 26.[7] Indeed, the 19 Squadron ORB recorded that was 'the first of this type shot down by Duxford'.[8] Unwin had actually destroyed – in concert with a 242 Squadron Hurricane – the 1/JG 26 Me 109 of *Leutnant* Erhard Scheidt.[9] Another 19 Squadron pilot, Sergeant David Cox, remembered a combat involving the misidentification of a twin-engined German aircraft, occurring on 19 August:

> Green Section comprised Haines, Steere and myself. We were given a vector of about ninety degrees, which was in the direction of the East coast. We flew at about 2,000 feet under 10/10ths cloud. As we approached the coast near Aldeburgh, the cloud started to break up and I, who was flying on the left and looking out to sea, saw a twin-engined aircraft. As was the rule, being the pilot who had the enemy in sight, I took over the lead. At about 300 yards I opened fire with my cannons in a quick burst of about three seconds. I then broke away, allowing Haines and Steere to attack. On making my second attack I saw the port engine catch fire, which rapidly enveloped the whole aircraft. *Three* of the crew bailed out. Haines said it was a 110 bomber. I had my doubts as I thought they only had two crew members, but as Leonard Haines was a senior Flying Officer I entered it my log book as an Me 110.[10]

Cox was right. The enemy machine destroyed by Green Section was not an Me 110, but a Do 17Z-2 of 7/KG 2, which was shot down off the Essex coast at 6.40 p.m – the crew of three baled out but remain missing.[11] Another experienced British fighter pilot who misidentified a twin-engine type was Flight Lieutenant Ian 'Widge' Gleed. On 30 September, he was flying Hurricanes with 87 Squadron and intercepted 'seventy Ju 88s' over Lyme Bay.[12] Gleed attacked the right-hand bomber, which broke away and spiralled down into cloud. These were not 'Ju 88s', however, but the He 111s of KG 55, which was fighting its way inland towards the Westland Aircraft Factory at Yeovil. *Flieger* Robert Götz was actually the nose-gunner in one of the bombers:

> The Hurricane came so close that at first I thought that he was trying to formate on us. We were stunned, but the other gunners and I rapidly recovered and opened fire! The Hurricane was hit and went into a vertical dive. Our *Staffelkapitän* ordered that a radio message be sent to our rescue service so that if the British pilot crashed in the sea he might be rescued. We all admired the British pilot's audacity.[13]

Fortunately, however, Gleed did not require the enemy *Seenotdienst* that day: although hit several times, his Hurricane was not seriously damaged and he returned safely to Exeter. Gleed's was far from the only misidentification that day, however.

The foregoing evidence indicates just how difficult it is to confirm exactly who shot down whom. The greater the number of aircraft involved, the more chaotic the reporting – not least due to over-claiming and aircraft misidentification. Also, as many combats took place above cloud, pilots rarely saw their victims actually crash, so geographic locations are often merely approximates. This is not always the case, however. On 5 September 1940, for example, 603 Squadron's Spitfires were embroiled over the Thames Estuary in a great air battle involving many fighters of both sides. Pilot Officer Basil 'Stapme' Stapleton reported that:

> I was diving to attack them (the bombers) when I was engaged by two Me 109s. When I fired at the first one I noticed glycol coming from its radiator. I did a Number Two attack and as I fired was hit by bullets from another Me 109. I broke off downwards and continued my dive. At 6,000 feet I saw a single-engined machine diving vertically with no tail unit. I looked up and saw a parachutist coming down, circled by an Me 109. I attacked the 109 from the low quarter, he dived vertically towards the ground and flattened out at ground level. I then did a series of beam attacks from both sides, and the enemy aircraft turned into my attacks. He finally forced-landed. He tried to set his radio on fire by taking off his jacket, setting fire to it and putting it into the cockpit.[14]

The enemy fighter crashed at 10.10 a.m., at Loves Farm, Winchett Hill, Marden, and was a machine of the II/JG 3 *Stabschwarm*;[15] the pilot was none other than *Oberleutnant* Franz von Werra, later to become infamous as 'The One That Got Away', through the book and film of that name, after becoming the only German prisoner of war to escape from Allied custody in the Second World War. Stapleton's description of the location of his combat and the events after the pilot crash-landed leaves no doubt whatsoever who the vanquished enemy pilot was on that occasion. This is, however, a rare example of the loose ends being so easily tied up.

From all of the foregoing, the essential point is also that there is an enormous gulf between a combat claim and the actuality of a confirmed enemy loss. Problems connected with over-claiming have previously been mentioned, which complicates the scenario further still. John Foreman wrote that, 'The over-claim rate was higher in 1940 – 1941, around 5:1'.[16] This is not helpful to the Battle of Britain historian. One explanation for the inevitably inflated balance sheet, and already explained, is multiple accreditation, i.e. where a number of pilots attack and claim the same enemy aircraft destroyed. Just one example of this occurred on 18 September, when Squadron Leader Bader's Big Wing intercepted the Ju 88s of III/KG 77 south of the Thames Estuary. Bader himself claimed to have destroyed a Ju 88, but research suggests that this machine, of 8/KG 77, was also attacked by Spitfires of 92 Squadron and at least two Hurricane pilots of 310 Squadron. In that engagement – in which 11 Group squadrons were also involved – a total of eight Ju 88s were actually lost. The Big Wing, however, claimed the destruction of twenty-four. Research indicates that in reality the Big Wing had a hand – no doubt with 11 Group fighters – in the destruction of six of the bombers. On that occasion the over-claim was 4:1. Interestingly, the reason that III/KG 77 suffered so badly was because it was escorted not by Me 109s on that occasion but by Me 110s – to which the Hurricane was markedly superior. The point of all this is, however, is to illustrate the inherent difficulties – and frequent impossibilities – involved with confirming combat claims against losses.

Primary sources are obviously of crucial importance in any attempt to cross-reference combat claims against losses. In the case of Fighter Command, historians have access to many primary sources preserved at The National Archives. These include group, squadron and pilots' personal combat reports, ORBs, details of losses and intelligence reports. German records, however, are inevitably incomplete. The principal source concerning losses is the *Luftwaffe* Quartermaster General's Loss Returns, or more accurately *Oberbefehlsaber der Luftwaffe Genst. Gen. Qu./6 Abteilung/40.g.Kdos.I.C.*, which is available to researchers at the Imperial War Museum. These records are complete and not for propaganda purposes but internal audit and as such they are considered accurate. German fighter combat claims can be found in the OKL records of the *Chef für Ausz. und Dizsiplin Luftwaffen-Personalamt L.P. (A) V*, preserved in Germany. The information contained, however, comprises basic details regarding the victory claimant's identity, unit, time, date and place of the combat concerned, and the type of enemy aircraft involved. Unfortunately German pilots' individual combat reports – comparable to Fighter Command's 'Form "F"', have not survived. Moreover, the majority of records belonging to *Luftflotte* Three, based around Paris and Cherbourg, were destroyed in 1945. Some unit war diaries of *Luftlotte* Two survive, again preserved in Germany. Overall, though, sources are incomplete and require supplementing with local defence and other records. Much of the surviving information concerning the losses and claims of both sides has been published, in fact, during recent years, so is now readily available to all.

This area of research could be described as a particular 'minefield', though, with numerous pitfalls awaiting the unwary or inexperienced. The compilation of accurate statistics concerning the losses and claims of both sides during the Battle of Britain is relatively straightforward, however. My own research with German combat claims, for example, reveals the following:

Table One

German Claims for Hurricanes and Spitfires Destroyed 10 July – 31 October 1940

(Source: *Chef für Ausz. und Dizsiplin Luftwaffen-Personalamt L.P. (A) V*)

10 July – 31 July 1940

Hurricanes Destroyed by 109s:	33
Hurricanes Destroyed by 110s:	9
Total Hurricanes Destroyed:	42
Spitfires Destroyed by 109s:	68
Spitfires Destroyed by 110s:	13
Total Spitfires Destroyed:	81

1 August – 31 August 1940

Hurricanes Destroyed by 109s:	262
Hurricanes Destroyed by 110s:	30
Total Hurricanes Destroyed:	292
Spitfires Destroyed by 109s:	362
Spitfires Destroyed by 110s:	88
Total Spitfires Destroyed:	450

1 September – 30 September 1940

Hurricanes Destroyed by 109s:	238
Hurricanes Destroyed by 110s:	11
Total Hurricanes Destroyed:	249
Spitfires Destroyed by 109s:	458
Spitfires Destroyed by 110s:	104
Total Spitfires Destroyed:	562

1 October – 31 October 1940

Hurricanes Destroyed by 109s:	127
Hurricanes Destroyed by 110s:	1
Total Hurricanes Destroyed:	128
Spitfires Destroyed by 109s:	129
Spitfires Destroyed by 110s:	7
Total Spitfires Destroyed:	136

Overall Total of Hurricanes Destroyed by Me 109s:	660
Overall Total of Hurricanes Destroyed by Me 110s:	51
Total Hurricanes Destroyed:	711
Overall Total of Spitfires Destroyed by Me 109s:	1,017
Overall Total of Spitfires Destroyed by Me 110s:	212
Total Spitfires Destroyed:	1,229
Total Number of Spitfires & Hurricanes Destroyed:	1,940

Table One is illuminating. Firstly, Dowding's fighter force comprised more Hurricanes than Spitfires. Taking the usually quoted figure of thirty-three Hurricane squadrons and given an operational number of twelve aircraft per unit, we arrive at the figure of 396 Hurricanes. Using the accepted number of nineteen Spitfire squadrons, applying the same calculation arrives at 228 Spitfires. This means that the overall ratio of Hurricanes to Spitfires was 1.7. It must actually be remembered, though, that when the foregoing figures are often quoted, what is not taken into account is the fact that this relates to all of Dowding's force – not just 11 Group and the two that reinforced it, 10 and 12, but also 13 Group in the North of England. Although 13 Group's squadrons intercepted the isolated mass raid against north-east England on 15 August, and chased around lone or very small formations of enemy bombers, the Battle of Britain was principally fought by 10, 11 and 12 Groups. It is really the squadrons in those groups, therefore, to which the German claims overwhelmingly relate. On 8 August 1940, for example, the Fighter Command Order of Battle indicates fifteen Spitfire squadrons and twenty-one of Hurricanes in 10, 11 and 12 Groups.[17] This represents a total (again assuming an operational strength of twelve aircraft per unit) of 180 Spitfires and 252 Hurricanes: a ratio of 1.4 in the Hurricanes favour. The German claims, however, confirm that their Me 109 and Me 110 crews were 1.7 times more likely to claim a Spitfire than a Hurricane. Given the Spitfire's technical superiority over the Hurricane, and evidence provided by following tables, this is impossible. It does, however, confirm Peter Townsend's suggestion of 'Spitfire

Snobbery' and the fact that greater prestige was attributed to the destruction of a Spitfire. The Order of Battle referred to is also of interest, confirming as it does that all but two of Dowding's Spitfire squadrons were in 10, 11 and 12 Groups, whilst 13 Group was also equipped with eight Hurricane squadrons. This confirms the fact that, because of their superior performance, it was Spitfires that Dowding required in the front line – not Hurricanes.

Next, actual Hurricane losses are examined.

Table Two

Hurricane Losses 10 July – 31 October 1940

N.B: Number of German Combat Claims shown in brackets.
(Source: *The Battle of Britain Then & Now, Mk V*)

10 July – 31 July 1940

Total Destroyed in Combat:	25 (German claims = 42)
Total Damaged in Combat:	24
Total Destroyed by Me 109s:	14 (33)
Total Damaged by Me 109s:	10
Total Destroyed by Me 110s:	NIL (9)
Total Damaged by Me 110s:	4
Total Destroyed by Bombers:	9
Total Damaged by Bombers:	9
Total Destroyed by Friendly Fire:	NIL
Total Damaged by Friendly Fire:	1
Misc:	1 Destroyed in collision with an Me 109.
	1 Destroyed by He 115.

1 August – August 31 1940

Total Destroyed in Combat:	124 (292)
Total Damaged in Combat:	100
Total Destroyed by Me 109s:	77 (262)
Total Damaged by Me 109s:	38
Total Destroyed by Me 110s:	24 (30)
Total Damaged by Me 110s:	18
Total Destroyed by Bombers:	20
Total Damaged by Bombers:	42
Total Destroyed by Friendly Fire:	3
Total Damaged by Friendly Fire:	2

1 September – 30 September 1940

Total Destroyed in Combat:	200 (249)
Total Damaged in Combat:	149
Total Destroyed by Me 109s:	113 (238)

Total Damaged by Me 109s:	63
Total Destroyed by Me 110s:	21 (11)
Total Damaged by Me 110s:	22
Total Destroyed by Bombers:	35
Total Damaged by Bombers:	28
Total Destroyed by Friendly Fire:	2
Total Damaged by Friendly Fire:	5

Misc: 29 destroyed in combat but unable to account for loss by enemy aircraft type.
31 as above.

1 October – 31 October 1940

Total Destroyed in Combat:	57 (128)
Total Damaged in Combat:	24
Total Destroyed by Me 109s:	45 (127)
Total Damaged by Me 109s:	23
Total Destroyed by Me 110s:	5 (7)
Total Damaged by Me 110s:	0
Total Destroyed by Bombers:	3
Total Damaged by Bombers:	1
Total Destroyed by Friendly Fire:	0
Total Damaged by Friendly Fire:	0

Misc: 4 destroyed in combat but unable to account for loss by enemy aircraft type.

Total number of Hurricanes lost 10 July – 31 October 1940:	406
Total number of Hurricanes claimed by the Luftwaffe:	711

Table Two indicates an over-claiming factor of 1.75 in the case of Hurricanes.

Table Three
Spitfire Losses 10 July – 31 October 1940

N.B: Number of German Combat Claims shown in brackets.
(Source: *The Battle of Britain: Then & Now, Mk V*)

10 July – 31 July 1940

Total Destroyed in Combat:	20 (81)
Total Damaged in Combat:	39
Total Destroyed by Me 109s:	19 (68)
Total Damaged by Me 109s:	16
Total Destroyed by Me 110s:	NIL (13)
Total Damaged by Me 110s:	NIL
Total Destroyed by Bombers:	1
Total Damaged by Bombers:	22
Damaged by unknown enemy aircraft type:	1

1 August – 31 August 1940

Total Destroyed in Combat:	108 (450)
Total Damaged in Combat:	86
Total Destroyed by Me 109s:	78 (362)
Total Damaged by Me 109s:	52
Total Destroyed by Me 110s:	6 (88)
Total Damaged by Me 110s:	7
Total Destroyed by Bombers:	12
Total Damaged by Bombers:	21
Destroyed by unknown enemy aircraft type:	8
Damaged by unknown enemy aircraft type:	6
Total Destroyed by Friendly Fire:	2
Total Destroyed by Seaplanes:	2

1 September – 30 September 1940

Total Destroyed in Combat:	111 (562)
Total Damaged in Combat:	100
Total Destroyed by Me 109s:	86 (458)
Total Damaged by Me 109s:	60
Total Destroyed by Me 110s:	6 (104)
Total Damaged by Me 110s:	11
Total Destroyed by Bombers:	10
Total Damaged by Bombers:	22
Destroyed by unknown enemy aircraft type:	9
Damaged by unknown enemy aircraft type:	17
Misc:	1 Destroyed in Collision with Me 110.

1 October – 31 October 1940

Total Destroyed in Combat:	37 (136)
Total Damaged in Combat:	38
Total Destroyed by Me 109s:	33 (129)
Total Damaged by Me 109s:	26
Total Destroyed by Me 110s:	NIL (7)
Total Damaged by Me 110s:	3
Total Destroyed by Bombers:	7
Total Damaged by Bombers:	2
Total Destroyed by Friendly Fire:	1
Destroyed by unknown enemy aircraft type:	2
Damaged by unknown enemy aircraft type:	2
Total Spitfires Lost 10 July – 31 October 1940:	276
Total Spitfires claimed by Luftwaffe:	1, 229

Table Three indicates an over-claim of 4.45 in respect of Spitfires. Given the actual losses and size of the Spitfire force, the number of Spitfires claimed destroyed by the Germans are impossible. The combined number of Spitfires and Hurricanes lost, ironically given the year involved, was 1, 940, indicating an actual *Luftwaffe* over-claiming factor of 2.84. This figure concerns the claims of both German fighters and bombers, however. This book, however, is principally concerned with the situation concerning the British fighters and the Me 109. The 109 pilots claimed a total of 1, 017 Spitfires destroyed, whereas 216 were actually destroyed by them. This represents an over-claim of 4.7. The 109s claimed 660 Hurricanes but destroyed 249 – an over-claim of only 2.6. The predominance of Spitfire claims is again immediately apparent – even though there were thirty-three less Spitfires actually destroyed. In total, the 109 pilots claimed to have destroyed a combined total of 1,667 Spitfires and Hurricanes. Only 465 of both types were actually destroyed by 109 pilots, representing an overall over-claiming factor of 3.58 where single-engined fighters are concerned. This, however, is more accurate than Fighter Command's overall average, according to Foreman, of 5:1. It could be argued that the Big Wing disproportionately increased Fighter Command's claims, but that formation only went into action, in fact, on a handful of occasions. Moreover, the German fighters frequently operated in similarly sized *gruppe* formations. An explanation for the greater overall accuracy of the German claims could be that the *Schwarm* was geared up to the leader of each *Rotte* being the killer, the second aircraft in each pair protecting his leader's tail. This meant that the leader's kills were often corroborated by their wingmen – and as per the OKL requirement for a second witness. Due to the total unsuitability of the RAF Vic, conversely, Fighter Command pilots would break upon being attacked, fighting individually. Hence a confused situation became even more so for the RAF pilots – and indeed their Intelligence Officers who, like historians today, tried to make some sense out of the reams of combat reports. In sum, although this study of German claims against RAF losses indicates an inaccurate and disproportionate inclination towards claiming Spitfires, the information is of little use in trying to confirm which of the two British fighter types was actually more effective during the Battle of Britain.

It is next necessary to reverse the foregoing process and consider RAF combat claims against German losses.

Table Four
German Combat Losses July – October 1940

N.B. The Nil return on *Stukas* in September and October is because this type was withdrawn from operations after the heavy losses suffered in August.
(Source: *The Blitz Then & Now, Volumes One & Two*)

July 1940

Bombers:	76
Me 110s:	19
Me 109s:	34
Stukas:	12

August 1940

Bombers:	183
Me 110s:	114
Me 109s:	177
Stukas:	47

September 1940

Bombers:	165
Me 110s:	81
Me 109s:	187
Stukas:	NIL

October 1940

Bombers:	64
Me 110s:	10
Me 109s:	104
Stukas:	NIL

Totals

Bombers:	488
Me 110s:	224
Me 109s:	502
Stukas:	59

Grand Total:	1,273
Total Claimed by Spitfires and Hurricanes:	2,051

The overall over-claim represented by Table Four is 1.6. The actual losses of 1, 273 did not arise simply from combat with Spitfires and Hurricanes, however. Other RAF aircraft types, such as the Defiant and Blenheim, also contributed to this figure, as indeed did General Pile's anti-aircraft defences. Much more research is therefore required before a definitive figure can be provided regarding the over-claiming factor applied to Spitfire and Hurricane pilots overall. Moreover, it is impossible to say from the information available to researchers today exactly how many of each enemy type was lost to Spitfires or Hurricanes. It will never, therefore, be known how many enemy aircraft, and of which type, Spitfires and Hurricanes actually destroyed. Nonetheless, it is interesting to review the *claims* of both sides.

Table Five
Hurricane Combat Claims: 10 July – 31 October 1940

(Source: Foreman, J., *Fighter Command Air Combat Claims 1939-45: Volume One*)

10 July – 31 July 1940

Bombers:	34
Me 110s:	15
Me 109s:	29
Stukas:	13

1 August – 31 August 1940

Bombers:	94
Me 110s:	132
Me 109s:	148
Stukas:	77

1 September – 30 September 1940

Bombers:	156
Me 110s:	140
Me 109s:	188
Stukas:	NIL

1 October – 31 October 1940

Bombers:	23
Me 110s:	10
Me 109s:	65
Stukas:	NIL

Totals

Bombers:	297
Me 110s:	292
Me 109s:	430
Stukas:	90
Grand Total:	1, 109

Table Six
Spitfire Combat Claims: 10 July – 31 October 1940

(Source: Foreman, J., *Fighter Command Air Combat Claims 1939-45: Volume One*)

10 July – 31 July 1940

Bombers:	17
Me 110s:	5
Me 109s:	36
Stukas:	6

1 August – 31 August 1940

Bombers:	99
Me 110s:	68
Me 109s:	174
Stukas:	33

1 September – 30 September 1940

Bombers:	152
Me 110s:	65
Me 109s:	193
Stukas:	NIL

1 October – 31 October 1940

Bombers:	13
Me 110s:	6
Me 109s:	85
Stukas:	NIL

Totals

Bombers:	271
Me 110s:	144
Me 109s:	488
Stukas:	39
Grand Total:	942

Although the foregoing are claims, as opposed to actual victories, there are some interesting facts arising. Firstly, if the old legend was true regarding the more numerous Hurricanes having destroyed more enemy aircraft than all other British defences combined, it could reasonably be expected that the pilots of that type would have claimed substantially more kills than the less numerous Spitfire pilots. They did not. The total number of enemy aircraft claimed by Hurricane pilots was 1, 109, only 167 more than the Spitfire pilots. This strongly suggests that the Hurricane did not, in fact, destroy more enemy machines than the other combined defences. In fact the Spitfire's record, considering that on 8 August there were sixty-two more Hurricanes and 168 more of that type in Fighter Command overall, is beginning to look distinctly impressive – even allowing for an over-claiming factor of 5:1. Applying that formula to the Hurricane claims reduces the number of claims to 221 confirmed kills, the Spitfire 188 – just thirty-three less than the more numerous Hurricanes. If the generally accepted Fighter Command totals are used, of nineteen Spitfire squadrons and thirty-three of Hurricanes, 228 and 396 aircraft, the respective figures are 0.87 and 0.55 – 0.32 in the Spitfire's favour. Although these figures are essentially hypothetical, arguably they are likely to be fairly accurate. The less numerous Spitfire emerges in the lead – firmly challenging the Hurricane myth.

Statistics, however, must always be treated with great caution. As John Tosh and Sean Lang wrote, 'Disraeli once spoke as statistics as a form of lying, but there is no denying that as statistical analysis has grown in importance, especially with the development of ever-more sophisticated information technology, no historian can ignore its importance to historical study. Statistics can give an impression of precision and accuracy, but major pitfalls await the unwary student who approaches them in a spirit of blind faith. Statistics may or may not be lies, but they are as open to bias, distortion, unsupported inferences or plain error as any other type of historical source'.[18] This is fair advice to any student of statistics.

In 1996, John Alcorn published his 'statistical study of the Battle of Britain'.[19] Alcorn claimed that 'By collating information regarding times, locations and targets, it was possible to link German losses and RAF claims'. Alcorn established an *average* over-claiming factor of 2:1. His statistics indicated that the nineteen Spitfire squadrons destroyed 521 enemy aircraft, the thirty-three Hurricane squadrons 655. This represented an average of twenty-seven kills per Spitfire squadron, and twenty-two per squadron of Hurricanes. According to Alcorn, therefore, Spitfires were 1.25 more successful in combat than Hurricanes. Further, Alcorn concluded that of the top-scoring six RAF fighter squadrons, four were equipped with Spitfires (603, 609, 41 and 92). Indeed, the first three were Spitfire squadrons: 603 (57.8 victories), 609 (48) and 41 (45.33). The two Hurricane squadrons were 303 (44) and 501 (43.5). The latter, however, was engaged for longer than any other squadron (35 days), so would arguably be expected to have accumulated a substantial number of victories. Although Alcorn's figures were approximations, this work provided the first attempt at a statistical survey of Fighter Command's combat claims and, therefore, the effectiveness of both individual squadrons and aircraft types. That the significantly less numerous Spitfires emerged as more successful on average per aircraft than the Hurricane was illuminating. Moreover, writing of his own findings whilst researching the events of 18 August 1940, Alfred Price wrote that 'the two fighter types were roughly equal in their ability to shoot down enemy aircraft. However, compared with the Spitfire, in combat, the Hurricane with its lower performance stood nearly twice the risk of being shot down'.[20]

In 2000, Alcorn updated his original work.[21] Of his methodology, Alcorn wrote that '… my primary goal has been to establish credits due to each of the fifty odd Hawker Hurricane, Supermarine Spitfire and Boulton-Paul Defiant squadrons actively deployed'. This was based upon a comparison of official German loss records and certain published sources. 'Credits', Alcorn explained, were allowed as 'per the published sources … and, beyond this, on a circumstantial statistical basis'. In only thirty-four cases was Alcorn unable to 'hazard a credit assignment'. At first this claim – given the immense difficulties in establishing exactly who shot down whom – appears most unlikely, until the depth of work undertaken by Alcorn is appreciated. More recently Alcorn defended his research:

> I challenge anyone to significantly improve on my findings. After all, I spent 2,000 hours performing the study, using just about all of the references available. No-one can be certain exactly how many *Luftwaffe* aeroplanes were lost to individual squadrons. I believe, however, that my "Circumstantial Statistical Credit" (CSC) methodology was as good as could be done … During the past two months I have again been working on the study … during this time, about 150 hours, I have further reviewed my results, yielding some detail refinements and changes. These now indicate that:
> 1. The nineteen Spitfire squadrons accounted for about 530 *Luftwaffe* aeroplanes, versus 655 by the thirty active Hurricane units.
> 2. My study as summarised in the July 2000 issue of *Aeroplane Monthly* gave 529 to Spitfires and 656 to Hurricanes.
> 3. Thus my recent review changed these numbers very little – one less Hurricane credit and one more to Spitfires.
> 4. However, the nineteen Spitfire squadrons averaged about twenty-eight, whilst the thirty Hurricane squadrons averaged about twenty-two-and-a-half.
> This does indicate that the Spitfires were somewhat more successful on average.[22]

Further analysis of Alcorn's final data indicates that the Spitfire destroyed 2.32 enemy machines per aircraft (530 ÷ 228 = 2.32), the Hurricane (taking thirty engaged squadrons) 1.81 (655 ÷ 360). The Spitfire was accordingly 0.51 more successful than the Hurricane. Thus the conclusion drawn from Alcorn's data is very similar to my own estimate of 0.32 in he Spitfire's favour.

In the final summing up, of course, the measure of the Spitfire and Hurricane's respective combat effectiveness has to concern their performance against the Me 109. For the first time Alcorn's work has enabled an approximate analysis to be reached: '… 529 *Luftwaffe* aircraft were shot down by Spitfires … some 282 of which were Me 109Es … 656 aircraft downed … by Hurricane squadrons, of which about 222 were 109s. Thus Spitfire squadrons accounted for about fifteen Me 109s on average, compared with around 7.5 for Hurricane units'.[23] On this basis, therefore, the Spitfire was twice as successful against the Me 109 than the Hurricane. It could be argued that this was because the Spitfire was used to engage the fighter screen, and therefore had greater opportunity for combat with the 109s. Such a view, however, only reinforces the fact that this was because the Spitfire's overall performance was superior to the Hurricane.

The New Zealander Alan Deere flew Spitfires during the Battle of Britain, achieving twenty-two kills – all made in Spitfires – by the war's end. He wrote that, 'There can be no doubt that victory in the Battle of Britain was made possible by the Spitfire. Although there were more Hurricanes than Spitfires in the Battle, the Spitfire was the RAF's primary weapon because of its better all-round capability. The Hurricane alone could not have won this great air battle, but the Spitfire could have done so'.[24] There is no question that this extremely experienced Spitfire pilot and fighter leader was absolutely right. As has been explained, the Spitfire was able to perform at all altitudes, even as high as 30,000 feet, whereas the Hurricane could not. Had Fighter Command only been equipped with Hurricanes, therefore, it would have been decimated by the high-flying 109s. The Hurricane was, however, able to attack bombers because the Spitfire engaged the high-flying enemy fighter screens. The Spitfire was able to do both. To put the late Air Commodore Deere's comment into context, however, it is not believed that he meant Fighter Command did not need the Hurricane, as some have interpreted this remark, including Gordon Mitchell, the son of and biographer of Spitfire designer 'R. J.'. Dowding made it clear that he required a minimum of fifty-two squadrons with which to defend the British Isles. Nineteen of Spitfires and thirty-three of Hurricanes gave him exactly the required fifty-two. Nineteen Spitfire squadrons alone were not enough, therefore, although fifty-two squadrons of Spitfires would undoubtedly have caused the *Luftwaffe* tremendous problems. So, whilst the claim that the Hurricane executed greater damage upon the enemy whilst the Spitfire walked away with the glory is largely a myth, the fact is that in 1940 the Hurricane was essential to the defence of this country.

The Spitfire, however, undoubtedly earned and deserves its place in Battle of Britain history. Any accolades it has received in the seventy years since are totally deserved – if not more so now than was hitherto believed. The Spitfire also contributed immeasurably to the nation's morale. The Spitfire captured the public's imagination and affection in a unique way. The so-called 'Spitfire Fund' provides evidence of this enough. During the summer of 1940 there was a spontaneous outbreak of support for Fighter Command in which people strove to raise or donate the sum of £5,000 to Lord Beaverbrook to cover the cost of a Spitfire.[25] Contributors ranged from school children sacrificing their pocket money to millionaires and corporations writing substantial cheques. In total, Spitfire Funds contributed a total of £14,000,000, paying for around 1,500 fighters.[26] The Spitfire Fund was also an incredible indicator of popular support for Churchill and the decision to fight on alone – in spite of the people's fear of German bombers and the dreaded 'knock out blow'. During the summer of 1940, Fighter Command showed the world that the bomber would *not* always get through. Both the Spitfire and Hurricane made an invaluable contribution to the defence of Britain and, indeed, the free world. But to all of those people who watched the criss-crossing vapour trails over south-east England that Indian summer, and to all who dug deep for Spitfire Funds both large and small, the Spitfire was, quite simply, supreme. The evidence available perfectly justifies that view.

Appendix 1
Supermarine Spitfire Mk I & II

A total of 1, 583 Spitfire Mk Is were built, all at Supermarine's factory at Woolston near Southampton. Although the Nuffield Organisation began producing the new Mk II at the Castle Bromwich Aircraft Factory in June 1940, the first of these did not reach the squadrons until August. Indeed, the Mk II did not actually replace the Mk I completely until the winter of 1940/41. The Battle of Britain was, therefore, largely fought by the Spitfire Mk IA, which was machine-gun armed. A handful of Mk IBs, equipped first with only two cannons but later with two cannons and four machine-guns, saw action with 19 Squadron, but these were unsuccessful and Mk IAs replaced them in early September. The basic specification of the Spitfire Mk IA and IIA are as follows:

Spitfire Mk IA

Wing span:	36 feet 11 inches
Length:	29 feet 11 inches
Power-plant:	Rolls-Royce Merlin III, twelve-cylinder, liquid cooled engine delivering 1,030 hp
Armament:	Eight Browning wing-mounted .303 machine-guns with 300 rounds per gun
Maximum speed:	355 mph
Range:	395 miles
Airscrew:	Originally manufactured with a fixed-pitch propeller, this was changed to a variable (two) pitch unit in time for the fighting in 1940. Superior Constant Speed propellers were fitted to all operational Spitfires and Hurricanes in August 1940.

Spitfire Mk IIA

As above but with the following improvements:

Power-plant:	Rolls-Royce Merlin XII, providing 1,175 hp. The Mk II also had an automatic Coffman engine starter.
Maximum speed:	370 mph
Airscrew:	Rotol CS propeller.

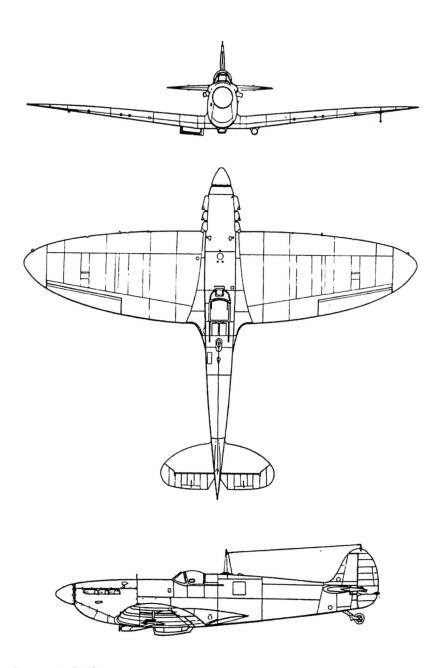

57. Supermarine Spitfire.

Hawker Hurricane Mk I and Mk II

The Hurricane Mk II also began reaching the squadrons in August 1940. Like the Spitfire, however, it was the Mk I that saw most action. Also like the Spitfire, the variable pitch airscrew was changed in service as an emergency measure to the Constant Speed unit in August 1940. The Hurricane Mk II had the new propeller fitted as standard.

Hawker Hurricane Mk I

Wing span:	40 feet 0 inches
Length:	31 feet 4 inches
Power-plant:	Rolls-Royce Merlin III, twelve-cylinder, liquid cooled engine producing 1,030 h.p.
Armament:	Eight Browning wing-mounted .303 machine-guns with 300 rounds per gun.
Maximum speed:	328 mph
Range:	505 miles
Airscrew:	Originally manufactured with a fixed-pitch propeller, this was changed to a variable (two) pitch unit in time for the fighting in 1940. Superior Rotol Constant Speed propellers were fitted to all operational Spitfires and Hurricanes in August 1940.

Hurricane Mk II

As above but with the following improvements:

Power-plant:	Rolls-Royce Merlin XX, providing 1,185 hp
Maximum speed:	342 mph
Airscrew:	Rotol Constant Speed Propeller

Messerschmitt Bf 109-E

Wingspan:	32 feet 4 inches
Length:	26 feet 8 inches
Power-plant:	D.B.601A inline engine producing 1,150 hp
Armament:	Two nose-mounted 7.92 m.m. MG 17s and two wing-mounted 20 mm Oerlikon cannons. The E-4/B and E-7 variants were fitted to carry one SC 250 kg bomb.

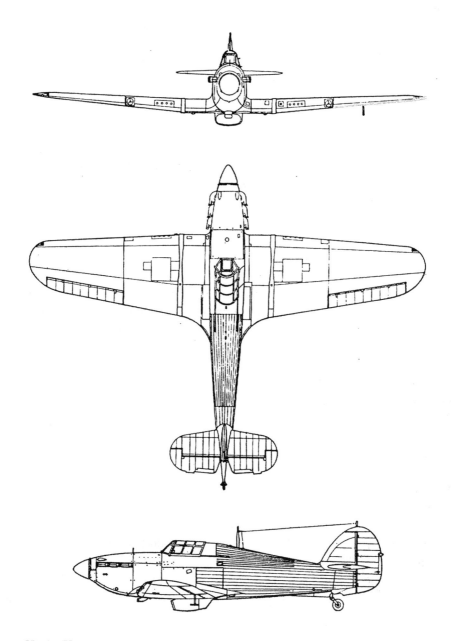

58. Hawker Hurricane.

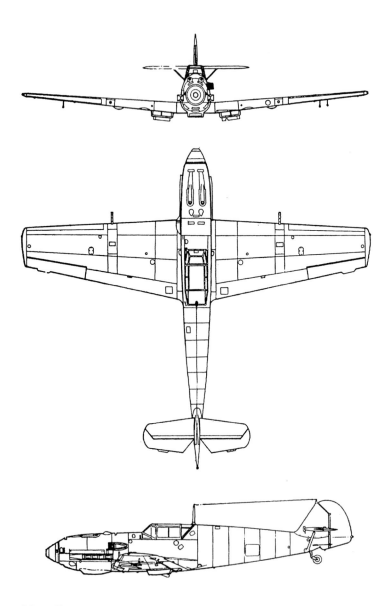

59. Me 109E.

Appendix 2
The Fighter Command 'Vic'

An RAF fighter squadron consisted of twelve aircraft, divided into two flights, 'A' and 'B'. Each flight was then divided into two colour coded sections, each of three aircraft: Red and Yellow in 'A', and Blue and Green in 'B'. The Leader in each section was, for example, Red One, the other two aircraft being Red Two and Three. It was intended that such a formation could bring twenty-four guns to bear simultaneously instead of the eight of a single fighter, and so was flown in close formation. This meant that pilots concentrated too much on keeping station and not enough on searching for the enemy. It was also far too inflexible for the high speed manoeuvres of fighter-to-fighter combat. Although some squadrons learned from bitter experience during the Battle of Britain and experimented with alternative formations, it was not until 1941 that the RAF's interpretation of the *Schwarm* – the 'Finger or Crossover Four' was adopted. Typically during 1940, however, squadrons flew sections flew in line astern, although some squadrons used one section, or a pair of fighters, to weave to and fro above and behind the main formation in an effort to prevent a surprise attack. Unfortunately it was these 'Tail-end Charlies' that were often the first to be picked off by German fighters attacking from high altitude and out of the sun.

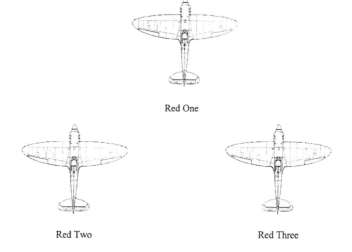

Red One

60. Red Section.

Red Two

Red Three

Appendix 3
The *Luftwaffe Schwarm*

Some 200 yards separated each aircraft, enabling the enemy pilots to search the sky for the enemy. When battle was joined, the formation would break into two pairs – each known as a *Rotte* – aircraft 1 & 2, and 3 and 4. Aircraft 1 is the overall *Schwarm Führer* and remains leader of the left-hand *Rotte* after the break. Aircraft 3 then becomes *Rotte Führer* of the second pair. Aircraft 2 and 4 are wingmen – *Katschmarek* – protecting their leaders' tails. The *Staffel* of twelve aircraft would fly in either *Schwarm* in line abreast or astern, with each *Schwarm* stepped up, each protecting the other.

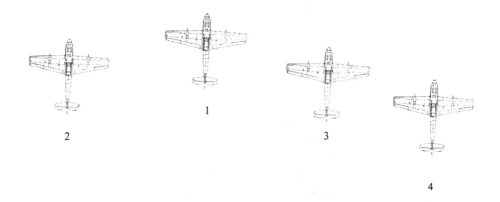

61. *Schwarm.*

Appendix 4
German Bomber Tactical Formations

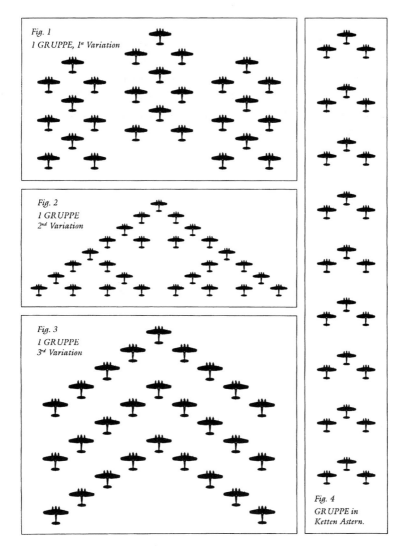

Fig. 1
1 GRUPPE, 1st Variation

Fig. 2
1 GRUPPE
2nd Variation

Fig. 3
1 GRUPPE
3rd Variation

Fig. 4
GRUPPE in
Ketten Astern.

62. German Bomber Formations.

Notes

Abbreviations:

AHB: Air Historical Branch
ORB: Operations Record Book
TNA: The National Archives

Introduction

1. Townsend, P., *Duel of Eagles: The Classic Account of the Battle of Britain*, p. 154

1. The Bomber Will Always Get Through

1. Mowat, C. L., *Britain Between the Wars: 1918-1940*, p. 1
2. Mowat, C. L., ibid, p. 1
3. Clapson, M., *The Routledge Companion to Britain in the Twentieth Century*, p. 23
4. Mason, F. K., *Battle Over Britain*, p. 13
5. Mason, F. K., ibid, p. 13
6. Calder, A, *The People's War: Britain 1939-45*, p. 21
7. Calder, A., ibid, p. 21
8. Bialer, U., *The Shadow of the Bomber: The Fear of Air Attack and British Politics*, 1932-39, p. 2
9. Dempster, D. and Wood, D, *The Narrow Margin*, p. 21
10. Dempster, D. and Wood, D., ibid, p. 21
11. Dempster, D. and Wood, D., ibid, p. 21
12. Dempster, D. and Wood, D., ibid, p. 21
13. Orange, V., *Dowding of Fighter Command: Victor of the Battle of Britain*, p. 66
14. Townsend, P., op cit, p. 61
15. Dean, Sir Maurice, *The Royal Air Force in Two World Wars*, p. 59
16. Dean, Sir Maurice, ibid, p. 41
17. Dean, Sir Maurice, ibid, p. 42
18. Calder, A., op cit, p. 26
19. Priestley, J. B., *English Journey*, pp. 397-403
20. Calder, A., op cit, p. 27
21. Dean, Sir Maurice, op cit, p. 41
22. Dean, Sir Maurice, ibid, p. 49
23. Dean, Sir Maurice, ibid, p.49
24. Dean, Sir Maurice, ibid, p. 40

25. Anon., *The Second World War, RAF 1939-45, Flying Training: Volume One, Policy & Planning*, p. 18
26. Anon., *The Second World War*, ibid, p. 18
27. Smith, M., The RAF. In Addison, J., & Crang, J. A. (eds), *The Burning Blue: A New History of the Battle of Britain*, p. 26

2. Schneider Trophy Racers

1. Orange, V., *Dowding*, op cit, p. 31
2. Orange, V., *Dowding*, ibid, p. 36
3. Ferris, J., British Strategic Air Defence 1915-40. In Cox, S., & Gray, P. (eds), *Air Power History: Turning Points from Kitty Hawk to Kosovo*, p. 40.
4. Orange, V., *Dowding*, p. 69
5. Orange, V., *Park: The Biography of Air Chief Marshal Sir Keith Park*, p. 41
6. Mitchell, G., *R.J. Mitchell. World-Famous Aircraft Designer: From Schooldays to Spitfire*, p. 32
7. Mitchell, G., ibid, p. 33
8. Mitchell, G., ibid, p. 33
9. Mitchell, G., ibid, p. 37
10. Mitchell, G., ibid, p. 50
11. Mitchell, G., ibid, p. 52
12. Mitchell, G., ibid, p. 55
13. Michtell, G., ibid, p. 63
14. Mitchell, G., ibid, p. 69
15. Mitchell, G., ibid, p. 81
16. Bader, Group Captain Sir Douglas, *Fight for the Sky: The Story of the Spitfire and Hurricane*, p. 35
17. Bader, Group Captain Sir Douglas, ibid, p. 35
18. Mitchell, G., op cit, p. 95
19. Mitchell, G., ibid, p. 97
20. Mitchell, G., ibid, p. 100
21. Mitchell, G., ibid, p. 102
22. Orange, V., *Dowding*, op cit, p. 64
23. Wright, R., *Dowding and the Battle of Britain*, p. 53

3. Monoplanes & Machine-guns

1. Wood, D. and Dempster, D., op cit, p. 31
2. Bungay, S., *The Most Dangerous Enemy: A History of the Battle of Britain*, p. 70
3. Orange, V., *Dowding*, op cit, p. 70
4. Orange, V., ibid, p. 70
5. Price, A., *The Spitfire Story*, p. 12
6. Mitchell, G., op cit, p. 122
7. Mason, F. K., *The Hawker Hurricane*, p. 15
8. Mitchell, G., op cit, p. 123
9. Price, A, op cit, p. 12
10. Price, A., ibid, p. 14
11. Wood, D. and Dempster, D., op cit, p. 33
12. Mitchell, G., op cit, p. 124
13. Mitchell, G, ibid, p. 124
14. Price, A, op cit, p. 17
15. Orange, V., *Dowding*, op cit, p. 73

16. Orange, V., *Dowding*, ibid, p. 69

4. The Hawker Hurricane

1.   Dean, Sir Maurice, op cit, pp. 51-52
2.   Dean, Sir Maurice, ibid, p. 52
3.   Bungay, S., op cit, p. 74
4.   Hough, R., & Richards, D., *The Battle of Britain: The Jubilee History*, p. 36
5.   Mason, F. K., *Hurricane*, op cit, p. 19
6.   Mason, F. K., *Hurricane*, ibid, p. 22
7.   Hough, R. and Richards, D., op cit, p. 37
8.   Mason, F. K., *Hurricane*, op cit, p. 28
9.   Mason, F. K., *Hurricane*, ibid, pp. 28-29
10. Bungay, S., op cit, p. 75
11. Gillan, Squadron Leader J.W., Tests to be Made to Determine the Operational Characteristics of the Hurricane Aircraft, 14 January 1938
12. Mason, F. K., *Hurricane*, op cit, p. 34
13. Townsend, Group Captain P., *Duel of Eagles: The Classic Account of the Battle of Britain*, p. 152
14. Townsend, Group Captain P., ibid, pp. 153-154
15. Townsend, Group Captain P., ibid, p. 155
16. Townsend, Group Captain P., ibid, p. 153
17. Townsend, Group Captain P., ibid, p. 155
18. Brothers, Air Commodore P. M., interviewed by Sarkar, D., 12 September 1992
19. Hough, R. and Richards, D., op cit, p. 38
20. Hough, R. and Richards, D., ibid p. 37
21. Grice, D., IWM Sound Archive, tape 10807
22. Mason, F. K., *Hurricane*, op cit, p. 36
23. Mason, F. K., *Hurricane*, ibid, p. 36
24. Wood, D., and Dempster, D., op cit, p. 30
25. Calder, A., op cit, p. 25

5. The Supermarine Spitfire

1.   Mitchell, G., op cit, p. 123
2.   Price, A., op cit, p. 36
3.   Mitchell, G., op cit, p. 131
4.   Price, A., op cit, p. 38
5.   Price, A., ibid, p. 38
6.   Price, A., ibid, p. 61
7.   Price, A., ibid, p. 67
8.   Price, A., ibid, p. 69
9.   Overy, R., *The Air War 1939-45*, p. 21
10. Handling Trials of the Spitfire K5054, p. 6
11. Ibid, pp. 9-10
12. Anon., The Spitfire, *The Aeroplane*, 12 April 1940, Vol. LVIII. No. 1507, p. 524
13. Ibid, pp. 517 – 524
14. Unwin, Wing Commander G. C., interviewed by Sarkar, D., 8 November 1989
15. Lyne, Air Vice-Marshal M. D, letter to Sarkar, D., 1 October 1989
16. Brinsden, Wing Commander F. N., letter to Sarkar, D., 25 July 1989
17. Woodhall, Group Captain A. B., *Soldier, Sailor, Airman Too* (unpublished memoir), p. 22
18. Bader, Group Captain Sir Douglas., op cit, p. 18

19.   Bader, Group Captain Sir Douglas., ibid, pp. 13-14

20.   Allen, Wing Commander H. R., *Fighter Squadron: A Memoir 1940-42*, pp. 31-32

21.   Morris, R., interviewed by Sarkar, D., 1 October 1986

22.   Hillary, R., *The Last Enemy*, pp. 82-84

23.   Crook, D., *Spitfire Pilot*, p. 20

24.   Hillary, Flying Officer R., op cit, p. 85

6. The System of Air Defence

1.   Overy, R., *Air War*, op cit, pp. 14-15

2.   Dean, Sir Maurice, op cit, p. 66

3.   Dean, Sir Maurice, ibid, p. 66

4.   Smith, M., op cit, p. 27

5.   Orange, V., *Dowding*, op cit, p. 85

6.   Hough, R. and Richards, D., op cit, p. 53

7.   Overy, R., *Air War*, op cit, p. 15

8.   Overy, R., *Air War*, ibid, p. 17

9.   Quoted by Terraine, J., in 'The Dowding System', *Battle of Britain* (Part One), The Daily Telegraph Editorial Supplement, 16 June 1990, p. XI

10.   Orange, V., *Dowding*, op cit, p. 84

11.   Anon., *The Battle of Britain*, Air Ministry Pamphlet 156, pp. 4 – 12

12.   Bungay, S., op cit, p. 250

13.   Orange, V., *Park*, op cit, p. 68

14.   Orange, V., *Park*, ibid, p. 71

15.   Orange, V., *Park*, ibid, p. 71

16.   Orange, V., ibid, p. 71

17.   Orange, V., ibid, p. 72

18.   Walker, Flight Lieutenant W. L. B., interviewed by Sarkar, D., 8 May 1988

7. German Military Aviation Between the Wars, and the Me 109

1.   Anon., *The Rise and Fall of the German Air Force (1933 to 1945)*, Air Ministry Pamphlet 248, p. 1

2.   Deist, W., *The* Wehrmacht *and German Rearmament*, p. 54

3.   Maier, K. A., The *Luftwaffe*. In Addison, P., and Crang, J. A. (eds), The *Burning Blue*, p. 15

4.   Deist, W., op cit, p. 57

5.   Air Ministry Pamphlet 248, op cit, p. 11

6.   Feist, U., *The Fighting Me 109*, p. 9

7.   Townsend, Group Captain P., op cit, p. 92

8.   Hough, R., and Richards, D., op cit, p. 43

9.   Bungay, S., op cit, p. 50

10.   Mason, F. K., *Battle Over Britain*, p. 48

11.   Corum, J. S., The *Luftwaffe* and Lessons Learned in the Spanish Civil War. In Cox, S., and Gray, P. (eds), *Air Power History: Turning Points from Kitty Hawk to Kosovo*, p. 66

12.   Galland, General A, *The First and the Last: Germany's Fighter Force in the Second World War*, p. 27

13.   Johnson, Air Vice-Marshal J. E., interviewed by Sarkar, D., 1 March 1996

14.   Corum, J. S., op cit, p. 70

15.   Air Ministry Pamphlet 248, op cit, p. 17

16.   Corum, J. S., op cit, p. 80

17.   Corum, J. S., ibid, p. 71

18.   Corum, J. S., ibid, p. 71

19. Harvey-Bailey, A., *The Merlin in Perspective*, p. 155
20. Anon., *D.(Luft)T.3601 A u. B., D.B.601 A u. B Motoren-Handbuch*, Mai 1942, p. 18
21. Air Ministry Pamphlet 248, op cit, p. 17
22. Orange, V., *Dowding*, op cit, pp. 69-70
23. Bungay, S., op cit, p. 257
24. Orange, V., *Dowding*, p. 88
25. Air Ministry Pamphlet 248, op cit, p. 19
26. Overy, R., *Air War*, op cit, p. 21
27. Air Ministry Pamphlet 248, op cit, p. 209
28. Air Ministry Pamphlet 248, ibid, p. 45
29. Air Ministry Pamphlet 248, ibid, p. 22

8. The Battle of France

1. Calder, A., op cit, p.33
2. Roberts, F., *Duxford to Karachi: An R.A.F. Armourer's War*, p.p. 59-60
3. Calder, A., op cit, p. 35
4. Calder, A., ibid, p. 33
5. Roberts, F., op cit, p. 60
6. Overy, R., *Air War*, op cit, p. 26
7. Mason, F. K., *Battle Over Britain*, op cit, p. 78
8. Anon., *Destiny Can Wait: The History of the Polish Air Force in Great Britain*, p. 17
9. Ibid, p. 17
10. Saunders, A., Fighter Command's First Casualty. In Ramsey, W. (ed), *The Blitz Then and Now: Volume One*, p. 27
11. Lane, B. J. E., *Spitfire! The Experiences of a Battle of Britain Fighter Pilot*, p. 23
12. Ayerst, Wing Commander P., interviewed by Lawson, N., 25 October 2008
13. Orange, V., *Dowding*, op cit, p. 158
14. Halahan, Squadron Leader P., Report on Comparative Trials of Hurricane versus Messerschmitt 109, 7 May 1940, TNA, AIR 35/121
15. Cox, Wing Commander D. G. S. R., interviewed by Sarkar, D., 1 November 1994
16. Peach, S. W., Air Power and the Fall of France. In Cox, S., and Gray, P. (eds), *Air Power History: Turning Points from Kitty Hawk to Kosovo*, p. 162
17. Bingham, V., *Blitzed! The Battle of France May – June 1940*, p. 21
18. Wright, R., *Dowding and the Battle of Britain*, p. 98
19. Wright, R., ibid, pp. 120-121
20. Orange, V., *Dowding*, op cit, p. 159
21. Wright, R., op cit, p. 110
22. Wright, R., ibid, p. 113
23. Wright, R., ibid, pp. 111-112
24. Orange, V., *Dowding*, op cit, p. 160
25. Wright, R., op cit, p. 122
26. Collier, B., *Leader of the Few*, pp. 192-194
27. Wright, R., op cit, p. 123
28. Caldwell, D., *The J.G. 26 War Diary: Volume One 1939-45*, p. 25
29. Foreman, J., *Fighter Command Air Combat Claims 1939-45: Volume One*, p. 38
30. ORB, 19 Squadron, 18 May 1940, TNA, AIR 27/252
31. Donaldson, Air Commodore E. M., letter to Sarkar, D., 25 November 1989
32. Hamar, Pilot Officer J. R., Combat Report, 18 May 1940, T.N.A., AIR 50/63
33. Edge, Group Captain G. R., interviewed by Sarkar, D., 10 February 1992
34. Brothers, Air Commodore P. M., letter to Sarkar, D, 26 January 2000
35. Terraine, J., The Battle of France. In Probert, H., and Cox, S. (eds), The Battle Re-thought:

A Symposium on the Battle of Britain, p. 15

36. Terraine, J., ibid, pp. 15-17

9. Dunkirk: Operation DYNAMO

1. Dean, Sir Maurice, op cit, p. 134
2. Bekker, C., *The Luftwaffe War Diaries*, p. 158
3. Hough, R., and Richards, D., op cit, p. 387
4. Foreman, J., op cit, pp. 59-60
5. Bingham, V., op cit, p. 232
6. Bingham, V., ibid, p. 212
7. Hough, R. and Richards, D., op cit, p. 92
8. Caldwell, D., op cit, p. 30
9. Freeborn, Pilot Officer J. F. C., Combat Report, 24 May 1940, TNA, AIR 50/32
10. Gray, Group Captain C.F., *Spitfire Patrol*, p. 27
11. Bingham, V., op cit, p. 213
12. Foreman, J., op cit, pp. 63-64
13. Lane, B .J. E., op cit, p. 23
14. Lane, B. J. E., ibid, p. 26
15. Orange, V., *Park*, op cit, p. 86
16. Lyne, Air Vice-Marshal M. D., letter to Sarkar, D., 1 October 1989
17. Lane, Flight Lieutenant B. J. E., Combat Report, 26 May 1940, TNA, AIR 50/10
18. Lyne, Air Vice-Marshal M. D, letter to Sarkar, D., 1 October 1989
19. Unwin, Wing Commander G. C., letter to Sarkar, D., 14 November 1988
20. Orange, V., *Park*, op cit, p. 87
21. Mermagen, Air Commodore H. W., letter to Sarkar, D., 26 January 1989
22. Mermagen, Air Commodore H. W., letter to Sarkar, D., 26 January 1989
23. Orange, V., *Park*, op cit, p. 87
24. Roberts, F. R., interviewed by Sarkar, D., 1 September 1990
25. Orange, V., *Park*, op cit, pp. 88-8
26. Morgan, E. B. and Shacklady, E., *Spitfire: The History*, p. 99
27. Deere, Air Commodore A. C., Spitfire v Messerschmitt – A First Encounter. In Bader, Sir Douglas, op cit, pp. 46-50
28. Orange, V., *Park*, op cit, p. 89
29. Peach, S. W., op cit, p. 164
30. Peach, S. W., ibid, p. 142
31. Scott-Malden, Air Vice-Marshal F. D. S., letter to Sarkar, D., 12 May 1987

10. The Lull

1. Donnelly, M., *Britain in the Second World War*, p. 14
2. AHB Narrative, The Battle of France, p. 150, TNA, AIR 14/41
3. Ibid
4. Calder, A., op cit, p. 128
5. Priestley, J. B., *Postscripts*, p. 27
6. Overy, R., *The Battle of Britain*, p. 15
7. Calder, A., *The Myth of the Blitz*, p. 255
8. Air Ministry Pamphlet 248, op cit, p. 73
9. Townsend, Group Captain P., op cit, p. 194
10. Messerschmitt 109 Fighter: Brief Handling Trials, A&AEE, 10 June 1940, TNA, AVIA 18/763

11. Stainforth, Wing Commander G. H., Report on the Investigation of Turning Circles of Me 109, Spitfire and Hurricane, 9 June 1940

12. Comparison Flight Between Me 109E, Me 110C, Spitfire, Hurricane and Curtiss, *E-Stelle Rechlin*, 9 August 1940.

13. Price, A., *Spitfire Mk I/II Aces*, p. 61

14. Brinsden, Wing Commander F. N., letter to Sarkar, D., 15 June 1989

15. 19 Squadron ORB, TNA, AIR 27/252

16. James, T. C. G., *The Battle of Britain*, p. 17

17. Price, A., *The Hardest Day*, p. 36

18. Price, A., ibid, p. 52

19. Brinsden, Wing Commander F. N., letter to Sarkar, D., 3 May 1989

20. 19 Squadron ORB, TNA, AIR 27/252

21. 19 Squadron ORB, TNA, AIR 27/252

22. Brinsden, Wing Commander F. N., letter to Sarkar, D., 3 May 1989

23. Roberts, F. R., interviewed by Sarkar, D., 1 September 1990

24. Dowding, Sir Hugh, Air Chief Marshal, letter to Sinclair, Sir Archibald, 24 July 1940, TNA, Trials of Cannon Armed Spitfires, AIR 16/142

25. James, T. C. G., op cit, p. 21

26. Brinsden, Wing Commander F. N., letter to Sarkar, D., 3 May 1989

27. Unwin, Wing Commander G. C., letter to Sarkar, D., 13 October 1988

11. The Battle of Britain

1. Fighter Command, Operational Strength of Squadrons and Order of Battle, TNA, AIR 16/365

2. Ibid

3. Ibid

4. Overy, R., *Air War*, op cit, p. 33

5. Mason, F. K., *Battle Over Britain*, op cit, p. 93

6. Overy, R., *Air War*, op cit, p. 33

7. Overy, R., *Air War*, ibid, p.33

8. Fighter Command, Operational Strength of Squadrons and Order of Battle, TNA, AIR 16/365

9. Overy, R., *Air War*, op cit, p. 21

10. Price, A., *The Spitfire Story*, op cit, pp. 107-109

11. Wood, D., and Dempster, D., op cit, p. 276

12. Wood, D., and Dempster, D., ibid, p. 276, 283 and 295

13. OKW Directives for Invasion of the UK, Operation *Seelöwe*, Summer and Autumn 1940

14. Air Ministry Pamphlet 248, op cit, p. 76

15. OKL, German Intelligence Appreciation of the RAF and Comparison with current *Luftwaffe* Strength, 16 July 1940

16. Hamar, Pilot Officer J. R., Combat Report, 14 July 1940, TNA, AIR 50/63

17. James, T. C. G., op cit, p. 394

18. James, T. C. G., ibid, pp. 394-395

19. Wood, D., and Dempster, D., op cit, p. 115

20. Cox, S., RAF and Luftwaffe Intelligence Compared. In Handel, M. I. (ed), *Intelligence and Military Operations*, p. 439

21. Kelly, Flight Lieutenant D. P. D. G., Combat Report, 28 July 1940, TNA, AIR 50/32

22. Bennions, Pilot Officer G. H., Combat Report, 28 July 1940, TNA, AIR 50/18

23. Pinkham, Squadron Leader P. C., Pilot's Flying Log Book, 11 August 1940

24. 19 Squadron ORB, TNA, AIR 27/252

25. Ibid

26. Unwin, Wing Commander G. C., letter to Sarkar, D., 8 September 1989
27. Report on German Fighter Tactics, TNA, AIR 16/300
28. Report on German Bomber Tactics, TNA, AIR 16/300
29. Ibid
30. Ibid
31. Galland, General A., *The First and the Last*, p. 51
32. Price, A., *The Hardest Day*, p. 61
33. Galland, General A., op cit, pp. 52-53
34. Quill, J. K., letter to Sarkar, D., 26 January 1988
35. Denholm, Group Captain G. L., letter to Sarkar, D., 27 May 1991
36. Brinsden, Wing Commander F. N., letter to Sarkar, D., 25 July 1989
37. Walker, Flight Lieutenant W. L. B., letter to Sarkar, D, 1 May 1987
38. Ibid
39. Dundas, Group Captain Sir Hugh, letter to Sarkar, D., 25 April 1987
40. Ibid
41. Walker, Flight Lieutenant W. L. B., letter to Sarkar, D., 1 May 1987
42. Ibid
43. Ibid
44. Gillam, Flight Lieutenant D., Combat Report, 26 August 1940, TNA, AIR 50/176
45. Walker, Flight Lieutenant W. L. B., op cit
46. ORB, 616 Squadron, TNA, AIR 27/2126
47. James, T. C. G., op cit, p. 172
48. Hutchinson, J. I., interviewed by Sarkar, D, 12 September 1992
49. ORB, 222 Squadron, TNA, AIR 27/2475
50. Johnson, R. B., letter to Sarkar, D., 3 March 1989
51. ORB, 242 Squadron, TNA, AIR 27/1471
52. Ibid
53. James, T. C. G., op cit, pp. 170-184
54. Fighter Command Combat Report, Form 'F', 501 Squadron, 30 August 1940, TNA, AIR 16/956
55. Fighter Command Combat Report, Form 'F', 1 Squadron, 30 August 1940, TNA, AIR 16/956
56. Ibid
57. Ibid
58. Ibid
59. ORB, 56 Squadron, TNA, AIR 27/528
60. Form 'F', 1 Squadron, op cit
61. Fighter Command Combat Report, Form 'F', 242 Squadron, 30 August 1940, TNA, AIR 16/956
62. Ibid
63. Bader, Group Captain Sir Douglas, interviewed by Price, A., 1980
64. Trials of Cannon Armed Spitfires, TNA, AIR 16/142
65. Woodhall, Group Captain A. B., *Soldier, Sailor, Airman Too*, p. 31
66. Unwin, Wing Commander G. C., interviewed by Sarkar, D., 1 May 1990
67. Whitbread, Pilot Officer H. L., Combat Report, 31 August 1940, TNA, AIR 50/51
68. Hillary, Pilot Officer R., Combat Report 2 September 1940, TNA, AIR 50/167
69. Air Ministry Pamphlet 248, p. 85
70. Ibid
71. Bekker, C, op cit, p. 221
72. Bekker, C., ibid, p. 220
73. Boog, H., The Luftwaffe and the Battle of Britain. In Probert, H., and Cox, S. (eds), *The Battle Re-Thought: A Symposium on the Battle of Britain*, p. 27
74. Galland, General A., op cit, p. 56

75. Steinhilper, U. and Osborne, P., *Spitfire on My Tail*, p. 286
76. Galland, General A., op cit, p. 56
77. Galland, General A., ibid, p. 51
78. Whitbread, Pilot Officer H. L., Combat Report, 7 September 1940, TNA, AIR 50/51
79. Hall, Flight Lieutenant R. M. D., *Clouds of Fear*, p. 72
80. No 11 Group, Instructions to Controllers, No. 16
81. Air Ministry Pamphlet 248, op cit, p. 34
82. Park, Air Vice-Marshal Sir Keith, Report on German Attacks on England 11 September – 2 November 1940, TNA, AIR 16/635
83. Edge, Group Captain G. R., interviewed by Sarkar, D., 12 September 1992
84. Park, Air Vice-Marshal Sir Keith, op cit, AIR 16/635
85. Fighter Command Combat Report, Form 'F', 92 Squadron, 11 September 1940, TNA, AIR 16/957
86. Ramsey, W (ed), *The Blitz Then and Now, Volume II*, pp. 79-81
87. Park, Sir Keith, AVM., op cit, AIR 16/635
88. Air Ministry Pamphlet 248, op cit, p. 86
89. Galland, General A., op cit, p. 59
90. Price, A., Battle of Britain Day, *RAF Historical Society Journal*, 2002, 29, pp. 5-23
91. Ramsey, W. (ed), *Blitz Volume II*, op cit, p. 96
92. Price, A., *Battle of Britain Day*, op cit, p. 14
93. Price, A., *Battle of Britain Day*, ibid, p. 14
94. Price, A., *Battle of Britain Day*, ibid, p. 14
95. Price, A., *Battle of Britain Day*, ibid, p. 14
96. Ramsey, W (ed), *Blitz Volume II*, op cit, p. 96
97. Jones, R. L., interviewed by Sarkar, D., 14 August 2010
98. Bekker, C., op cit, pp. 223-224
99. ORB, 310 Squadron, TNA, AIR 27/1683
100. Unwin, Flight Sergeant G. C., Combat Report 15 September 1940, TNA, AIR 50/10
101. Cox, Sergeant, D. G. S. R., Combat Report 15 September 1940, TNA, AIR 50/10
102. ORB., 611 Squadron, TNA, AIR 27/2109
103. Lane, Squadron Leader B. J. E., Pilot's Flying Log Book, TNA, AIR 4/58
104. ORB, 611 Squadron, op cit
105. Lane, Squadron Leader B. J. E., Combat Report, 15 September 1940, TNA, AIR 50/10
106. Unwin, Flight Sergeant G. C., Combat Report, 15 September 1940, TNA, AIR 50/10
107. Ibid
108. Bekker, C., op cit, p.227
109. Wood, D., and Dempster, D., op cit, p. 233
110. Hough, R., and Richards, D., op cit, p. 283
111. Galland, General A., op cit, p. 67
112. Johnson, Flight Lieutenant R. B., letter to Sarkar, D., 3 March 1989
113. ORB, 72 Squadron, TNA, AIR 27/624
114. ORB, 605 Squadron, AIR 27/2089
115. Wright, Group Captain A. R., letter to Sarkar, D, 1 October 1992
116. Wade, Pilot Officer T. S., Combat Report, 20 September 1940, TNA, AIR 50/40
117. Sanders, Squadron Leader P. J., Combat Report, 20 September 1940, TNA, AIR 50/40
118. Rolls, Sergeant W. T. E., Combat Report, 20 September 1940, TNA, AIR 50/30
119. Wellum, Squadron Leader G. H. A., letter to Sarkar, D., 20 January 1992
120. Lane, Squadron Leader B. J. E., *Spitfire!* Op cit, p. 15

12. Spitfire Ascendant

1. Park, Air Vice-Marshal Sir Keith, op cit, AIR 16/635

2. Ibid
3. Ibid
4. Ibid
5. Galland, General A., op cit, p. 63
6. Bader, Group Captain Sir Douglas, op cit, p. 19
7. Greenwood, Flight Lieutenant J. P. B., interviewed by Lawson, N., 5 June 2010
8. Palliser, Flight Lieutenant G. C. C., interviewed by Lawson, N., 30 July 2010
9. Bartlett, Group Captain L. H., interviewed by Lawson, N., 11 July 2010
10. Pickering, Flight Lieutenant T. G., interviewed by Sarkar, D., 5 May 1987
11. Messerschmitt 109. Handling and Manoeuvrability Tests, September 1940, AVIA 6/2394
12. Feist, U., op cit, pp. 31-32
13. Johnson, Air Vice-Marshal J. E., interviewed by Sarkar, D, 12 March 1996

Conclusion

1. Boog, H., The *Luftwaffe* and the Battle of Britain, op cit, p. 32
2. Air Ministry Pamphlet 248, op cit, p. 87
3. Air Ministry Pamphlet 248, ibid, p. 86
4. Townsend, Group Captain P., op cit, p. 263
5. Townsend, Group Captain P., ibid, p. 263
6. Knocke, H., *I Flew for the Fuhrer*, p. 23
7. Unwin, Flight Sergeant G. C., Combat Report, 5 November 1940, TNA, AIR 50/10
8. ORB, 19 Squadron, op cit
9. Caldwell, D., *The J.G. 26 War Diary: Volume One 1939-42*, p. 85
10. Cox, Wing Commander D. G. S. R., letter to Sarkar, D., 30 October 1988
11. Mason, F. K., *Battle Over Britain*, op cit, p. 228
12. Gleed, Flight Lieutenant I. R., Combat Report, 30 September 1940, TNA, AIR 50/37
13. Götz, R., letter to Sarkar, D., 10 January 1994
14. Stapleton, Pilot Officer B., Combat Report, 5 September 1940, TNA, AIR 50/167
15. Ramsey, W. (ed), *Blitz Volume One*, op cit, p. 310
16. Foreman, J., op cit, p. 8
17. James, T. C. G., op cit, p. 338
18. Tosh, J., with Lang, S., *The Pursuit of History*, p. 257
19. Alcorn, J., Battle of Britain Top Guns, *Aeroplane Monthly*, September 1996, pp. 14-18
20. Price, A., In Alcorn, J., ibid, p. 18
21. Alcorn, J., Battle of Britain Top Guns Update, *Aeroplane Monthly*, July 2000, pp. 24-29
22. Alcorn, J. Email to Sarkar, D., (25/08/10)
23. Alcorn, J, Top Guns Update, op cit, p. 29
24. Deere, Air Commodore A. C., In Mitchell, G., op cit, p. 265
25. Beckles, G., *Birth of a Spitfire*, p. 78
26. Boot, H., and Sturtivant, P., *Gifts of War*, p. 11

Acknowledgements

As ever, I must firstly thank all of those veterans of our 'Finest Hour' who have supported by research over the last twenty-five years or so. Sadly their number gets fewer every year, but thankfully their august deeds remain unforgotten.

John Alcorn kindly gave permission to quote from his statistical survey on Fighter Command's combat claims during the Battle of Britain, and provided updated information in a lively email exchange. Nick Lawson – nephew of Battle of Britain Spitfire pilot Sergeant John Gilders – helped with interviews. His efforts to record the last surviving few on film are commendable, his enthusiasm and friendship a tonic. Mike Williams was also most helpful in helping to source contemporary documents and I commend to the reader his website on the comparative performance of various aircraft of the Second World War (see Bibliography). My publisher, Jonathan Reeve of Amberley Publishing, always deserves a mention – not least for his single-minded tenacity in persuading me that I need to produce yet another book!

Writing is a solitary pursuit. It takes many hours to produce a work such as this, time spent in archives, interviewing, corresponding and – eventually – analysing and writing up the results. Working from home, this can often be an imposition on family life, so I can only thank my wife, Karen, and our children who live at home, James, Hannah and George, for supporting me – as all do in different ways. To Karen, though, goes the lion's share of my appreciation – and not just for helping me extract data from lists of combat losses and claims, which is clearly above and beyond the call of duty!

Bibliography

Primary Sources
Personal interviews and correspondence of Dilip Sarkar

Air Vice-Marshal J. E. Johnson CB, CBE, DSO**, DFC**, DL
Air Vice-Marshal M. D. Lyne CB, AFC
Air Commodore P. M. Brothers CBE, DSO, DFC*
Air Commodore E. M. Donaldson, CB, CBE, DSO, AFC**
Air Commodore H. W. Mermagen CB, CBE, OBE, AFC
Group Captain G.L. Denholm DFC
Group Captain Sir H. S. L. Dundas KCB, DSO*, DFC
Group Captain G. R. Edge OBE, DFC
Wing Commander F. N. Brinsden
Wing Commander D. G. S. R. Cox DFC
Wing Commander G. C. Unwin DSO, DFM**
Group Captain A. R. Wright DFC, AFC
Squadron Leader I. Hutchinson
Squadron Leader G. H. A. Wellum DFC
Flight Lieutenant R. B. Johnson
Flight Lieutenant R. L. Jones AE
Flight Lieutenant T. G. Pickering AE
Flight Lieutenant W. L. B. Walker AE
Mr J. K. Quill OBE, AFC, FRAeS
Mr R. Morris
Mr F. R. Roberts
Herr R. Götz

Interviews by Nick Lawson of *www.battleofbritain.tv*

Group Captain L. H. Bartlett DSO
Wing Commander P. Ayerst DFC
Flight Lieutenant J. P. B. Greenwood
Flight Lieutenant G. C. C. Palliser DFC, AE

Contemporary Documents (TNA references shown where appropriate)

AHB Narrative, The Battle of France: AIR 14/41
Report on German Fighter Tactics, AIR 16/300

Report on German Bomber Tactics, AIR 16/300

OKW Directives for Invasion of the U.K., Operation *Seelöwe*, Summer and Autumn 1940

OKL German Intelligence Appreciation of the RAF and Comparison with current *Luftwaffe* strength, 16 July 1940

ORBs:

19 Squadron: AIR 27/252

56 Squadron: AIR 27/528

222 Squadron: AIR 27/2475

242 Squadron: AIR 27/1471

Pilots' Personal Combat Reports:

19 Squadron: AIR 50/10

41 Squadron: AIR 50/18

72 Squadron: AIR 50/30

74 Squadron: AIR 50/32

87 Squadron: AIR 50/37

92 Squadron: AIR 50/40

151 Squadron: AIR 50/63

222 Squadron: AIR 50/51

603 Squadron: AIR 50/167

616 Squadron: AIR 50/176

Fighter Command Combat Report Form 'F', 1 Squadron, 30 August 1940: AIR 16/956

Fighter Command Combat Report Form 'F', 222 Squadron, 30 August 1940: AIR 16/956

Fighter Command Combat Report Form 'F', 242 Squadron, 30 August 1940: AIR 16/956

Combat Losses and Claims

Fighter Command Victory Claims and Casualties: AIR 16/960

Fighter Command, Operational Strength of Squadrons and Order of Battle, AIR 16/365

German fighter combat claims can be found in the OKL records of the *Chef für Ausz. und Dizsiplin Luftwaffen-Personalamt L.P. (A) V* (available online from various sources)

Oberbefehlsaber der Luftwaffe Genst. Gen. Qu./6 Abteilung/40.g.Kdos.I.C., Imperial War Museum

Pilots' Flying Log Books

Squadron Leader B. J. E. Lane DFC: AIR 4/58

Squadron Leader P. C. Pinkham AFC

Reports on Aircraft Performance

Report on 'Tests to be Made to Determine the Operational Characteristics of the Hurricane Aircraft', by Squadron Leader J. W. Gillan, 14 January 1938

Halahan, Squadron Leader P., Report on Comparative Trials of Hurricane versus Messerschmitt 109, 7 May 1940, TNA, AIR 35/121

Report on the Investigation of Turning Circles of Me 109, Spitfire and Hurricane, 9 June 1940

Handling Trials of Spitfire K5054, AVIA 18/636

Trials of Cannon Armed Spitfires: AIR 16/142

Messerschmitt 109 Fighter: Brief Handling Trials, A&AEE, 10 June 1940: AVIA 18/763

D.(Luft)T.3601 A. u. B., D.B.601 A. u. B Motoren-Handbuch, Mai 1942

Comparison Flight Between Me 109E, Me 110C, Spitfire, Hurricane and Curtiss, *E-Stelle Rechlin*, 9 August 1940

Messerschmitt 109: Handling and Manoeuvrability Tests, September 1940: AVIA 6/2394

Personal Memoirs

Allen, Wing Commander H. R., *Fighter Squadron 1940-1942*, first edition, William Kimber & Co. Ltd., St Alban's, 1979

Bader, Group Captain Sir Douglas, *Fight for the Sky: The Story of the Spitfire and Hurricane*, first edition, Sidgwick & Jackson, London, 1973

Crook, Pilot Officer D. C. M., *Spitfire Pilot*, first edition, Faber & Faber Ltd., London, 1942

'Ellan', Squadron Leader B. J. E., *Spitfire!*, first edition, Faber, London, 1942

Galland, General A., *The First and the Last: Germany's Fighter Force in the Second World War*, first edition, Fontana, London, 1954

Gleed, Wing Commander I. R., *Arise to Conquer*, first edition, Victor Gollanz Ltd, London, 1942

Gray, Group Captain C. F., *Spitfire Patrol*, first edition, Random Century, London, 1990

Hall, R. M. D., *Clouds of Fear*, first edition, Bailey Brothers & Swinfen Ltd, London, 1969

Hillary, Flying Officer R., *The Last Enemy*, second edition, MacMillan & Co. Ltd., London, 1950

Knocke, *Hauptmann* H., *I Flew for the* Führer, first edition, Evans, London, 1953

Lane, Squadron Leader B. J. E., Sarkar, D. (ed), *Spitfire!*, (new illustrated and uncensored edition), Amberley Publishing, Cirencester, 2009

Roberts, F. R., *From Duxford to Karachi: An RAF Armourer's War*, first edition, Victory Books International, Worcester, 2006

Woodhall, Group Captain A. B., *Soldier, Sailor, Airman Too*, unpublished

Secondary Sources

Addison, P., and Crang, J. A. (eds), *The Burning Blue: A New History of the Battle of Britain*, first edition, Pimlico, London, 2000

Alcorn, J., Battle of Britain Top Guns, Aeroplane Monthly, September 1996

Alcorn, J., Battle of Britain Top Guns Update, *Aeroplane Monthly*, July 2000

Anon., *Battle of Britain*, Air Ministry Pamphlet 156

Anon., *The Battle of Britain: An Air Ministry Account of the Great Days from 8ᵗʰ August – 31ˢᵗ October 1940*, HMSO, London, 1941

Anon., *The Battle of Britain: An Air Ministry Account of the Great Days from 8ᵗʰ August – 31ˢᵗ October 1940*, illustrated edition, HMSO, London, 1941

Anon., *Destiny Can Wait: The History of the Polish Air Force in Great Britain*, first edition, William Heinemann Ltd., London, 1949

Anon., *The Second World War, RAF 1939-45, Flying Training: Volume One, Policy and Planning*, first edition, M. L. R. S. Books, Smalldale, 2009

Anon., *The Rise & Fall of the German Air Force 1933-45*, Air Ministry Pamphlet 248, first edition, Public Record Office, London, 2001

Anon., The Spitfire. *The Aeroplane*, 12 April 1940, pp. 517-524

Bekker, C., *The Luftwaffe War Diaries*, sixth edition, Corgi, London, 1972

Bialer, U., *The Shadow of the Bomber: The Fear of Air Attack and British Politics 1932-39*, first edition, Royal Historical Society, London, 1980

Bingham, V., *Blitzed! The Battle of France May – June 1940*, first edition, Air Research Publications, New Malden, 1990

Bungay, S., *The Most Dangerous Enemy: A History of the Battle of Britain*, first edition, Aurum Press Ltd., London, 2000

Calder, A., *The People's War: Britain 1939-45*, thirteenth edition, Pimlico, London, 2008

Calder, A., *The Myth of the Blitz*, eighth edition, Pimlico, London, 2008

Caldwell, D., *The J.G. 26 War Diary: Volume One 1939-1942*, first edition, Grub Street, London, 1996

Clapson, M., *The Routledge Companion to Britain in the Twentieth Century*, first edition, Routledge, London, 2009

Cox, S., and Gray, P. (eds), *Air Power Turning Points From Kitty Hawk to Kosovo*, first edition, Frank Cass & Co. Ltd., London, 2002

Cox. S., and Probert, H. (eds), *The Battle Re-Thought: A Symposium on the Battle of Britain*, first edition, Air Life Publishing, Shrewsbury, 1991

Dean, *Sir Maurice, The Royal Air Force and Two World Wars*, first edition, Cassell Ltd., London, 1979

Deist, W., *The Wehrmacht and German Rearmament*, first edition, The MacMillan Press Ltd., Basingstoke, 1981

Dempster, D., and Wood. D., *The Narrow Margin: The Battle of Britain*, first edition, Arrow Ltd, London, 1969

Donnelly, M., *Britain in the Second World War*, first edition, Routledge, London, 1999

Feist, U., *The Fighting Me 109*, first edition, Arms & Armour Press Ltd., London, 1988

Foreman, J., *RAF Fighter Command Victory Claims of World War Two*, first edition, Red Kite, Walton-on-Thames, 2003

Handel, M. I. (ed), *Intelligence and Military Operations*, second edition, Frank Cass & Co. Ltd., Abingdon, 2004

Harvey-Bailey, A., *The Merlin in Perspective – the Combat Years*, first edition, Rolls-Royce Heritage Trust, Derby, 1983

Hough, R., and Richards, D., *The Battle of Britain: The Jubilee History*, first edition, Hodder & Stoughton Ltd., London, 1990

James, T. C. G., *The Battle of Britain*, first edition, Frank Cass, London, 2000

Mason, F. K., *The Hawker Hurricane*, first edition, MacDonald, London, 1962

Mason, F. K., *Battle Over Britain*, second edition, Aston Publications, Bourne End, 1990

Mitchell, G., *R.J. Mitchell. World Famous Aircraft Designer: From Schooldays to Spitfire*, first edition, Nelson & Saunders, Olney, 1986

Mowat, C. L., *Britain Between the Wars*, tenth edition, Methuen & Co. Ltd, London, 1976

Murray, W., *Strategy for Defeat: The Luftwaffe 1933-1945*, first edition, Eagle Editions, Royston, 2003

Orange, V., *Park: The Biography of Air Chief Marshal Sir Keith Park GCB, KBE, MC, DFC, DCL*, second edition, Grub Street, London, 2001

Orange, V., *Dowding of Fighter Command: Victor of the Battle of Britain*, first edition, Grub Street Publishing, London, 2008

Overy, R., *The Air War 1939-1945*, first edition, Europa Publications Ltd., London, 1980

Overy, R., *The Battle of Britain*, first edition, Penguin, London, 2004

Pallud, J. P., *Blitzkrieg in the West: Then and Now*, first edition, After the Battle, London, 1991

Price, A., *Battle of Britain: The Hardest Day 18 August 1940*, first edition, MacDonald & Jane's Publishers Ltd., London, 1979

McKinstry, L., *Hurricane: Victor of the Battle of Britain*, first edition, John Murray, London, 2010

Morgan, E, and Shacklady, E, *Spitfire: The History*, first edition, Key Publishing, Stamford, 1987

Price, A., *The Spitfire Story*, revised second edition, Arms & Armour Press, London, 1995

Price, A., Battle of Britain Day, *RAF Historical Society Journal*, 2002, 29, pp. 5-23

Priestley, J. B., *English Journey*, new edition, Mandarin, London, 1994

Priestley, J. B., *Postscripts*, first edition, Heinemann, London, 1940

Ramsey, W (ed), *The Battle of Britain: Then & Now*, Mk V Edition, After the Battle, London, 1986

Ramsey, W (ed), *The Blitz Then & Now: Volume One*, first edition, After the Battle, London, 1989

Ramsey, W (ed), *The Blitz Then & Now: Volume Two*, first edition, After the Battle, London, 1990

Robinson, A, *RAF Fighter Squadrons in the Battle of Britain*, first edition, Arms & Armour Press Ltd, London, 1987

Sarkar, D., *Spitfire Squadron: 19 Squadron at War 1939-41*, first edition, Air Research Publications, New Malden 1990

Sarkar, D., *Angriff Westland: Three Battle of Britain Air Raids 'Though the Looking Glass'*, first edition, Ramrod Publications, 1994

Sarkar, D., *Bader's Duxford Fighters: The Big Wing Controversy*, second edition, Victory Books International, 2006

Sarkar, D., *The Few: The Battle of Britain in the Words of the Pilots*, first edition, Amberley Publishing, 2009

Sarkar, D., *Duxford 1940: A Battle of Britain Base at War*, first edition, Amberley Publishing, 2009

Sarkar, D., *Last of the Few: Eighteen Battle of Britain Pilots Tell Their Extraordinary Stories*, first edition, Amberley Publishing, 2010

Sarkar, D., *The Spitfire Manual*, first edition, Amberley Publishing, 2010

Sarkar, D., *Spitfire Voices: Life as a Spitfire Pilot in the Words of the Veterans*, first edition, Amberley Publishing, 2010

Steinhilper, U. and Osborne, P., *Spitfire On My Tail: A View From the Other Side*, first edition, Independent Books, Bromley, 1989

Terraine, J., in 'The Dowding System', *Battle of Britain* (Part One), The Daily Telegraph Editorial Supplement, 16 June 1990, p. XI

Tosh, J, with Lang, S., *The Pursuit of History*, fourth edition, Pearson Education Ltd., Harlow, 2006

Townsend, Group Captain P., *Duel of Eagles: The Classic Account of the Battle of Britain*, third edition, George Weidenfeld & Nicolson, London, 1990

Wood, A, *The True History of Lord Beaverbrook*, first edition, Heinemann, London, 1965

Wright, R., *Dowding and the Battle of Britain*, third edition, Corgi, London, 1970

Wynn, K., *Men of the Battle of Britain*, first edition, Gliddon Books, Norwich, 1989

Websites

http://www.spitfireperformance.com – Mike Williams' site from which many original documents can be downloaded as P.D.F. files.

http://www.battleofbritain.tv – Nick Lawson's site of interviews with survivors.

http://aces.safarikovi.org - Jan Šafařík's site about air aces and from which German combat claims can be downloaded as Microsoft Word or P.D.F. files.

www.dilipsarkarmbe.co.uk – the author's personal website.

http://www.the-hawker-hurricane-society.com/1.html - The Hawker Hurricane Society

http://www.spitfiresociety.demon.co.uk – The Spitfire Society

http://www.raf.mod.uk/bbmf – The RAF Battle of Britain Memorial Flight

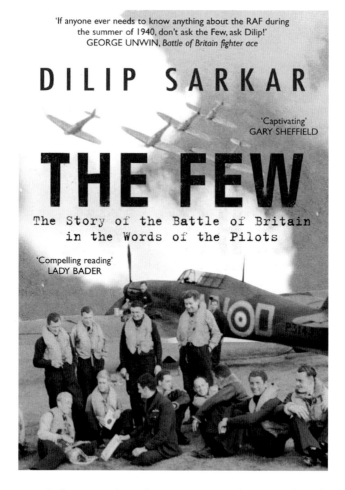

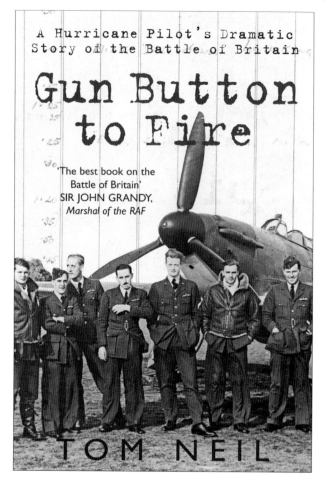

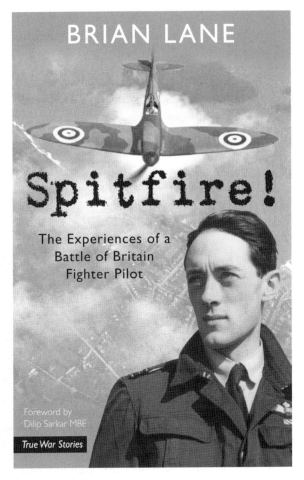

Also available from Amberley Publishing

How to fly the legendary fighter plane in combat using the manuals and instructions supplied by the RAF during the Second World War

An amazing array of leaflets, books and manuals were issued by the War Office during the Second World War to aid pilots in flying the Supermarine Spitfire, here for the first time they are collated into a single book with the original 1940s setting. An introduction is supplied by expert aviation historian Dilip Sarkar. Other sections include aircraft recognition, how to act as an RAF officer, bailing out etc.

£9.99 Paperback
40 illustrations
264 pages
978-1-84868-436-2

Available from all good bookshops or to order direct
Please call **01285-760-030**
www.amberleybooks.com

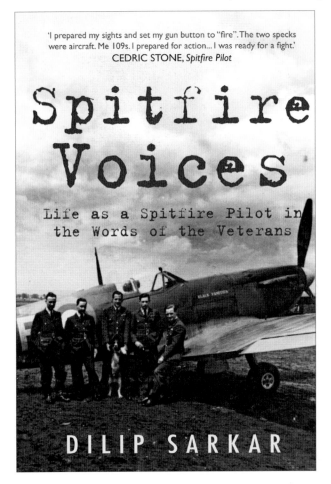

Also available from Amberley Publishing

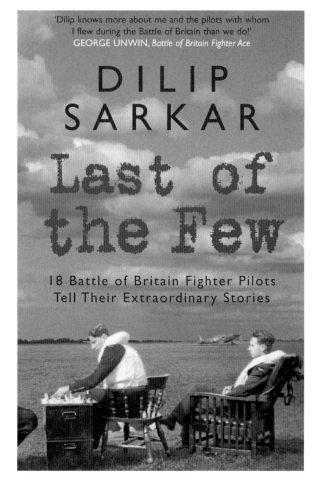

'Dilip knows more about me and the pilots with whom I flew during the Battle of Britain than we do!'
GEORGE UNWIN, *Battle of Britain Fighter Ace*

DILIP SARKAR

Last of the Few

18 Battle of Britain Fighter Pilots Tell Their Extraordinary Stories

18 Spitfire and Hurricane fighter pilots recount their experiences of combat during the Battle of Britain

'Dilip knows more about me and the pilots with whom I flew during the Battle of Britain than we do! If anyone ever needs to know anything about the RAF during the summer of 1940, don't ask the Few, ask him!' GEORGE 'GRUMPY' UNWIN, Battle of Britain fighter ace

£20 Hardback
60 illustrations
240 pages
978-1-84868-435-5

Available from all good bookshops or to order direct
Please call **01285-760-030**
www.amberley·books.com